[handwritten inscription: March 26, 2017 Dear Jennifer(?) You are a Pure Light in our world]

Praise for
For Time and All Eternity
Love Never Dies

"There are hundreds of inspirational and moving stories out there and this is one of the most powerful I've read."

—*Sandra Martin, President, Paraview, Inc.*

"...For Time and All Eternity, is a deeply touching and triumphant story that assures us that the soul survives and that love is eternal. It reminds us that we are not here by chance, we are never alone, and that life is full of miracles."

—*Christopher Naughton, Executive Producer & Host of PBS's* New World *and NPR's* New World Radio

"This journey is an inspiration to others."

—*Charles Thomas Cayce, Executive Director of the Association for Research and Enlightenment, Edgar Cayce Foundation*

"Few books have moved me as this book has. Reading through my own tears and giggles this writing has ignited my own slow burning flame to find spirituality into a dancing fire ready to cross a higher bridge of consciousness. Many thanks for sharing your pain, joy, laughter and tears."

—*PJ Wenger, MFT, NCC*

"Beautiful and inspiring, this story had me sobbing in places and laughing out loud in others."

—*Reverend Luanna Pierce*

"For Time and All Eternity, represents a riveting personal account, no fiction writer could ever hope to duplicate. A powerfully written, unforgettable story."

—*Vitae Bergman, author of* Take Sylvia's Case

"A beautiful book, mesmerizing, difficult to put down, very powerful and thought provoking. Film worthy."

—*Vaune Peck, Director of Performing Arts at Monmouth University*

"For Time and All Eternity – From tragedy to triumph. One soul's incredible journey that once again proves there are no coincidences in this life; that God's ever-present love surrounds every one of us; and that, thankfully, love is eternal."

—*Denise Conti*

"For Time and All Eternity, touched my heart in a profound way. After reading this courageous story, I realize the time is now for me to stop hiding behind the fear that holds me back from shining my Divine Light."

—*Angela Minervini, Chaplain, Unity Church by the Shore*

"A powerful, emotional journey: eloquent and inspiring. Hands down one of the best books I've ever read."

—*Karen English, Mom Execs, Mentor/Director*

"If you have ever wondered whether there is life after death, LaVoie's story of loss and her spiritual struggle after the death of her husband will assure you that there is no death, that our loved ones have just gone on ahead. Her personal journey through grief and rebirth is so powerfully written that she makes the reader feel every single emotion she has as she moves through the shock and pain of her loss to the realization that love never dies. As she presents compelling proof that our loved ones live on, LaVoie also provides inspiration for anyone who has ever experienced grief and loss."

—*Venture Inward: The Magazine of Edgar Cayce's A.R.E.*

"This was truly a cosmic journey of unconditional love, forgiveness, compassion. Rock solid proof that our love, our souls do go on for the greater evolution of God's Divine Plan."

—*Maria Dempsey*

"For Time and All Eternity, encourages us to listen to the still, small, voice within. It reminds us to cherish the earth and all of her creatures. It proves that we are not alone."

—*Reverend Alanya Lee*

"In her magnificent book, Karla Lee LaVoie tells us about her journey through her own pain and loss into the Beyond. She shows us the healing that she experienced there and has brought back for us to help us find our own way. A must-read for anyone exploring or questioning their own spirituality."

—*Kenneth Kinter, MA, UMDNJ: University Behavioral HealthCare, The Center for Excellence in Psychiatry*

For Time and All Eternity
Love Never Dies

Karla Lee LaVoie, creator of the highly acclaimed meditations *Garden of Light* and *Earth Mother* is a facilitator of the Bonny Method of Guided Imagery and Music and a Reiki master teacher. Her passion is creating customized imagery and empowerment recordings that inspire others to move toward greater peace and healing. In her presentations she helps audiences open to higher levels of consciousness while creating a bridge to the other side. Karla's greatest joy is playing with her granddaughter Sophia and spending time in nature. An avid supporter and volunteer for animal groups she lives at the Jersey Shore with her rescued felines Joshua, Gabriel, Ellie, Apricot and Mufasa.

For Time and All Eternity

Love Never Dies

Karla Lee LaVoie

Copyright © 2006 by Karla Lee La Voie

Book Design by Leslie Nolan Design

Author Photograph by Matt Denton

ISBN 978-0-7414-3247-6

Published by:

INFINITY
P U B L I S H I N G

1094 New DeHaven Street, Suite 100
West Conshohocken, PA 19428-2713
Info@buybooksontheweb.com
www.buybooksontheweb.com
Toll-free (877) BUY BOOK
Local Phone (610) 941-9999
Fax (610) 941-9959

Printed in the United States of America

Published October 2013

For my son Tom,
My constant joy and shining light,
With all my love

Acknowledgements

I am deeply grateful to the following: My book manager Janet Grosshandler, for keeping the fire burning. My editor Kathryn Gordon, for her inspired guidance and editing. A special thank you to all of the proofreaders, Leslie Nolan, for her amazing patience and beautiful design, Matt Denton for his creative photography, and the many helpers along the way: Jennie Meares, a true angel, Christopher Naughton, Eve Sicurella, Maria Dempsey, Dr. Roger Jahnke, Marlene Satter, and Vivian Basalari for her great encouragement and intuition. Deep gratitude also belongs to Sherry Kennedy-Cameron and Hilda McCoy for holding the sacred space in the early years.

Gratitude belongs to Dr. Raymond Moody for his courageous pioneer work and book *Life After Life*. His research and amazing generosity has increased belief in the afterlife journey of the soul and eased the hunger of millions who have longed for that knowledge.

This story would not be told were it not for the amazing courage of Josephine Matullo, Ron, Bruce, and the entire DeVizia family. Thank you for entrusting me with the sacred material and cherished memories that have made this story come alive.

It would also not be told without Edgar Cayce's valiant life, work and readings. I am very appreciative to have been part of the A.R.E. family.

I am very grateful to my son Tom and my sister Sharlene, for her loving care of us during the difficult years, and grateful for my family, friends, clients and students, who have supported me and have understood my need for focus and retreat.

A heartfelt thank you to my first spiritual teacher Sondra Craig-Piniak, and to my guides and mentors: Ram Dass, Elisabeth Kübler-Ross, Carol Bush and Ken Brusica, who each in their own unique way opened doors to infinite possibilities.

Most of all, thank you Mom for always believing in me and for your continued presence in my life, even beyond the veil.

Foreword

It is a privilege and honor to introduce this enthralling book by an old friend, Karla La Voie. I first met her through our mutual connection with one of the first spiritual organizations in the nation, the Association for Research and Enlightenment. Later on, I encountered her again when lecturing for other groups. She always impressed me as a vibrant, happy, bright person who had it all together.

Little did I know at that time, which was the mid 1980's that she had struggled through some of the most formidable difficulties that can beset human beings, and bounced back magnificently. What is more, she had accomplished all this with grace and unwavering determination. Primarily her calm demeanor, kind smile, and sparkling eyes struck me. And, although I am a trained psychiatrist, I never once sensed or suspected the daunting history of agony and trauma that forged her character. That she has turned these seemingly unbearable travails into a first-rate autobiographical account of spiritual transformation makes her life story even more remarkable. For all those reasons, it is a pleasure to recommend this book to everyone who is concerned with the nature of human spirituality. I believe that it will be especially helpful to those who are in the throes of grief and as a result are questing what life is all about. Indeed, in addition to being a sensitive chronicle of spiritual struggle, the book is also a powerful statement about the ultimate meaning of life.

For Time and All Eternity is replete with heart-wrenching themes that will be painfully familiar to many. Troubling changes in a spouse's personality due to an encroaching debilitating illness. Tragic loss of that spouse by a horrible suicide. Prolonged estrangement from a beloved child. Helping a dear friend through a frightening, stigmatizing terminal illness. And then, above all, redemption, forgiveness, renewal, and inner peace through a determined, personal, spiritual quest. Karla's book will comfort many and encourage them to keep on plugging through awful external circumstances and many discouraging setbacks.

The book is an excellent remedy for the common misconception that enlightenment is a quick, immediate, one-way ascent to nirvana. It is only for very few of us that happiness and fulfillment come in a single, profound episode of mystical consciousness. Rather, for most of us, it is a long, painful, laborious process of ups-and-downs, and hard, hard work. Karla's struggle, as she shows in these pages, is an excellent example of the latter, more common variety of spiritual awakenings.

Along the way, she paints charming and revealing portraits of some of the most influential figures in the contemporary consciousness movement. For example, she brings the famous Ram Dass vividly alive in the minds of those of us who have never met him. Nor does she neglect influential figures who are not so widely known, but who ought to be. For example, her word-picture of one of my own favorites—Dr. Mark Thurston, a fine, endearing man affiliated with the Association for

Research and Enlightenment—is truly memorable.

Karla is a good writer. And her work deserves a place on the bookshelf of anyone who cares about the enduring verities with which the great religions of the world are concerned. It is also a valuable, practical guide to personal transformation. I believe that many who read it will be inspired to keep on trying through their own hard and dark times. And discovering that they are not alone will refresh them.

Raymond A. Moody, M.D., Ph.D.
Author of Life After Life

For Time and All Eternity Love Never Dies

Introduction

The inspiration for this book was birthed out of great tragedy, which ultimately became great joy and triumph. Although the impulse to write came in 1976, it has taken many years for me to complete this story. The second inspiration, part two of the book, flooded my awareness in 1987 after many miracles and glorious realizations.

So what have I been doing all of these years? Procrastinating, for one thing, further developing myself and waiting for Divine timing and order to assist with the birth and dissemination of this work.

Many times in these last years I have questioned that apparent procrastination. In the early spring of 2000, while on a spiritual quest at Genesis, I pondered it again. Genesis, a wonderful spiritual retreat center nestled at the foot of the

Berkshires in Westfield, Massachusetts was the perfect place for quiet contemplation.

At that time the director was Sister Elizabeth Oleksak, a gentle yet powerful Sister of Providence. Sister Elizabeth and the other Sisters had created a space where all could come, regardless of their religion, to ponder life, deepen spirituality and heal. Emphasis was placed on healing the healer and awakening inner creativity. The holistic classes offered, in subjects like Reiki, massage, focusing and sacred dance, hardly matched my picture of a convent. A Universalist myself, I was deeply touched by the open-heartedness of Sister Elizabeth and all those I encountered at Genesis. Although devout Catholics, they honored and respected, as did I, all paths to God.

Genesis fed my soul in many ways. Long contemplative walks along prayer and nature trails helped me to connect more fully with Gaia, our earth mother. Small and simple living quarters and beautiful surroundings offered the soul nourishment I very much needed at that busy time in my life. A mystic's corner on the top floor of an old rustic red barn offered solitude, a place for inspirational reading, journaling or quiet meditation.

Embraced by this place, I felt at home. My small room, with its one window opening onto a beautiful garden filled with daffodils, hyacinths and tulips invited contemplation. Warm rays of the morning sun poured through the window and I became distinctly aware of the sweet fragrance of hyacinth. Flowers of red, yellow and purple still touched with morning dew glistened as the sun bathed them. As I met each day with such beauty it was easy to become still. Early one morning, while listening to the calls of the birds, I turned within to the question that lived always at the back of my awareness: *What about the book? It has been years now and I only have an outline sitting in a drawer. Why don't I write it? Why am I not living my Divine purpose? Am I such a procrastinator, or is this about timing greater than my own?*

I felt disturbed, as I often did when contemplating my soul's mission; I worried that I wasn't fully living the deep vision that had been given to me. Often I had to remind myself to lighten up. But the questions were always there at the back of my mind, yanking at me in those moments when stillness triumphed over my much too busy life.

Years before while in meditation I experienced a powerful vision. I was shown a Golden City with a great auditorium where many gathered to awaken to higher consciousness. I felt it to be part of "the call" to that higher knowing, that my life and work in some way could make a difference in the coming of a new age, in the remembrance of our true nature as spiritual beings.

Even with my teaching and healing ministry I still felt like I was not fully realizing the "work," the vision of that Golden City. At Genesis, I called out to God in prayer,

"Please show me the way, Lord. What would you have me do? What ever happened to that book I was going to write? If that is what I am to do then please guide me."

I placed the prayer in my journal and the next day, bidding Sister Elizabeth a loving goodbye, I made my way home. Never could I have guessed in a million years what was waiting for me. As soon as I arrived I checked my phone messages. The first call nearly dropped me to my knees. It was from Janet, a woman who had attended a monthly women's support group at my home for many years. Lovingly called the Upper Astrals, they were six women who had come together searching for higher truth and understanding.

Though dear to me, Janet was not privy to my inner world; I was the facilitator of the group and kept my deep soul questioning to myself. Janet knew there was a book on the back burner but did not know of my agonizing over the unrealized manuscript. I had not seen her for many months. As I listened to her words I was filled with gratitude, for they were God's instant answer to my prayers. She said,

"Karla, while I was running yesterday I put out a question to God. Running is my form of meditation, and I asked when was I going to write my book, my personal story? I heard a voice loud and clear; it said, 'Help Karla write her book.' I don't know what I am to do for you but perhaps we can talk about it."

Flabbergasted, I played the message over and over to be sure I was hearing it correctly. On Saturday at Genesis I put my prayer out to Spirit and on that same day Janet heard and became God's angel for me.

Janet, an avid, published writer, became my book manager, taskmaster and guiding light. She has been my major source of support and encouragement. Without her this story might still be sitting in a drawer or locked up somewhere in the back of my mind.

During our first meeting I shared my concerns about exposing my personal life and deep soul journey with the world.

"Will people think I am crazy or making it up? Maybe it's not the right time."

Placing her hand gently on mine she responded, "It's time, Karla, it's time."

With the exception of a few name changes, all of what you are about to read is true, each vision and each miracle. Memories and actual dialogue were retrieved from journals, videos, newspaper articles, and therapy transcripts. My deepest desire is that it will awaken in you a remembrance that all life is One and that we are on a journey back from whence we came.

May it help all those who have suffered loss to know that the seeming coincidences that happen in life may indeed be messages from the "other side," for the veil is truly very thin.

May it help all to know that we can move from tragedy to triumph. There is no cross that is too great to bear and we are never alone. And most importantly, may it help all to invite and accept the still small voice within until it expands into a solid voice for God.

This is my mystical journey, a journey that began when I was a small child and continues still. The voice and the knowing come to me when I allow myself to be quiet and when I am most in need. I do not herald myself as a psychic, but just one with a deep yearning for truth. It is my hope that I have now made greater progress on my pilgrimage to the Golden City, the place of remembrance within. It is my ardent prayer that this story will inspire you to move further along on your own spiritual quest.

These words from *A Course in Miracles* have guided my life.

"I am the light of the world
How holy am I who have been given the function
Of lighting up the world
Let me be still before my holiness
In its calm light, let all of my conflicts disappear
In its peace, let me remember Who I am."

May we all remember that we are indeed the light of the world. This story is humbly offered from my heart to yours.

"And this that we call death, it is no more

Than the opening and closing of a door—

And in Your house how many rooms must be

Beyond this one where we rest momently."

———*James Dillet Freeman*

Part One

For Time and All Eternity

Chapter 1
The Last Days

I can still hear my screams. They echo through my body and mind like razors, sharp and piercing. Was it really thirty years ago that my husband Lucky died? Sometimes it feels like an eternity, and sometimes it feels like someone else sat on that couch waiting for the gun to fire.

Lucky . . . hardly a name befitting one who had endured so much. He suffered for many years with a horrific head injury. His body was breaking down slowly and painfully; each trip to the doctor revealed another malady. The seizures had become debilitating and after each major breakdown he had to be hospitalized, sometimes for as long as six weeks. The violent episodes in his brain left him confused, unsteady and unstable. Toward the end, the seizures became very violent. After having one, he would drop into an unconscious state with no memory after of what had happened. During the final stage of his illness he unknowingly hurt me and my young son Tommy, the stepson he loved.

How could this happen to such a strong, compassionate, exciting and healthy man?

Lucky might as well have been orphaned. His father developed peritonitis after a simple surgical procedure and died without warning. Completely unable to cope with the loss his mother suffered a nervous breakdown. She became unable to care for him, so Lucky and his sister Nancy were sent to relatives when he was only five-years-old. He developed a rebellious streak in his early adolescence, getting into trouble at every turn. Eventually he was placed in foster homes, one after the other, until he landed with a family noted for very strict discipline.

The patriarch was a tyrant. Abusive and violent, this pathetic excuse of a foster father chained him to the iron post of his bed and beat him unmercifully at the slightest provocation. At times while chained he was given only mustard sandwiches to eat and was forbidden to speak or even go to the bathroom. He witnessed horrific cruelty to the other young boys that had the grave misfortune of being placed in this deadly home. It's hard to imagine the fright and pain he must have endured during his childhood.

Fleeing from this brutal man he took to the streets. It was only a matter of time before he was placed in a juvenile detention home where he spent the rest of his troubled youth, constantly bucking the system. It was there that he vowed to be the strongest and best at whatever he did. He took on the name Lucky, for he had survived the unimaginable.

His need for competition became great. He took on dares and fights with the older bullies, constantly seeking to prove his superior strength. Lucky declared that no one would ever hurt him again. At the same time he developed a deep caring for the underdog, for the oppressed and the abused, never condemning anyone weaker than himself, for he had witnessed so much.

Lucky's presence filled a room. He was often misunderstood, and many feared him. Yet those who grew close loved him for his loyalty, courage and commitment to helping those less fortunate than himself. He had a way with women, a hopeless flirt; he could sway the ladies with his captivating good looks and devilish charm. In spite of his harmless shenanigans, his heart was always mine. Never did I doubt his love or devotion. No one would have believed that this strong brave man wept in my arms like a small child as he shared the brutal stories of his youth and the tragic loss of his father.

When I first laid eyes upon him, I saw past the persona, deep into him, where the soft and gentle soul resided. At first he tried to lock it back up, away from my gaze, but he was joined with me as I was with him in a place that was greater than both of us. We were deeply in love, attuned to one another's thoughts and feelings, as if joined by one mind and one heart.

Lucky was the love of my life, beautiful and brave beyond words. In his early twenties he was the lone dock builder/pile driver who climbed to the highest point on the New York Verrazano-Narrows Bridge during its construction to make it safe for the engineers that followed. Helicopters flew beneath him, shooting pictures of his daredevil maneuvers as he set the highest steel in place. His picture was in Time and Life Magazines as the construction story of this magnificent bridge unfolded.

He was the anonymous and courageous man who went into the Staten Island oil tanks in 1973 after a devastating explosion stole the lives of many men. Moving through the dangers, he ignored his own welfare. Lucky worked around the clock with a pain in his belly and a heart heavy with grief, while the families of the men waited outside the tank for their loved ones. He wept as he carried out the charred, unrecognizable bodies, reproaching those in charge for their lack of safety. As always, he put others first and his own welfare last, donating his entire paycheck to the survivors. Whatever he owned was yours for the asking; even without asking it was fully given.

Lucky truly walked to the beat of a different drummer, often saying that he belonged somewhere else, in an earlier time perhaps. He reminded me of an historical western character, one that would swagger into a saloon, capture the hearts of the women and the respect of the men as he cleaned up the town. Lucky had no fear, until his last days.

During our early years together, my husband defended a frightened man who was being harassed by loan sharks. As he guided this man out of harm's way, placing his own body in the way of the collectors, he was gunned down. He took a bullet in his back for this stranger, and nearly lost his own life. Lucky, a rescuer of the timid, caretaker for the hurt and abandoned animals, and a supporter of Father Flanagan's Boys Town could not bear to see anyone abused, especially the weak and frightened. Still to this day when I see the Boys Town logo—the picture of the stronger boy carrying the weaker one—I think of Lucky. "He ain't heavy, he's my brother" could certainly have been his personal motto. He would help anyone in need.

I remember our first meeting. My closest friend Gail had introduced us. She and Lucky had just shared dinner and were about to enter a favorite pub when I spotted them from across the street. I rushed over to greet Gail and as she made the introduction I was mesmerized.

While gazing into his crystal blue, twinkling eyes I drank in his golden skin, his blond hair, his mischievous smile, and strong, tall, muscular frame. He was an Adonis to me. Yet, in the moment that I lost myself in him, a veil opened. In an instant I knew that he was my heart's joy and my long-awaited love. Somehow I knew that we would marry, love intensely, and I also knew in that moment that he would die. He would only be with me for a short time. In just a few seconds all these truths were revealed to me. I was in a moment of timelessness, drinking him in and at the same time being made ready by some unknown force to walk this path of love and joy, tragedy and death.

We had a whirlwind courtship, married and purchased a home in the quaint seafaring town of Keyport, New Jersey and settled into our new life. On a clear day you could see the Verrazano-Narrows Bridge across the bay, always a reminder of his amazing courage.

But early in our marriage, while setting steel sheeting some distance in the air, Lucky was struck with a steel wrecking ball in the right temporal-parietal area of his skull. He fell unconscious, yet miraculously was caught in the leads, dangling by one ankle until help arrived. Fellow dock builders came to his aid, removed him from the steel sheeting and rushed him to the hospital. A subdural hematoma was suspected but tests were not conclusive. Lucky remained in the hospital for six weeks, until he was stable again. The doctors warned him about returning to work too soon, but he didn't listen. After that long and grueling hospitalization, he came home, shaken and forever changed. The prophecy I saw in his eyes when we first met was about to unfold. His decline began.

Many problems beset him as he attempted to resume his livelihood. Headaches were severe, blackouts unpredictable. His equilibrium and speech would falter and soon he realized that driving the car was impossible. Yet Lucky refused to give up. He would work four to six weeks at a time, then recuperate at home for a month to two months, or when he was totally unstable, in the hospital for many weeks.

Shortly after his horrific injury we were involved in a minor automobile accident. We were thrown forward in the car. Under normal circumstances this would not have been severe, but it aggravated the head injury. Lucky was admitted to the hospital again; many different neurologists, neurosurgeons, and psychiatrists saw him, all with different opinions.

He was released at thirty-six-years old, with the understanding that he would not work again since his local union would no longer insure him. Lucky tried to keep himself busy. He studied locksmithing, worked in the yard, had a garden and did most of the cooking when he felt well enough.

My days were consumed with taking care of Lucky, doing the best I could for Tommy, and teaching. I loved my job at the high school. Years prior, I had been a hair designer and manager of a popular and progressive hair salon, when the Matawan-Aberdeen school superintendent, the high school principal and vocational director approached me. I was asked to design and implement a program in Cosmetology that would be offered in the public school setting, very different from other schools that transported vocational students to another location. This bussing felt like segregation, separating very creative and intelligent kids from the college bound.

The government was funding vocational education and looking for innovative career programs. Thrilled to be part of this, I designed a three-year career program, which later expanded into a Personal Development program for students with special needs. Two groups of cosmetology students were with me two to three hours a day, learning the related sciences including anatomy and physiology as well as all aspects of hair and skin care, with licensure at the completion of their study.

Time at school brought a welcome relief. I could put aside the chaos and drama of my home life and be with the students that I loved. They blessed me in many ways and this experience opened the door to what would become my life long passion, teaching.

The weeks and months passed and the once strong, intelligent and passionate man could no longer concentrate. He could not perform any task without risk of blackouts, dizziness and seizures followed by amnesia. Many times I returned home from work to find him slumped over the locksmithing home-study course. Papers were strewn all over the table and the floor. Even this simple study was beyond his capability. My heart ached for him.

The pain in his head was unbearable at times, and insomnia tormented him. Watching my husband deteriorate over the years was nearly as unbearable for me as it was for him. Hard as I tried, there was nothing that I could do to ease his suffering. This proud man was losing himself. He was slipping away into a gripping dark oblivion, his power usurped by the head injury at every turn.

During Christmas week in 1975, after an overdose of pain medication, I rushed him to the hospital for what must have been the fifteenth visit. I begged his physician to refer us to a new neurologist. The doctor explained that the specialist he would recommend was on vacation and had a long waiting list. We would have to wait. The usual tests were done; petit mal epilepsy, post concussion syndrome and bleeding of the cerebrum were suspected, yet the tests returned inconclusive. My husband was released ten days later feeling disgusted with himself and useless.

His depression became worse. Again I reached out to his doctor by phone, in person and by letter, pleading with him to get us started with the new physician. Lucky would not seek out a new specialist on his own, because he didn't want to hurt his long-time doctor's feelings. He said he cared for him and respected him too much. My hands were tied.

How could I blame him for wanting to leave? The doctors had no solutions. Pumped with pills for pain, sleep, blood pressure, and anxiety he made it through the days. He continued to try to make something of his life, but repeatedly failed. His judgment was off, and the psychological problems of his tormented youth were now magnified, as he lost more and more of himself.

One afternoon I returned home from work and found him screaming at Tommy, who was then ten-years-old. Lucky was trying to construct a fence in the backyard as a surprise for me. Tommy was unable to carry out the hard task of lifting and holding the poles in place as Lucky pounded them into the ground. By this time in his illness he could not tolerate even the slightest stress, as it would cause his blood pressure to rise followed by excruciating pain in his head.

In those aberrant states he would lose his capacity for judgment and become violent, usually just pounding the wall or whatever inanimate object was in sight. But this time was different. Hearing the commotion in the backyard, I ran down the driveway and saw him throwing the poles and screaming at Tommy, who was fighting to hold back tears.

Furious, I yelled,

"Leave him alone, he's only a little boy, this work is much too hard for him."

"Tommy," I shouted. "Get in the house!"

Then I turned back to Lucky, hoping to ease his stress, my voice softening,

"It's okay honey, the fence is great, I love it and I'll even help you build it."

I saw the look in his eyes change; he became like a madman. My once-loving husband appeared not even to know me as I attempted to soothe him. With fury in his eyes, he picked up one of the fence poles and approached me.

"Lucky, put it down, try and calm yourself." But it was too late.

My husband was gone, and in his place a monster charged at me. Terrified, I fled down the long sloping hill at the back of our property. I heard the thud of the pole hitting the ground just behind me. It then crashed into my legs, knocking me down. As I tumbled down the hill, pain shot through my chest and side. One of my ribs had broken.

Near panic, I heard another thud, and turned to see Lucky sprawled on the ground, his face in the dirt. My heart pounding and my chest aching, I cautiously moved toward him. He was unconscious. I was afraid that he had suffered a stroke.

Fleeing into the house I called the first aid, calmed my shaken child and returned to my husband. Lucky was beginning to stir yet was confused and unable to speak coherently. Through his weak mutterings I was able to decipher,

"What happened?"

"You're okay, honey, just be still."

I held him until the first aid arrived and off to the hospital we went for yet another long stay. As in past episodes, his brain was scrambled; attempts to speak or comprehend what was going on were diminished, and the pain in his head excruciating. Doctors were compassionate yet offered little hope. In those days there wasn't much that could be done for severe head injuries.

The hospital stay seemed endless. It took weeks for him to recover his mental capacity and reason. He had no idea what had happened to Tommy and me, as I was able to hide the wrapped rib under my clothes. I couldn't bear to tell him what had transpired during that episode. I prayed that it would never occur again. Perhaps the new medication would control the seizures.

One night, after leaving the hospital exhausted from my work at school, the daily long hospital hours with him, and my feeble attempt to care for my son and my home, I fell into bed. Just as I was drifting off to sleep, the phone rang.

"Quick put on the Tonight Show," Lucky said, "There is a song I want you to hear. This is how I feel, I always will. I need you to know."

I turned on the television to hear Johnny Mathis singing *The Twelfth of Never*.

You ask how much I need you, must I explain
I need you oh my darling, like roses need rain
You ask how long I'll love you, I'll tell you true
Until the twelfth of never, I'll still be loving you

Hold me close, never let me go
Hold me close, melt my heart like April snow

I'll love you till the blue bells forget to bloom
I'll love you till the clover has lost its perfume
I'll love you till the poets run out of rhyme
Until the twelfth of never and that's a long, long time

My heart melted. My husband's clear mind had returned; he was back. Through my tears I whispered,

"I love you Lucky, more than you could ever know. Please come home soon."

The tears soaked my pillow as I fell off to sleep praying that the new medication would help.

Soon after that call he returned home, holding a beautiful long stem red rose in his hands, a constant symbol of our love. The rose graced my table, opening each day to its exquisite beauty and filling the air with its fragrant perfume. He'd given me so many cards and single red roses, but this one stood out. As it opened to its full bloom, it petrified in that state, never wilting, never fully dying. A reminder of our life together, it remains with me still, pressed forever in my heart and in the Bible that preserves it.

For a short time he was stable, yet I sensed the memory of the violent episodes that had threatened my son and me were breaking through into his awareness. The amnesia was lifting. I could see that pain in his eyes but we couldn't speak of it, it was just too horrible. How excruciating that must have been for him, to know that he was causing us harm. There was nowhere to go, no one to help, no solution; just more and more pills.

On Tuesday, March 16, 1976, he made his last visit to the compensation doctor. For some unknown reason this doctor made wisecracks about his symptoms and my being married to him. He insisted that his complaints were all in his head and I was a fool to put up with it. They certainly were in his head but not in the merely psychological way that this very uncaring and brutal doctor was suggesting.

Lucky was not feeling well to begin with and this only caused more anguish. That evening he begged me to call his doctor. That was unusual, as I always had to drag him to the hospital. After a number of blackouts the pain in his head became excruciating and he was not stable on his feet. Lucky told me he was afraid, and that he could not snap out of the depression. He asked to be admitted right away. I again contacted the doctor only to be told that no hospital beds were available and that nothing could be done until the new neurologist saw him. I pleaded, but he said no, his hands were tied.

My final desperate phone call to his doctor that fateful week was devastating. I was crying for help. He said the only avenue left was to commit him to an institution. I gasped in horror: not another institution; he had suffered far too much with that as a child. I didn't tell Lucky about that conversation. Instead we spoke of his going to El Salvador to live in the rain forest. At some level, we both knew that he had to get away from those he loved, before we were severely hurt.

A fantasy at best, but if anyone could have lived that way, it would have been him. My husband would have found a way to help the indigenous people; he would have lived a solitary and primitive life until a stroke or a violent brain episode killed him. I bought the tickets, a round trip for me and one way for Lucky. Plans were being made for Tommy, who had turned eleven by then, to stay with my mother until the heart ripping yet necessary departure day arrived.

But the seizures were too frequent, the confusion and pain too great. During his long sleepless nights he began to see dark hooded figures hovering in a corner watching him. The ghosts of his past also frequented the painful nights. What fear he must have endured during those last days.

March 20, 1976, was the first day of spring. Lucky was very disturbed, in terrible pain. He was drinking far too much alcohol along with the many mind-altering prescriptions. The week had been very hard and we were both exhausted. I was up most nights with him in an effort to ease his fear and anxiety. He was drinking excessively now, in an attempt to escape the physical and psychological pain of his life and wounded spirit, but there was no escape; the alcohol only caused further deterioration, ultimately exacerbating the symptoms and the seizures.

Just a few days before that fateful last night, I returned home from work and found him drunk and staggering. At my wits end I screamed,

"Stop it! You're killing yourself with this alcohol! Why don't you just blow your head off, instead of this slow and agonizing death? "

He was bent over in gripping pain, vomiting as he held his throbbing head. How could I have said such a thing? I didn't mean it, I was so tired and exasperated, and years of caring for him, sometimes at the expense of my son, had left me feeling completely drained and helpless.

There was nothing I could do to stop his agony. I had just wanted to shock him into some kind of reality, make him stop drinking. I helped him into bed, then caressed his beautiful face, until he fell off to sleep.

I had planned a baby shower for my sister that final evening and had to go to my mother's. I felt a terrible uneasiness about leaving him that night, but he said he was going to our neighbors next door and would be all right. I knew, though, that he didn't really want me to go. At that point he never wanted me to be anywhere away from him. I was torn. He monopolized all of my time now, never wanting me to leave his side. It was my hope that he would return from our friends' house and fall asleep, as he had a few nights before after being so distraught. I prayed that the medication would eventually give him some respite from his agony. I was very wrong.

When I returned that evening, Lucky was literally bouncing off the walls, yelling, cursing, and making no sense. He was in the midst of a violent seizure. Tommy had come home from the baby-sitter next door and was asleep upstairs. It was only by the grace of God that this gentle child was spared the sight and sounds of the horror to come.

Coming through the back door into the kitchen, I saw Lucky standing there; the wild look in his eyes terrified me. He was bald now, and I could see the blood coursing through the engorged veins of his head, which rose up from his skin like small ropes. He was frantic, his body was out of control. He tried to move toward me, but inadvertently turned and crashed into the wall. I could not understand what he was shouting; it was incoherent. I rushed for his medication, begging him to try to calm down.

"Please take your pills," I cried. The pain in his head was too loud to let my pleading in.

"Lucky, please take your pills."

He stumbled past me into the dining room, to the hutch,

where a shotgun was kept. I tried with all of my might to grab it from his determined hands. He pushed me away. I rushed towards him again; this time I held on, not letting him push me off. With all of my strength, I tried to pull the gun away. As I clung to him pleading, he loaded the bullets.

"Oh no! Please, not like this."

I screamed about El Salvador, my last and only hope.

"You can go there . . . you can go there . . . it will be okay."

With a swoop, he pushed me off and I landed hard on the floor.

How could my baby still be sleeping? Had he found a way to tune out the pain, the horror we'd been experiencing? I thanked God that he was not seeing this, that he was safe.

Pulling myself up, I ran out through the back door for my neighbor Gilbert, screaming,

"He is going to kill himself. Please come . . . please help me."

As we ran back to the house, Lucky was sitting on the dining room chair in the corner of the room. The barrel of the gun was centered between his eyebrows; his head rested down upon it. Terror gripped every cell and fiber of my being; my heart was pounding, caving in upon itself. I pleaded one more time.

"I love you so, please don't leave me. Things will change, you'll get better, it will be okay."

In my terror and his insanity we both knew I was wrong. It would never get better, and he would rather die than risk hurting us again. Rising up from somewhere deep inside me were the words that he had whispered and written to me a hundred times.

"For time and all eternity, I will love you."

There was nothing more I could do. Gilbert took my place,

standing in front of him, begging.

"I love you man, please don't do this."

In a low and emphatic voice, Lucky replied,

"I just can't take it anymore . . . Don't touch me . . . don't touch me."

I went to the couch in the living room, where I could not see what was about to happen. I was frozen in a timeless moment, waiting for the gun to fire. The prophecy held in his eyes from when we had first met eight years before was unfolding. It seemed like forever, but it was only seconds. I heard muffled sounds, I was sitting on the couch but I was also somewhere else far away. From that place I could see my body so frozen, so scared.

The gun fired and I was transported into a scream, I was only the scream, there was nothing else. In the far distance I heard Gilbert crying and screaming too.

"Oh no . . . Oh no . . . My God no!"

Did I hear him fall to the floor? I am not sure. The gun was firing within my scream, throughout my body. I could not look; I could not see him that way. My beautiful man, my love.

Gilbert came to me splattered with the flesh and blood of my beloved. I heard myself ask,

"Is it over?"

I was still in the scream although it was silent now. It had found its way into me, into every cell. It would live with me for a very long time.

Through my stupor, I saw Tommy run down the stairs. I got to him quickly, before he looked into the dining room. I raced, screaming, "Look at me, look at me."

I covered his face and pulled him into my body. Holding him close we moved away from the view of death and horror.

My precious son and I were cowering on the couch. What seemed like an instant and yet an eternity passed. The police arrived and asked questions that I could not comprehend. It was all very, very loud and at the same time very distant. I seemed to be in more than one place. I was holding and loving my son. I was frozen in a scream and I was hovering somewhere above myself in the distance. It all happened at once. Time was moving yet time was standing still.

The police called a local doctor, telling him of the suicide. They asked him to come immediately, to aid this hysterical, yet frozen young wife and her son. The response to this day rings loud and clear within me. It brought me back to a sense of some reality. The doctor said,

"I don't make house calls."

In that moment I knew that I would have to walk this tragic path alone. I would have to take care of my son and myself. Why did I expect it to be any different? It had always been that way.

The last thing I remember before my brother-in-law Wayne came for us was my son crying,

"Mommy, is it my fault?"

Years of having to tread softly around Lucky had left its mark. My dear child was afraid he had done something to upset him.

"No, no, my baby," I said as I held him close to me,

"Lucky was so afraid that he would hurt us, that he took his own life. He loved us that much."

As I gently spoke those words to him, I asked myself, *Is it my fault?*

Guilt-ridden and demolished I could not possibly foresee that this seemingly insane act by my husband would catapult me on a journey of healing and truth. This horrific tragedy, the darkest time of my life would open a door for great Light. Dreams, visions and miracles would manifest over the next days, weeks, months and even years. They would show me that there was indeed no death but merely a change in form. I would learn that life is a continuum moving us from one dimension into the next. I would come to realize that love never dies; it goes on in all of its beauty and splendor, for once we are joined we remain so forever.

Chapter 2
The Light

Wayne gently drew Tommy and me into the safety of his arms as he led us to his car for the trip back to my mother's house. He kept his eyes steadfast on the road, barely able to look at us. His hands tightly gripped the steering wheel, as if every muscle was choking in a desperate attempt to hold back the emotion. He didn't speak. Tears filled his eyes and although unspoken, I felt his love. Wayne's deep and quiet strength permeated the car as he maneuvered us to my mother's. In that silence, some comfort reached out from him and touched Tommy and me.

As we drove I wondered how it must have been for him to witness that devastating death scene and what he must have been feeling as he stoically drove us to safety. I found out much later that the police had only told him that there had been a shooting. He was terrified as he drove to our home, fearing the worst that Tommy and I had been killed. This one act from my brother-in-law endeared him to me forever.

Was it just a few hours ago that we were all at the baby shower celebrating the upcoming birth of his and my sister's first child? *Joy to tragedy, tragedy to joy.* As I have moved through life, I have seen this all too often: in a flash everything changes. I didn't know then that I would eventually come to a center place where joy and tragedy dance together and become one within me. I would learn to feel the richness of all life's emotions and understand the Divine purpose in all things, love and pain, tragedy and joy. Ram Dass, who would become my beloved teacher, taught me that it is all One. If we embrace the pain it will bring us closer to God.

But this night in my disheveled state I was unaware of the One. I was split within myself, ripped apart. Many levels of consciousness bore down upon me. Some were present in the moment, focused on the headlights of cars speeding by us and the tops of the trees as they reached up into the dark night sky, and some were with my little boy, who seemed smaller now, smaller than he had been just a morning ago. There was one frightening vision of myself plastered against an imaginary wall in my mind, in the frozen place.

Once we were at my mother's, everything started moving quickly. We all sobbed and sobbed. As I began to make calls to those who needed to know, I heard my dearest mother with my son. She held him and let him cry his heart out. *My poor child,* I thought, *how will we ever get through this?* I was feeling a strange pulling in and away, as if I was lost inside myself. Babbling incessantly on the phone, I told the same story over and over, keeping it as simple as I could in an attempt to mask its pain and horror.

As I told the story I was also hearing myself speak it, as if I were in a far away place. But there was one lie: I could not bring myself to tell Lucky's ex-wife and daughters that he had killed himself. Instead I told them it was a massive brain hemorrhage; I wanted to spare them that excruciating pain.

Did I actually think that it would go unnoticed? I was not in my right mind.

I wish I could have held my child all night long, but I was pulling away deep inside myself, into a dark place. Unable to reach out to him or anyone, I had never felt so alone. Sleep swallowed me up. I felt as if I traveled into a dark cave, hearing over and over again the words I would never be able to call back,

Why don't you just blow your head off?

I was plummeting in and down. The words wouldn't give me rest; they pierced through me, tearing at every fiber of my being. My body was spinning and falling until I was pressed up against a cold wall curled into myself. It was a place without light, just darkness, but then a welcome sweet quiet gently laid itself down upon me. Here I could forget what I had said to my lover just a few days before, at least for a little while.

Morning came all too soon. I felt drugged, heavy and thick in my body. Speaking and even breathing took great effort. I still felt strangely detached, as if I was walking on a plane of existence just slightly removed from everyone else. My sister Sharlene guided me, telling me what to do,

"We have to make arrangements," she said.

Numb, I let her bring me to the funeral parlor. On the exterior I seemed calm, but inside it was all so strange. The funeral director led me through the necessary papers and steps, and then he said,

"You need to choose a casket."

As I stood in the doorway that led into the cold casket room, I froze. The scream that now lived inside my body was coming up and I couldn't stop it. It took over. It had a life of its own, ruling mine. It slid up from the deepest part of my belly, burning my chest as it moved and then exploded out of my throat.

"No! . . . No! . . . I can't do this!" They want me to pick a box my lover will look good in. Are they crazy?

"No!" . . . I felt wedged there in the door, unable to move. My shaken, young, and very pregnant sister was at my side trying to hold me up. Everything was buckling underneath me.

"No!" . . . I screamed, "I can't go in there!"

Then from somewhere else within me, a place deeper and wiser than the scream came another voice. I heard myself begin to pray, calling out like a frightened child, lost in the thick dark woods, without light.

"God, please help me, please, I can't do this."

My mother had always taught me never to pray for myself, just for others. All of my life I had done that. Even as a child wishing on the first star I had to wish for another, not myself.

But here was the plea, finally,

"Lord, here I am, please help me."

The moment I said that, Light began to fill the casket room. It appeared close to the ceiling, hovering for a moment as my eyes adjusted to its Presence. It was a soft white, silvery mist that slowly swirled and moved, making its way down toward the floor. As I watched, it began to move out in front of me, creating a path of silver white light for me to follow. I felt a beckoning, and a quiet peace enveloped me. It seemed to lead me by the hand. The path of light moved beyond the first room that was filled with caskets of many colors, designs and sizes, caskets that too many broken-hearted would have to choose. The Light drew me into an adjacent room where, against the wall, stood a beautiful pale blue casket. It shimmered as I reached out my hand to touch it. From my mesmerized state, I finally spoke.

"This is it, he will rest in here."

As Sharlene and I left the funeral parlor, a strange thing

occurred. Dark, ominous clouds came billowing in from the north. Then suddenly without warning, the wind rushed in and whipped around us, nearly knocking us over as it stole our breath away. The sky was tumultuous, dark gray with groaning, rumbling thunder. I felt as if it were speaking to me. Sharlene and I were both captured by it and stunned. We turned and looked at one another and said in tandem,

"Lucky?"

As quickly as the clouds came, they parted, leaving a bright and beautiful sun that warmed us. A very odd and rapid storm disturbance had quickly moved through the town. It was mysterious, yet in an odd way comforting. We both felt something or someone was watching over us.

Calls were made to the local church, and to my horror the priest refused to do a blessing.

"A suicide does not deserve a church service." His words shocked us.

In the midst of all of this pain how could the church fail us? I was beside myself, aghast at being treated in such a cruel manner. I rummaged through my mind, trying to think of some way that Lucky could be honored. And then the memory of a dear and precious Monsignor came to mind.

Of course, I thought, that was it: the beautiful red church in a town called West End, just a short distance from our home. I had gone there often to pray. The large, stunning, white statue of Saint Michael that graced the front lawn always beckoned me to enter.

I called Monsignor Bradley. This robust, outspoken former Marine was the most loved and honored of all parish priests. As I cried to him and shared all that had happened, he calmed me with his loving and kind words.

"You bring your husband to me. I will take care of him."

My heart swelled with gratitude.

In our deep talks about death, Lucky had asked me to remember him with one red rose, as he had remembered me so often. The single red rose had become our touchstone. It whispered,

"For time and all eternity."

At the viewing I placed my one red rose in his hands and kissed his restructured, unfamiliar face goodbye. His gravestone would hold the symbol of the rose, our love etched in stone forever.

The church was packed to overflowing. To this day I still hold the picture in my mind of Tommy and me walking slowly down the very long aisle of the church, following the slow-moving casket. I look back upon that scene, remembering the young widow that I was and my courageous young son with such tenderness. No one should have to take that walk, not at such a young age. Yet the walk claimed us.

Standing at the altar, filled with genuine caring and love, was the Monsignor. His steady gaze drew me forward and at thirty-one years of age I took my place as the widow. I was captured by his words. He did not know Lucky personally yet had made it his business to find out about his life so he could honor him. Monsignor Bradley spoke of our loss, our love, the pain of separation and the forgiveness of Christ. He uttered words that would stay with me forever.

"This is a man who never condemned."

As he spoke those words, memories surfaced of Lucky helping the abused and downtrodden as he so often had done. It was as if the Monsignor reached deep into my heart and touched the essence of Lucky, the part that I loved the most. I would be eternally grateful.

A statue of Saint Michael watched over him at the cemetery. Saint Michael, Lucky and I would spend many hours there. *For time and all eternity* was inscribed at the base of the stone, close to his resting heart.

At least I thought he was resting.

I was wrong.

Chapter 3
Phenomena

It was nearly impossible to get through the customary pleasantries of the death reception. Food, coffee and cakes—was I really expected to eat? I had just buried my husband. I was demolished and others were eating cake. Oh be sure many times would come when I would submerge myself in chocolate and creamy substances, in an attempt to deaden the pain. But this was not one of those times. How odd it all seemed. Another wonderful friend also named Gail had offered her home for this event, and I was grateful beyond words. Nevertheless, I was bewildered as I watched people milling around, telling stories and laughing. How could they laugh?

My eyes fell upon my sweet son as he played pool with John, our host. I watched my boy standing at the pool table. The pool stick quivered in his hands just as John was about to shoot. On his face was a mischievous grin reminiscent of the one Lucky wore when he devilishly played pool. He had spent many hours watching Lucky play pool and though not his biological son, Tommy had been shaped by Lucky.

When playing pool, Lucky would deliberately throw his opponent off focus, quivering the pool stick just as he was about to make his shot. I had seen that so many times. Lucky would always win. He would distract his rival and then laugh uproariously when the shot was missed. All in good fun, but what a devil he was!

And now here was Tommy with that look on his face, playful and yet determined. It was as if Lucky was right there, conducting this competitive performance.

The moment stood out, like a child's pop-up book, a scene or character moving out in front of the rest as you turned the page. It demanded your full attention. Everything else faded away. My eleven-year-old was standing there in his power, just like Lucky had done. Strength, cleverness and sheer will seeped out of his pores.

Running through my mind was the song, *And When I Die,* sung by Blood, Sweat and Tears. It was a song that Lucky loved, one that he often sang.

I'm not scared of dying and I don't really care
For if it's peace you find in dying Lord
Then let the time be near...

And when I die, and when I'm gone
There will be one child born in this world
To carry on

As the lyrics moved through me they brought a calm feeling. I felt Lucky whisper to me. *This is the child I meant. He is mine, he is strong, I have loved him and I have molded him. You needn't worry.*

Feeling this I was able to excuse myself from this gathering of loved ones. Lucky's words assured me that my child, his stepson, would be all right.

I escaped into Gail's bedroom for what I thought would be just a short rest. As I laid my head down upon the pillow the remainder of the song ran through me.

Give me my freedom for as long as I live
All I ask of living is it have no chains on me
And all I ask of dying is to go naturally
I want to go naturally

"Dear Lord," I prayed, "Why did it have to be like this, so violent? Please watch over him. And Lucky, please watch over Tommy."

I fell once again into the deep dark oblivion of welcoming sleep. My dear friends John and Gail gave up their bed and I slept for nearly twenty hours. A gentle energy enveloped and held me.

Gail brought me home the following day. My steps going into the house were cautious, tiny baby steps. I held onto the walls, bracing myself for what, I didn't quite know. The last time I had come through this backdoor my husband was literally bouncing off the walls in anguish and pain. Now I was trembling, fearing I might find a piece of his flesh or bone. The thought terrorized and gripped me. Gail stayed close, not knowing what to say, but watched my every step.

Moving through the dining room I saw that everything was bright, clean and freshly painted. The chair where I had last seen and touched my beloved was moved from the corner, where it had sat for many years. It was as if nothing had occurred. I only wished that it could be that easy.

Steadying myself, I cautiously stepped toward the living room. My body felt like it was braced in steel. A frightened breath was suspended somewhere in the contracted tissues of my form. Perhaps the held breath shared temporary occupancy with the now-in-residence scream. Those few steps seemed like an eternity. Once in the living room, I fell onto the couch and released the tight breath, and allowed a deep full one to fill me. My body softened.

Looking back at this, it is amazing that I received no professional help, counseling, or medical care. I was teetering on the edge of this world, and on another one surely off center. But perhaps if I had been medicated I would not have experienced the wondrous phenomena. There *is* Divine Order in the midst of great tragedy.

For a few days I just wept, holding tightly on to myself as an excruciating pain ripped through my belly and heart. Music became my ally; the love songs on the soft rock station helped me to sob as I called out to my lover. Many questions were bleeding through me.

While washing dishes one afternoon, I was weeping and singing to Jim Croce's *Time in a Bottle* when the music from the living room stereo abruptly changed. *What is this country music?* I thought. *It doesn't seem to fit with this station.* I went to the stereo. To my amazement, the dial was on a different channel, far from my favorite 92.

What's going on? I moved the tuner all the way back to my favorite station and returned to the dishes.

A brief moment passed. My hands were soapy and wet, and

I was beginning to sing a new song, when the music changed to country again. *Whoa!* . . . I thought, *this is much too weird. What's happening?* I dashed back to the stereo. Again the dial was set on the country station. As I moved it slowly back, it hit me: *Oh my God, this is Lucky, this is his favorite station! But how impossible is that? Quite preposterous,* I thought, *it must be some quirk with the equipment. Yes, that's it. I will take the stereo to be repaired. Settled.*

I hadn't made it around the corner when it happened again. This time I giggled, for the mischievous grinning energy was with me.

Stopped in my tracks in the dining room, I felt the energy begin to wrap all around me. The feeling was intense and warm, yet chills ran through my body. My heart was beating wildly, as if it were leaping within itself.

"Oh, it is you." I felt him for a moment as he washed over me. More than anything, I wanted to touch him.

"Where are you? . . . I can feel it . . . I can feel you."

His love and playfulness were fully present, as when he had been well. Around and around I turned in the middle of the dining room. Joyful tears streamed down my face as my hands reached out hoping that I would feel something tangible, something I could hold onto. But there was only air.

I was experiencing a strange yet exhilarating heightened state. Every hair on my body was raised.

"It is you." My heart cried out to him. "I love you so!"

I wanted to hold him to me and sink into the safety of his strong arms. Stopped in the moment, by our love, I let it soak in. It filled me completely.

"All right you're here, but where? I can't see you, I can only feel you."

For a long time I just sat in amazement on the dining room floor, absorbing the sensation.

"Where are you?" I cried out again. "Are you okay?" With that the excruciating pain of his loss returned.

"I am so sorry for what I said, please forgive me." Sobs overtook me as I sputtered out the words. "I didn't want you to die; I didn't want you to leave me."

It was then that I felt a soft brush against my cheek, almost like a breeze, warm and gentle. My eyes shifted right then left. I turned my head in the hope that I would catch a glimpse of him. I knew he was with me, I just couldn't see him. I rested in his love for a very long time, until the feeling eventually faded.

Not knowing what to do next, I began to pray.

"What do I do now Lord? What do I do with all of this?"

Impressed upon me was the word, *Write.*

That day and in the days that followed, poetry and stories spilled out of me, speaking of my great sorrow. I wrote endless letters to him.

"Where are you?" I'd ask, looking up from the tear-stained pages of letters his physical eyes would never see. "Please come back to me. Let me know you're all right."

And then, within my despair and my longing, I remembered our promise, the last words, along with "I love you," that I had heard just before he died.

For time and all eternity.

Love never dies. Lucky was here with me. He had not left.

Chapter 4
Visitations

Time waits for no one; life continues to move forward, coaxing, pulling or screaming at you to step ahead.

Reluctantly and through necessity I returned to my job at the high school. I was merely going through the motions in an attempt to survive the day. Looking directly at anyone was impossible. I was afraid they would ask me something about Lucky's death. Since I was just barely holding it together, speaking about the trauma was simply out of the question. I would smile at well-wishers, but avert my gaze so as not to encourage any deep conversation.

One afternoon I was cornered in the teacher's lounge. A colleague approached me just as I was collecting my mail from the little cubby in the wall. I felt him coming, but was unable to escape. My head was down as I shuffled through the papers in the cubby. I thought, *if I just stay fixed here looking at this hole in the wall, maybe he will leave.*

But the voice broke through my concentration as Harry said, "I'm so sorry to hear about your husband. How did he die?"

Here it was: the question that most terrified me. Up until that moment the word suicide was unable to make its way out of my mouth. But now the moment trapped me.

Standing there in self-imposed stupor, I heard Margo, the drama teacher, utter a slow groan, and just under her breath the words,

"Oh no."

She apparently felt my discomfort, my nervousness.

As I stammered, it felt like everyone backed up just a bit. Perhaps I was feeling their energy move away from the place of terrible pain.

The word squeezed itself up and through the tight canal at the back of my throat. I could feel the inner mechanism trying to hold it in place. Yet it slid forward, over my tongue and finally birthed into the air,

"Suicide," I said. It seemed so loud, like clanging bells that bounced off the walls as they rang through the small room. Everyone waited.

My poor colleague cringed at the word, and a shudder ran through his body. Yet, he persisted.

"I am so sorry, how?"

Everyone backed away a little more. Now it was much too hard to handle.

I felt very small in that moment, like a little child craving a loving touch. I needed someone to rescue me out of the question, but no one stepped forward.

Ignoring him, I pulled further into myself, slinked out of the teacher's room, and moved back to class. The word had made its way out of my body for the first time. Years would pass however, before I could say "suicide" without my throat squeezing in upon itself, and my stomach and heart turning into a vicious vice.

For the next three months, until the end of the school year, I went through the motions of teaching, praying that the students were receiving something of value. However, I surely doubted it. I was a mess.

Home wasn't much different; I found that I couldn't cook dinners. Since he was unable to work, Lucky had prepared most of the meals. For some crazy reason cooking just made me cry even more, so Tommy and I spent nearly every night at the local diner. Vacantly we looked at each other over our meals. Very little was said now about the trauma. Some pleasantries were shared and school questions were answered, but an invisible barrier kept us apart. We each formed protective walls around ourselves. How horribly sad that was. Tommy turned to weight lifting, building muscles hard and strong to protect his delicate heart. I would find another way.

There were endless cups of coffee, too many cigarettes, and a young boy itching to go home while his mother sat looking into the distance, seeing nothing.

It was just as hard to be in the house. Aimlessly I walked from room to room. There was no respite from the anxiousness, unless I was writing. Then the emotions poured out. They found a place of belonging on the tear-stained pages.

One night, having finished yet another letter to my husband, I fell exhausted into bed. Sleep started to invite me in when I felt a strange pressure beside me. Someone had sat down right next to me. Startled at first, my heart began to race, but soon I knew it was Lucky. The gentle brush on my face spoke to me.

I felt his warmth, his kiss, and his tender caress. He was close to me; the feeling moved over my body, from my toes up, and caught in my throat until an expanded breath opened me fully to his love. It felt like an electrical charge; invisible energy giving me comfort and strength. Through my tears, I loved him right back. The energy coming from him was warm, beautiful, and real. We were completely present with one another.

"Please don't leave me," I said, "stay. I am so lonely and I miss you so." But the energy faded.

While in this experience, and in the many others like it that followed, I knew he was with me. There was no doubt in my mind. But in my normal consciousness, if there was such a thing, I began to question myself. Was I crazy? Since I wasn't sharing any of the bizarre occurrences, there was no one to give me a reality check. My close friends and family, though supportive in many ways, could not broach the subject of Lucky's death. It was just too painful and too hard for everyone. Protecting them from discomfort and from the fear they would feel if they believed I was coming unhinged, I kept it all to myself. Suicide is the most difficult of all transitions. No one knows what to say or what to do.

Am I crazy? The thought swirled through my mind. I made it through the work day, buoyed by the thought that he might come to me again in the night. More and more letters were written.

"Please show me where you are. Are you all right?"

To my amazement, he came one night just as I was about to fall off to sleep. This time, I had a visual impression of him. He swooped me up and out of our bed. Holding me in his strong and capable arms, he carried me off. We moved over plains, golden tan in color, almost like rolling hills, but more like clouds. These unusual clouds had color and texture, like nothing I had ever seen before. I knew I was still lying on the bed, but I was also with my husband. I didn't understand out of body experiences then, but it was most certainly that.

He brought me to a vast construction site where he was building something quite grand. Lucky was extraordinarily happy and proud to show me his work. Continuing to hold me he brought me to the massive cranes and dock building equipment. He was ecstatic! We were aware of each other's thoughts. There was no need to speak in the customary way; our minds were joined.

Before I knew it, my spirit body was returned to the bed and only a faint sense of him remained. I lay there for a long time, astonished and grateful. I thanked God over and over for letting me know my husband was safe.

But after the exhilaration passed, the nagging and frightening question returned.

Am I crazy? This can't be real. Please Lord help me with this.

My prayers were soon answered. God found a wonderful way to show me the truth.

Just a few days passed when a call came from Lucky's ex-wife Arlene, with her two daughters Karen and Laura close by her and joining in. Reluctantly, and with some trepidation in her voice, Arlene began,

"The other night, while I was sleeping, a loud noise downstairs woke me up. I went down, afraid, you know, and what I saw, I still can't believe it, was Lucky. I saw him clearly, Karla, as if he were alive! He was sitting in the chair smiling. I rushed to the chair. We spoke about the girls and then just as I reached out my hand to touch him, he vanished."

This was sweet music to my ears. Silently I sent out a new prayer.

Thank you God for helping me with my doubt. Oh dear Lord, I'm not crazy.

My attention returned to Arlene.

"You have no idea how much this means to me. I have been experiencing him too. How fortunate that you actually saw him. I can hear him and feel him. And from a place deep within me I see his spiritual body. Did he seem okay to you?"

"Oh yes," she responded with sort of a chuckle. "He had that mischievous grin on his face."

A long awaited sense of wondrous relief moved through me.

His daughter Laura got on the line then and told me that he visited her in dreams. The dreams would seem to last all night long. I knew then that he was helping all of us from the other side.

Over the years, through the dream state, Lucky has revealed his deep soul work to me. His words to his daughters, Karen and Laura, to Tommy, and to me have always carried the same message.

"I did not die. I am still with you, and I love you."

He has assured me that he has been with Christ, yet continues to stay close, to be of service to us.

This is not to romanticize suicide in any way. Those that are left behind experience pain that is at times beyond unbearable. It is to assure us that God watches over all His children. Those that have passed on, no matter what the circumstance, continue their soul's evolution. We are all deeply loved, we are never condemned.

Chapter 5
For Time and All Eternity

The scream found its way out. At unexpected times, with very little provocation, the bubbling inferno would rise. Often it erupted while I was in the kitchen. Lifting my head up and back I was like a howling she-wolf serenading the sky. But unlike the wolf's howl, my screech had no song, just a long, sustained and shrill release.

Once after one of those welcome bellows, I looked out the window and saw, to my horror and embarrassment, my neighbor watching. I'm sure she didn't know if she should call the police or the men in the white coats to take me away. My poor neighbors, what it must have been like for them to witness the wild woman I had become.

I ran next door and approached my unsure friend.

"Anna Mae, I'm so sorry that I scared you. I'm just trying to release the terrible tension in my body. Please don't be concerned. It's much better out than in."

Her eyes wet with tears, she placed her arm around my shoulder and said,

"I am so sorry, Karla. Is there anything I can do for you?"

"Just know that I am all right," I lied. "I am afraid that I can't stop the screaming. You see, it has a mind of its own. It just comes out at the craziest times. I feel much better after. Please don't worry about me."

"All right," she said hesitantly. I could hear the concern in her voice, but she continued. "Then I'll be happy for you when you're rattling the windows. I'll warn Joe and the kids too."

"Thanks, Anna Mae." My thoughts moved to Tommy. Oh no, now his best friend Paul would know that his mom was nuts. It was bad enough that he had to witness my craziness.

Once back in the house, I was able to grin just a little as I imagined what I must have looked like.

I managed through the school day and spent most afternoons at the cemetery, talking to God, Saint Michael and Lucky. My back resting against the cold concrete, I held a single red rose to my heart. Countless roses lay against the stone, marking our love.

The weeks turned into months and soon school was out. I still spent the nights weeping, tears soaking the T-shirt that I held close. I prayed that my tears would not wash away Lucky's scent. I needed it still. I clung to it as to a life raft. Memories transported me to happier times before he had been injured. I recalled our first night of love.

We frequently visited the pub that was just below his apartment. He had been pursuing me for some time and this evening he was determined to bring me to his bed.

"No," I insisted as we sat at the corner of the bar.

Since the outside door to his apartment was barricaded, the only way to get there was through the door across the dance hall.

"No," I repeated. "People will see and know where we're going."

"Oh sweet prim and proper Doris," he teased with his favorite nickname for me. "They don't care."

"No, I can't do that."

But then he had an idea. "Come on, we'll go outside."

"Why?" I asked.

"You'll see." I thought he had a plan to get through the blocked exterior door.

But when the mischievous grin emerged on his handsome face, I knew he was up to something devilish.

Out we went, assuming that our secret conversation had not been heard.

He brought me to the side of the building, where a huge sprawling tree sat just under his apartment window.

"Oh no! You're crazy, I can't get up there."

"Oh yes you can, Doris, watch me." Up he climbed, laughing as he went.

"Come on," he shouted. "Grab my hand, I'll pull you up."

There I stood, gazing at this crazy and beautiful man. Before I could protest, my arm involuntarily shot up to reach him. Caught in the moment, I let him lift me off the ground.

I was dangling in the air by one arm screaming, "I'm going to fall," when I heard laughter and applause. All his comrades had come out to cheer us on. There was nothing left to do but finish the climb.

With a quick and steady pull he had me up and balanced in the tree. He maneuvered us with ease to the roof and through the window.

Laughing uncontrollably, we fell into one another. Tenderly we transported each other that night into worlds new yet somehow remembered. It was clear to us that we had loved each other for what felt like forever. Lying in his strong arms, I gazed into his light blue eyes,

"All of my life, I have been looking for your face," he whispered. With tears in his eyes, his hand gently brushed across my cheek.

"Please Lucky, don't ever leave me. I have waited for you for so long."

"Never, Doris, I will be with you always. For time and all eternity, I promise."

With a deep sigh, I rested into him. We had finally found home in each other's arms.

Throughout our lives we had felt that deep longing, knowing that a piece of us was missing. But now we were together, our souls joined once again. Our love and our destiny culminated in that wondrous moment.

As I came out of my reverie, the words he had spoken tumbled over and over in my mind. *Who could ever take his place? No one.* Holding tightly to his fragrant T-shirt I fell off to sleep.

The evening visitations were becoming less frequent, so I lost myself in the love songs of the time. As I sang, I felt my song reach out into eternity and at times I heard *his* song, *The Twelfth of Never*, return. In those moments I was torn between wanting to hold him close to me and feeling that he might need to move on. To what and to where I was not sure. I missed him so very much; the longing was indescribable.

What could I do to ease this? First, I could get out of the house; I had been glued there. Then the thought came: *Go shopping, that will help.* Grabbing an outfit from the closet, unaware if it even matched, I made it out the door. Little did I know what was waiting for me at the mall.

Roaming through a department store, I fingered the items, soft, sweet and sexy things that Lucky would have bought for me, but I was unable to make any decisions. The stress of being in close quarters with the crowd of people was agitating. I felt myself start to percolate.

Oh no! The familiar rumbling was forming in my belly. It shook me side to side and then back and forth. My body felt like an old wringer washing machine with clothes lumped unevenly on one side ready to go tilt. I held on to the counter for support.

The scream was following its familiar route, up into my chest where it felt like it might explode, annihilating my heart. *I have to get out of here!*

My rocking stance became a hurried walk. I charged past fellow customers, apologizing as I nearly knocked them and their packages over. Soon I was on a mad dash for the door.

"Oh, God, help me." The force of the scream was at the back of my throat. Could I get out and to my car in time? No, it was too far away. Where could I go?

I ran as if my life depended upon it. As I bolted through the glass doors, past the alarmed shoppers, I saw it: a telephone booth just a few feet away. Without forethought, I raced to it and threw open the door. I was like Clark Kent about to spin my way into the garb and form of Superman. But unlike Superman, I was the Wild Woman. As I held on to the phone counter my head rose and the scream burst forth. Ah, what exhilarating relief it brought. My head dropped back down and a deep breath escaped from my body.

Approaching shoppers stopped dead in their tracks and then immediately backed up. This time, right beneath the outburst, there was a chuckle. Without a second thought I brushed myself off, shook my head and tossed my hair back. Smiling at the onlookers as if a person screaming inside a phone booth was completely normal, I exited.

Acknowledging shoppers in my path with a grinning nod, I walked deliberately and with a demeanor of great accomplishment to my car. Once there, laughter overtook me. The moment was like a wacky cartoon. Finally there was some humor in my insanity.

The scream became my ally. After each subsequent release I would envision myself in the phone booth and laugh. In some crazy way it was helping me become the wild, transformed superwoman who could surmount anything. I just prayed that I could get to the car or a phone booth in time.

As I was becoming acquainted with the scream and its wild ways, my dearest friend Gail, who had introduced me to Lucky, invited me to a holiday party. Still rooted in the house, I begged off.

"Please come," she implored, "It will do you good. You have to get out. There will be lots of nice people and delicious food. Bring Tommy and stay the night."

Oh great, lots of people, I thought. *What if the volcano decides to release and I can't get away? I'll be doomed.*

"Gail, I'm not sure if I'm ready. I'll let you know."

As if reading my thoughts, she insisted.

"Come on, Karla, the party is downstairs and outside. You can go into the house if you need to get away, and besides, Jennifer would love to see Tommy."

I agreed reluctantly. Gail had loved Lucky too and knew how hard this was for me.

Okay Karla, come on, I bolstered myself, *pull yourself together. You can handle a little party.*

As I dressed to go, I gazed into the mirror. The shining look that Lucky loved so much had changed. Once it was fresh and vibrant, with a smile that lit up my whole face and caused my eyes to dance.

"My dearest Doris," he fondly called me, referring to the wholesome girl-next-door look of Doris Day. No Doris, but a wild, howling, crazy woman with dead eyes stared back at me. With a shudder I reached for the makeup. I did my best to sparkle my face with blush and lighten my shadowed eyes. The smile however was reluctant to make its appearance. Doris was gone.

With Tommy at my side, I drove to the party. The house was near the ocean, and the scent of the sea was in the air. I breathed it deeply into my lungs, hoping it would energize me. It was a bright and sunny day and everyone was in good spirits, except me. The thought that no one here knew of my tragedy was helpful. At least I wouldn't be asked uncomfortable questions. Gathering my nerve, I joined the party.

Pushing myself into the festivities, I began to drink. One glass of wine after another was making me a bit tipsy. I had lost so much weight that my tolerance to alcohol was low. *Perhaps it will numb me a bit*, I thought.

While standing at the buffet table my eyes fell upon a man just across the room. I was taken aback at the sight of him. His resemblance to Lucky was astonishing; he was tall, blonde, tan and handsome and seemed very self assured. Seeing my gaze, he made his way toward me through the crowd. Gail stepped forward and introduced us.

"Karla, this is Joe. I met him through his mother Mildred. She comes to my salon."

"Oh," I stammered. "It's nice to meet you, Joe."

He apparently felt my nervousness and asked,

"Can I get you a drink?" Certainly not what I needed, but I nodded yes.

To my dismay, Gail left us to return to her other friends. Holding the drink tightly in my sweating hands, I tried to listen to what he was saying. But I couldn't get my mind off his uncanny resemblance to Lucky. For a moment I wanted to reach up and caress his face. Quickly gathering my wits about me, I mumbled,

"Will you excuse me? I have to check on my son."

I made a quick departure to the other side of the large room.

Tommy and Jennifer were playing with a prizefighter who had been invited to the party. He seemed a bit odd, but Gail assured me that he was fine. The kids were having a great time getting their picture taken with this so-called famous character. Seeing Tommy was all right, I milled around, attempting to be sociable with the other guests and doing my best to avoid Joe, but to no avail.

"Your son okay?" he asked with a twinkle in his eyes.

"Oh yes, he's fine."

Joe told me he had been a college professor once but had escaped the dark halls of academia for a life in the sun. He was a professional lifeguard, and, as he termed it, a "leisure-cologist." He made sure I knew he had coined the phrase. A marathon runner, he traveled the country attempting to break his own best race time. *What a life,* I thought. *Is he for real?*

The hours passed and I found myself relaxing in the presence of this very blonde and tanned leisure-cologist. He had a gift for good conversation and when it came to the wine, he was no slouch.

"How can you survive on just a lifeguard's salary?" I boldly asked.

"Oh I bartend too, and I've made some very good stock investments. I do just fine."

We laughed as I shared some of my funny stories from the amazing kids I was teaching. At one point he looked at my wedding ring and asked,

"Where is your husband?"

My eyes dropped away from his and my body shifted nervously. He caught that movement and said,

"I'm sorry, it's none of my business."

"No, it's okay, he died some months ago."

"I am very sorry. You don't have to talk about it if you don't want to."

As I thanked him, his hand came up to the side of my face and brushed across it ever so gently. As our eyes met I felt my knees begin to weaken. The tightly held drink nearly dropped out of my hands.

How could he know that gesture was the way to melt my heart?

"I have to go," I blurted out.

"No, stay, let's talk some more."

He persuaded me and placed a small kiss on my cheek. I didn't know if it was the wine or his presence that caused me to flush.

My mind began to race. *This is not right; I have to get out of here.* Tommy was upstairs sleeping and the party was breaking up. I needed to escape. Yet I was strangely attracted to him.

"Come to my house for a night cap." His words broke through my confused thoughts.

"Oh no, I couldn't, I'm visiting Gail."

Gail, standing nearby, overheard and called out,

"No, that's fine, you go ahead, I'll see you later."

Oh my God, what am I doing? I thought, as I walked with him to the van.

"It's just a short distance," he said, "I have a small cabin tucked away in the hills, you'll like it."

With a lump in my throat I sank into the seat. A mixture

of fear and anticipation filled me. I wanted to be with this stranger, but for the life of me I didn't know why. It had taken Lucky weeks of persuasion and here I was going home with this man on the first night. Oh Lord, where was prim and proper Doris when I really needed her?

No sooner did we get into the house, when he wrapped his arms around me. I sank into them. Real and tangible warmth enfolded me. Feeling very safe in his strong arms I succumbed and let him take me into his bed.

Lucky's gold chains and Saint Michael medal hung heavily on my bare chest, tangled in my necklace and cross. I touched these reminders of our undying love, then looked up into Joe's eyes. They were no longer his. It was Lucky there with me. I kissed and caressed his eyes, his face, his hands and fingertips. As he responded, I lost myself in him and our souls danced together once again. In those moments I felt that I was being given a last chance to feel my dearest husband and say goodbye. Tears of sadness and joy streamed down my face as our bodies joined. I whispered endearing words under my breath to my beloved,

"For time and all eternity I will love you, just you."

It was an endless night filled with tenderness and passion that only the deepest and most abiding of lovers could ever hope to share. Intertwined in one another, we fell into a deep sleep.

When we woke, Joe reached for me.

"I have never felt anything like this before. "He was astonished, as he asked, "What was that?"

Clearly shattering his mood, I stammered, "I don't know, I'm sorry. I have to go." I quickly covered myself with my clothes and rushed out of the bedroom.

"Can I have your phone number?" he called.

I felt like a woman of the night as I yelled out my number

and slammed the door behind me.

I sped back to Gail's, hoping I would arrive before everyone woke. I was embarrassed and ashamed, yet knew that something very powerful had happened. Here was another experience that I would have to keep inside myself. Who would understand such things? I wasn't sure that I understood. So with a mixture of embarrassment and joy, I slinked into the house.

Joe called the following day. "When can I see you?"

"I'm sorry, Joe; this is just too much for me right now. It's too soon. I need time to think."

"All right." I could hear the disappointment in his voice.

"I'll get back to you Joe. I promise."

I didn't get back to him. Emotionally I was on a roller coaster ride. Unsure of how I should feel after being with this man, I obsessed. The question would raise its shameful head. *Shouldn't I be feeling guilty? Wasn't it wrong?* Yet it was clear that it was Lucky who made love to me that night. How, I didn't know, but I was certain.

One evening, while in that obsessive state, a comforting peace came over me. It urged me to rest into it. As I sighed deeply, releasing the pent-up obsessive energy, I felt Lucky's reassurance. I sank into his presence and let his love envelop me. He was whispering that it was okay. I was unsure of what to make of it all, but knew that I was not ready to even consider seeing the lifeguard again. Putting that evening with Joe out of my mind, I moved back into the school groove, keeping busy with the normal details of classes and chores.

Two weeks after that fateful night with Joe I was returning home from work laden with papers to grade and bags of groceries. As I made my way from the car to the door, I heard the phone ringing. Fumbling with the keys I rushed into the house. The bags of groceries and papers dropped from my arms, their contents spilling everywhere. Oranges flew out of their protective plastic and hazardously rolled around on the freshly waxed floor. Nearly tripping, I grabbed the counter for support as my feet almost went out from under me. I made it through the orange obstacle course to the insistent ringing. Clinging to the counter and out of breath I grabbed the phone and yelled in frustration,

"Hello!"

"Has it been enough time?" A somewhat familiar voice questioned without the usual and normal salutation.

I was caught off guard, but then recognized Joe's voice. A laugh escaped, and before I had time to censor my words I heard myself say,

"Yes."

Oops . . . the word had flown out of my unguarded mouth. Too late now, I thought.

Our conversation was quick and easy and before I knew it I had agreed to attend a party at the infamous cabin in the hills. I actually felt like a silly schoolgirl. A new excitement was finding its way into my long-standing depression. A smile even found its way to my drawn face.

My life changed dramatically after that call. It felt like a hand had reached down into the dark pit where I had been hiding. It pulled me up and out, at least partially. The tremendous grief was still there, but now there were moments of respite. Joe was a party man; existence for him was about fun and he was inviting me to join him.

Up until that point my life had been about shouldering the burdens of others. It began with caring for a handicapped mother and going to work at twelve-years-old to help support our broken family. From there I entered a very troubled first marriage where the main goal was survival. I became a mom at the tender age of nineteen, yet even that joy was tainted. After a tumultuous divorce, I spent years working long hours just to survive as a single parent. There wasn't nearly enough time with Tommy. Add in those last few horrific years with Lucky, when he was in the worst depths of the illness and despair, and it made sense that I felt disintegrated.

Would I even know how to have fun?

So I allowed myself to be with Joe, and for a few years we played. I spent summers on the beach clad in teeny bikinis. When you're the lifeguard captain's girlfriend you must dress the part, and I did it quite well. Doris was gone and in her place was a sexy, tanned blonde. I grieved the loss of Doris. No one knew as I sat on my beach chair writing, glistening with suntan oil and smiling, that I was in mourning. I wrote endless poetry about the loss of my husband and the devastation of myself. I was able to hide the deep pain from others as long as I could be the scribe. Never did I share those words. I was living two separate lives.

There were constant parties at Joe's cabin, trips all over the country to marathons, and visits to Florida in the winter. I made new friends, friends who didn't know of my tragic past. Joe was also the resident lifeguard and bartender at an exclusive resort in Hobe Sound, Florida. There he hobnobbed with society's blue blood. He conjured up the best drinks in town and shared jokes with the millionaires. He had found a way to squeeze the best out of life. Always following the sun, he lived at the Jersey Shore in summer and Florida in winter. Joe's personal motto *carpe diem* (seize the day) was the antithesis of Lucky's, "He ain't heavy, he's my brother." But it worked for me, for awhile.

I still spent many nights at home in agonizing tears, but weekends brought a welcome relief. I needed to be with someone. More than anything, I ached to be held; it eased the tremendous pain. I could forget for a little while. It helped me put some of the deeper grief and shock that was anchored in my cells on hold.

Lovemaking between Joe and I never reached the heights of our first encounter. Little did he know that first night that I was not with him, but with my Lucky. Years later when he questioned me about it, I told him that he had been a proxy. To my great amazement he seemed to understand.

I have since learned that a spirit hovering close to the earth can enter another when there has been a soul agreement. Having a high degree of alcohol in the system also helps. Joe could consume a tremendous amount, yet still seemed to be unruffled and in full charge of his faculties. In spite of his idiosyncrasies, he was good for me at that time. He had pulled me up out of the darkness and taught me how to enjoy life. He was my friend and gentle lover. Unbeknownst to both of us, this party man would also become an unlikely but important teacher on my path to spiritual awakening. Yet it would be this very path that would ultimately move me away from him.

Chapter 6
A Great Miracle

In late fall of 1976, I suffered a terrible injury. Late for an appointment with a friend, I flew out the door, running into the road instead of the sidewalk. Why had I run into the street? Destiny was about to say "hello" again.

My left foot turned as I landed hard in a pothole. Down I went in the middle of the road.

"Yowsa!" I yelled out, thinking that I had sprained my ankle. It turned out to be far worse.

Limping back into the house, I felt an odd piercing pain shoot from my lower back all the way down my left leg. "Oh God, what's this? Ow! Ow! Ow!" I screeched out with each step. *Okay, Karla, calm down,* I instructed myself. *You just turned your foot; you'll be all right.* Settling in on the couch, I gathered my thoughts about me. *Just breathe.* After a short time, the pain began to lessen.

But not for long. As I made my way through the next few school days it sharpened. Each day my body was leaning a little more forward in an attempt to bargain with the pain. Standing up straight took my breath away. Barely making it home one afternoon from school, I entered the house and collapsed on the living room floor. *Oh, God,* my thoughts went to Tommy. *Poor kid, he's going to come home and find me lying here. What next?* I thought. *He must be so exasperated with my wild moods, depression and time away with Joe. And now he'll find me flat out on the floor.*

What now, Lord? What's happening? Any slight movement sent that shrilling pain up and down my leg and into my back. I couldn't make it up the stairs to my bed; I was stuck in the middle of the living room floor. The large hatch cover table just a few feet away strewn with papers and magazines called to me. I was crazy with pain; it looked inviting.

If I could just crawl under it, I would feel better; it would protect me. I began a slow agonizing crawl. My mind was certainly not intact; all I could think of was curling up into a ball and hiding under that table. I inched toward it. I was half under when I heard the back screen door slam shut.

Oh no, it's Tommy. I have to get a grip. What am I thinking? I'm under a table. I'm losing it. Quickly I rolled over, as an excruciating pain shot through my body again. *I can't let Tommy see this. Pull it together Karla.* I rolled away from the table. From my balled up position on the floor I managed a weak,

"Hi, honey."

With a look of disbelief on his face, Tommy approached me,

"Mom, what happened?" The concern in his sweet voice and all too wise eyes shot into my heart.

Tears overcame me, "I think my back is worse, I can't move."

"It's okay Mom, don't be upset, please don't be down. I'll help you. It will be all right."

How many times had he said that to me since Lucky died?

"Please, Mommy, don't be down."

From when he was just under three-years old this dear child

had been my savior. How unfair, that was not supposed to be his role. Thoughts flooded my mind of that earlier time.

A terrible fight had ensued with my first husband Pat, Tommy's father. He had become physically abusive and my tiny little boy rushed into the middle of the struggle. Grabbing at his father's leg he bit him and yelled at him to stop hitting me. Shocked, Pat released his grip and fled from the house.

I had pulled my baby into my arms and cried. As I wept, this special child placed his chubby little hands on each side of my face. His deep brown, knowing eyes locked into mine as he said,

"I'll never let him hurt you again, Mommy. I'll take care of you."

That day, I left his father for the last time, bolstered by the courage of my little hero.

And now, nearly drowned by the pain in my back and leg, I wondered as I had before: *Who is this child?* He seemed old and wise beyond his years. He deserved so much more than I felt capable of giving, and here he was again, having to support me. Would it ever end?

My sister Sharlene came to our aid. She brought me to an orthopedic surgeon. It didn't take him long to diagnose a herniated disc in my spine. He explained that it was affecting the nerves down my leg. By then I was completely hunched over and there were no reflexes when my foot was tapped with the doctor's little hammer.

"We'll try traction," he said.

Off to the hospital Sharlene and I went. I was beginning to feel like a living soap opera, a Calamity Jane.

The next month was spent in the hospital in traction, with medication to ease the pain. Valium helped the depression and sleeping pills got me through the long and lonely nights. I braved it through the EMG studies to determine nerve involvement and finally an epidural block. Here I had plenty of time to write, and it soothed my soul once again releasing more of the anquish I felt over Lucky's death.

The December birthdays passed, first Lucky's, then mine, and Christmas was fast approaching. Being in the hospital at that time was dreadful, yet it provided a way to escape the usual calendar of days. Hiding there in bed was looking like a good way to avoid Christmas day, my first without Lucky. But Tommy needed me, and the doctor felt it was better for my mental condition to be home for the holidays. So he released me, knowing full well that I would have to return.

Strapped in a large brace that covered my body from just under the bust to below my hips, I felt imprisoned. There were still no reflexes in my left leg, and I relied upon the drugs to get through the days and nights. Maybe I would have been better off hiding in the hospital. At the dinner table Christmas Day, the abundance of good food and loving family only made Lucky's absence all the more agonizing. My precious little nephew Joe, now seven-months old, Sharlene and Wayne, his parents, my mom and Tom all gathered around the festive table. Wayne sat across from me, keeping his gaze away from mine; the pain and horror of Lucky's death were still too great. I made an attempt to eat but dissolved into tears, with the rest of the family following. It was the first time since the funeral that we were all visibly in the pain together. In an odd way, it helped: I felt less alone.

The school granted me a leave of absence so I could heal, and after only a few short weeks at home the physical pain became unbearable again. It was time to return to the hospital. I endured more tests, more traction and physical therapy, but still without favorable results. Lucky frequented my nights; his love and tenderness brought me comfort, but still the agonizing sense of loss persisted. Joe was off in Florida, yet called frequently and promised a visit home to cheer me up.

One afternoon the good doctor presented me with some news. He wanted to do surgery. A test was needed to pinpoint the precise location of the herniated disc. However, I was allergic to iodine, the substance needed to perform the myelogram test. Because of that allergy the doctor suggested that I undergo an exploratory spinal laminectomy.

"What's that?" I asked. The sound of it was more than frightening.

Attempting to appear nonchalant, he explained,

"We will open an area of your spine where we *think* the disc is damaged and if it is not the exact spot, we will close that area and try slightly higher or lower."

His words shocked me. "You'll do what?" I screeched, "You must be joking!" In that moment I knew that I had to find another way.

"Dear Doctor, I'm out of here!"

It is said that when the student is ready the teacher appears, and I was blessed to have three at that time. Joe's mother Mildred was my first. She had been living with cancer and had found a way to use the power of her mind to control the disease and her life. She gave me a little orange book, *Consciously Creating Circumstances* by George Winslow Plummer. It was based on Rosicrucian philosophy and packed with metaphysical dynamite.

One evening lying home in my bed I began to read the book. It suggested that I had the power to heal my body and create my "Kingdom of Heaven" here upon the earth. The material instructed me to allow a thought form to come into my mind that depicted a whole and perfect self. It then suggested that I hold this thought form in meditation. I wasn't sure what meditation was, but I closed the book and instantly began to see myself running toward a group of people. In the imagery I was free of pain. My body was healthy and strong as I ran and there was a feeling of great victory and joy. As I reached this group of people, a man stepped out of the crowd and handed me a bouquet of flowers. There was even the sense of my husband's loving presence. It was a wonderful little thought form that took less than a minute to conjure up. It seemed to flow effortlessly without forethought from a place deep inside of me that knew the truth. In that moment I felt that something powerful had happened. I had been given hope.

With this new sense of power I began to meditate, at least what I thought meditation was. Each day I spent time quieting my mind, and focused on the thought form. There were many days that I sat outdoors imagining the light and strength from the sun moving along my spine fusing the disc. The meditations were always completed with the thought form: joyously running to the group of people, fully aware of my wholeness and perfection. With each imaging I thanked God that this had already manifested and for some unknown reason *I knew* that this would work for me.

The next teacher came into my life and offered me yet another way to heal. I had met Vic at the hair salon. We experienced an instant connection and over the course of numerous haircuts we shared many deep and personal stories. He told me about his spiritual awakening through yoga and I shared my mystical encounters with Lucky. Vic mentioned a six-week meditation course being offered in New York City, based on the Edgar Cayce readings.

"Who is that?" I asked.

Vic explained. "Edgar Cayce was our greatest modern psychic. He was a sweet country boy from Kentucky, a Sunday school teacher with a solid foundation in fundamental religion. He was born in 1877, long before the awakening of consciousness and psychic experimentation in our country. When he was a child, an angel told him that he would heal others in his lifetime. He embodied extraordinary gifts that would later help countless thousands. I really think this can help you, Karla, and answer many of your questions about psychic phenomena. You will be with people who can relate to your experiences."

I was mesmerized and excited by what Vic was saying. Finally someone might understand.

Laden down by my brace, but filled with a sense of adventure, I left for New York City. During the train ride, my mind moved to all of the many possibilities. I was stirred up with anticipation yet convinced myself to become still. Moving into grateful meditation I settled in on the thought form that had brought me so much comfort and healing, thanking God over and over again for my healing.

My hosts welcomed me at the door as if I was a long lost friend. As the instructor spoke of silencing the mind and concentrating on the Light of God, I knew I was in the right place. It felt like home. Being with these very loving and open people I began to feel more comfortable with the miracles and visitations that had been happening since Lucky had died. They were not at all shocked by my extraordinary stories.

Each week brought the next step in fine-tuning the meditation. There were head and neck exercises to open the higher chakras. The Lord's Prayer was used as a devotion to enter into the silence. We chanted as we called the name of God in many different languages. Affirmations were suggested to focus on when distracted. I resonated to "Be still and know that I Am God." These words became a way for me to surrender into the silence and the knowledge that Spirit was present within me. There was no need for imagery or phenomena, just quiet, and the gentle reminder, "Be still." Each week I sank deeper and deeper into the sublime peace.

The running thought form that I had once used as a touchstone was now laid aside, for all I needed was the quiet. As I had a sense of God's Light pouring down the front of my body and then back up my spine, I knew I was being healed.

The hospitalizations were over, and soon after completing the meditation course I was out of the large brace and wearing just a waist belt for support. No longer did I need the pain and sleeping medication; something else was managing my body. So positive was I that healing would take place that I proclaimed to my orthopedic surgeon that when I returned from a trip to Florida, where I would bask in the sun and meditate, the reflexes would be back in my leg. He was quite taken with me and very supportive of my newfound method of healing.

"Go for it, Karla," he said, bolstering my confidence.

So, with my doctor's blessing, off I went.

It was good to see Joe in Florida. He wined and dined me. His exuberant, playful spirit buoyed my own. Joe was not quite sure what I was doing in those quiet meditative times, nor did he really want to know. Nonetheless, while keeping his distance, he supported me. The sun and the water were healing, and his tenderness a welcome gift.

Upon returning, I made an appointment to see the good doctor. I was sure of my success, and boldly said,

"Check those reflexes, Doc."

With a grin, he grabbed for the little hammer and positioned himself in front of me on his doctor's stool. As I sat on the exam table, my legs dangling in front of him, he hit a spot just below my knee. Without warning my leg flew up, nearly knocking him over.

"Whoa!" he exclaimed. "Well done, Karla."

We were both ecstatic. I couldn't help hugging him. His support and genuine caring for me had made a marked difference in my healing. Blissfully I moved through the rest of the day with a smile locked on my face and the words repeating over and over in my mind. Thank you, Spirit, thank you.

Joe came home for the summer. He too was pleased with my progress. One night while having dinner he said,

"Hey, you're just doing simple stretching, what about walking? That would strengthen your whole body."

"Okay, that makes sense, and I can start slowly."

With that I secured a pair of good walking shoes and, still in the waist cinch, hit the pavement. The first walk was just to the corner and back. It felt so good that I increased it to a few more blocks and very soon I reached a mile. An energy within prompted me to move a little quicker and in just a few short weeks I was doing a slow jog. It felt great! By the end of the summer of 1977, I was jogging two and a half miles. The cinch belt was off, and I was clearly healed. But I wouldn't realize just how powerful that healing was until the following spring.

As Joe was leaving for Florida for his winter work, he had another suggestion,

"Karla, you're already running two and a half miles; why don't you train over the winter while I'm gone and do the five-mile Spring Lake Race with me next Memorial Day?"

"Why not?" was my response. Neither one of us knew that he was the third important teacher on my path to spiritual healing and awakening. I trained all winter, getting closer and closer to my five-mile goal with each practice session.

The long awaited day came. It was balmy and bright with the rays of my beloved sun, the same sun that had warmed my body and helped me to heal. Tommy joined me; he was on the cross-country team at school so running was natural for him.

The crowd was forming when we arrived. The feeling of excitement and nervousness in the air was tangible. Everywhere runners stretched, their shorts and shirts with logos of all kinds bright in the sun. The bumpers on cars supported their legs, while others were rolling around on the grass looking quite pretzel-like. Joe had given me the last set of instructions.

"Stretch out, then keep your muscles warm. Find a steady pace and increase a little as you pass others, keep your breath even. And don't forget to save a sprint for the end."

Since it was my first race I had no clue as to what I was doing. I was absolutely exhilarated just being there. And, what could be more perfect, I would be running with my son. Joe would certainly be way ahead of us. His best marathon time, in Boston, had been just under three hours, so I didn't expect him to be anywhere near us during this five-mile race. This was just a little jaunt compared to a twenty-six-mile marathon.

Tommy and I found a spot within the first group of a hundred runners. There had to be five hundred or more in all, and being mashed into this pack of perspiring, revved-up athletes was a thrill in itself. The gun went off, and the crowd began to move. I found a rhythm and a pace that worked for me. My body felt strong, healthy and whole. Tommy and I ran together for a little while, I'm sure a gesture of loving support on his part. Then he allowed the excitement, the energy of the moment and his youth to catapult him on.

As I ran along the boardwalk in Spring Lake, I could feel the delicious salt air fill my nostrils and move into my lungs. I was acutely aware of the different sensations provided by the boards as opposed to the pavement. The boards seemed to rise up to meet my feet almost as if I was bouncing, quite different from the hard pavement. I was ecstatic as I passed others! At strategic spots along the course, bystanders played the music from *Rocky*. What triumph I felt as the oranges and water were tossed to me. I picked up my pace. *I was an athlete!*

As I ran faster, a runner's stitch assaulted my side. *Breathe it through*, I thought. My breath had become a key in releasing stress and pain.

Karla, you can do this, the now familiar voice encouraged. It was as if an inner guide was constantly reminding me of my strength and conviction. The cramp passed, and I moved agilely through the crowd, amazed each time I passed someone. *I'm really doing this!* I was in the middle of the crowd of five hundred or more. Pretty good for a girl who could barely walk just a year before!

The sweating mass of runners turned inland, maneuvering through the streets until coming upon a beautiful shimmering lake. The ducks and geese floated aimlessly by. They were perfectly unaffected by the energy in the air and the steaming, adrenaline-surging swarm of runners blazing by. A blue and white church with a magnificent golden dome was nestled at the far end of the lake. Its colors were reflected in the water as the sun's rays shone down upon it. The gold seemed to spread out in an iridescent fashion, illuminating everything in its path. It was beyond beautiful. It was captivating. There was a surrealistic yet spiritual feeling. Gratitude poured through me as I gazed upon its immense beauty.

Endorphins were surging through my body. I was most definitely experiencing the famed runner's high. To avoid crashing into an unsuspecting comrade, I averted my gaze from the lake. As I looked ahead, a group of people came into view. Chills began to rush through my already heightened body. The crowd was clapping and excitedly cheering on the runners. The hair began to rise up from every pore on my skin as the group of people from the thought form came flooding into my mind.

No, I thought, *this can't be.* My feet seemed like they were not even touching the ground. Utter thankfulness, awe, and joy overcame me. Here I was, completely healed. Spirit had moved through me and had fused that disc. I had not realized, until that moment, just how powerful a healing it was. It had actually happened months before. Now I was in the *recognition* of that *glorious* miracle.

I thought my heart might burst.

Tears streamed down my face as my pace quickened. Closer and closer I came to the group of people, and as I did, Lucky moved into my awareness, his love and presence coaxing me on. I felt as if Spirit was carrying me. I knew then that I was not alone, I had never been alone. Just as I reached the crowd, a man stepped out and handed me a bouquet of flowers. In awe and amazement, I accepted them as from the hand of God, and hold them still in my heart.

In less than forty-seven minutes, my race was complete. I shot through the runner's chute across the finish line, where I crumpled to the ground. Rocking in Lucky's and God's love, I wept uncontrollable tears of gratitude and joy. First aid attendants with oxygen in hand rushed to my side. How could I tell them that I was in the middle of a spiritual experience?

In that moment I knew that I had to teach others the power of the mind to heal the body. There is a way to move through anything in life, even the unbearable. I had aligned myself with the Light of Spirit and a great miracle had occurred. I knew if it happened for me, it could happen for others. A new life purpose had dawned upon me. I agreed to be a teacher for God.

Chapter 7
The Brave Team

It didn't take long to get rolling. Filled with so much excitement, I felt like I would explode if the message wasn't shared.

Bursting with enthusiasm, I convinced a handful of my high school colleagues, and believe it or not, the Assistant Superintendent of Schools to take a look at meditation and the power of the mind. In 1978, that was certainly not in vogue or even accepted. Yet, with a sense of adventure and some apprehension, five brave souls agreed to attend the six-week study group at my home.

The first member of the student body was Judy, a beautiful, blonde science teacher who had become my cohort in fun. We spent numerous days at the beach and she frequented Joe's infamous summer parties with me. However, she wasn't quite ready for this new aspect of my life.

Michael came on board next, hardly what one would expect of the Assistant Superintendent. But he had an inquiring mind and a thirst for knowledge of the unseen. Michael was a perfect candidate for meditation.

Judy then convinced Steve, a conservative history teacher, and thinking that it might be fun, he signed up.

Along came Helen, our school nurse. She had always seemed quite prim and proper, yet to my great surprise she was interested in the subject matter.

Pulling up the rear was Pat, my friend and partner in the vocational program. With a bit of reluctance and trepidation she climbed on board. My first class was in place and ready to go.

On the first night I jumped in head first, sharing my miraculous healing experience. The group was amazed by that powerful story and became eager to learn.

Being a teacher, it was easy for me to instruct from the outline I had received the year before at the Edgar Cayce Meditation Course. Each week I taught an aspect of becoming still. I suggested practical ways to train the mind, such as meditating at the same time and place each day, and loosening resistance with head and neck exercises that also stimulated the higher chakras (the spiritual energy centers of the body).

We used affirmations and The Lord's Prayer to enter into the quiet. Each student found an affirmation that resonated with them and would use it to return to the stillness whenever they were distracted.

I created a guided meditation to a sacred garden, leading my newfound spiritual comrades to a place within themselves of deeper peace and connection. When I guided the meditation, the inner images appeared first then the words would clothe themselves around the image. Flowing through me effortlessly, it came from a place that was beyond my linear thinking. No pre-thought was needed, just a full and conscious breath opening me to God.

It was much like my running thought form, but now the images and words were for others. I felt deeply grateful to be of service in that way. The meditation, which I named *Garden of Light,* became my personal logo.

The courageous meditation team was becoming more peaceful, connected and joyous with each step. At our final meeting I introduced them to the power of chanting, to raise consciousness and to step more fully into Spirit. Little did I know that this was far too much for the brave team.

Standing in the center of the living room with my school chums circled around me, I began the *Om* chant, which I had learned at the Cayce meditation course. The sound of it vibrated through me as I reverently aligned myself with its vibration. As I returned my awareness to the group I noticed their mouths hanging open and their eyes wide with disbelief. The conservative history teacher, the inexperienced science teacher, the unsure vocational teacher and the daring school nurse looked at me as if I had lost my mind. Everything up to that point had been accepted; now I was just plain crazy.

Recognizing their discomfort, I attempted to tone it down.

"Look, this is just another way to open yourself further. *Om* is a universal sound for the name of God."

"It's not that weird. The ancient teachings and spiritual disciplines of many world religions have used chant throughout history."

"Yeah, but not my history," chuckled Steve, the conservative history teacher.

"Just try it," I implored.

Their boggling eyes had returned to their normal position and their mouths had closed. However, Pat's folded arms tightened across her chest. She then sank back into the couch in an attempt to disappear. Judy and Steve were sitting next to each other (definitely a mistake), with an astounded look on both their faces. Nurse Helen was surprisingly more courageous and serious about the new lesson. Michael was excited and ready to let it rip.

Steve and Judy decided to stand up next to me, while Helen and Pat remained sitting. Pat seemed to be further enmeshed into the back of the couch. Helen was sitting up straight, befitting a dutiful student. Michael assumed a cross-legged, lotus position on the floor. As I glanced at Steve and Judy I knew I was in trouble. They were giggling and clutching each other's arms for support.

"You can do this," I urged again. "It's just a sacred sound."

They nodded.

"Okay now, close your eyes and take a deep breath. Allow the sound of *Om* to come up from a deep place within. Let it be your own tone, your own personal sound, let it vibrate throughout your whole being. Follow my lead, I know you can do this."

Closing my eyes, I centered and allowed the deep breath to come.

"Om" . . . I chanted, feeling the vibration come up from my heart space, then spread out through the room.

Pat offered a timid and barely audible sound, a look of extreme discomfort on her face. Helen was clearly into it. Michael, my prize student, looked like a picture right out of a yoga magazine, hands resting on his lap, fingers touching.

On the second chant Steve and Judy could no longer contain themselves. Their giggling became explosive laughter.

"Judy," I pleaded. "Come on." She was my best friend; I had expected her to support me.

"Okay," she said, "I'll try, honestly."

Steve chimed in as he fought to hold it together.

"We can do it, Judy. It's a snap."

Judy just grinned.

Helen's face pinched up as she muttered, "Tsk, Tsk," in their direction. Upon feeling she had been heard, she reclaimed her serious meditative pose.

At that point Pat was nearly invisible. I'm certain she wished the door was closer so she could escape. Michael held his posture steady, waiting for the opportunity to raise his consciousness.

"Here we go," I raised my arms up toward the ceiling, as a cue for them to get ready.

In my most reverent and spiritual demeanor I moved into the deep breath.

"*Om*" . . .

My misbehaving students could no longer contain their emotion. Desperately holding on to their mouths in an attempt to keep the explosive laugh at bay, Steve and Judy flew out of the living room and into the kitchen. Uproarious, hysterical laughter ensued. They had lost it!

Intent on my lesson, serious teacher that I was, I ran into the kitchen after them, to find them holding their sides in uncontrollable outbursts.

"Now stop that! You're disturbing the others and they are trying."

"We're really sorry," Steve blurted out through his unsuccessful attempts to stop laughing.

"I can't help it," Judy added. "I'm *soooooo* sorry" she offered in her most apologetic and dramatic way, knowing full well that I was counting on her. "We had better just stay in the kitchen."

Tears streaming down their faces, they tried to pull themselves together.

"Okay, but be good now." It felt like I was with my high school kids.

In the living room, I apologized to brave Helen, apprehensive Pat, and very ready Michael.

"Let's try again."

The *Om* rang out from me, fuller this time as it resonated through the stillness of the room. Michael's tone met mine. Helen followed suit and Pat's obedient, yet reluctant voice joined in.

And again, on the second *Om*, the laughter bellowed from the kitchen. As I ran in, Judy was bent over gripping her legs tightly together as she hurried to the bathroom, nearly wetting her pants. Steve was clutching his side and leaning against the wall for support. Snorts leaked out as he held his hands tightly over his mouth, while his cheeks blew up looking like they might burst apart from the wild laughter.

There was nothing left to do but surrender into their joyous, uproarious shenanigans. Pat and Helen joined in the gaiety, a welcome relief for Pat. Michael was visibly disappointed.

The serious lesson was over. My new career as a spiritual teacher had birthed itself in that moment of pure joy and playfulness. I would never be the same.

Chapter 8
The Journey Home

A page in the book of my life had turned; the unbearable grief had lifted and I was beginning to see a reason for the pain. My two separate lives, though increasingly different, continued. Weekends with Joe still included the great parties, travel to races and white water rafting. I really enjoyed being with him, yet in my heart I knew my unfolding spiritual path was creating a distance between us. Joe could not step into my world of Spirit and contemplation, and I could not fully embrace his hedonistic lifestyle.

Our fun-filled excursions included Joe at the wheel, with Jack and Elayne, my beach buddies, drinking beers in the front of the van while I meditated in the back. I sat with my legs crossed attempting to hold my meditative posture as the van bounced me around—surely an odd picture.

I found an Edgar Cayce *Search for God* study group that continued to answer my deepest questions. The group members were kind and loving and I made beautiful new friends.

Sondra was a powerful healer with psychic gifts. Much of our time together was spent deepening intuition skills through meditation and hands-on healing. One afternoon when Sondra and I were alone, I asked her if she could contact Lucky. To my astonishment she said,

"Lucky is right behind you, on your left side, his arm is placed gently upon your shoulders. Ah . . . he's smiling at me, what a beautiful face . . . He's moving in front of you now; his hand is tenderly brushing across your cheek. Can you feel it?"

As she said those words, I softened and allowed myself to feel him once more.

My face was wet with tears as she went on to describe him: his looks, his demeanor, and personal things that only I could know.

"He loves you so very much. His spirit will always be with you."

"Thank you Sondra. Please let him know that I love him."

"Oh he knows."

Sondra's psychic gifts were astounding and she spent a great deal of time with our group helping us become more comfortable with our own innate abilities. She was a dedicated and inspired teacher and had a way of easily bringing us to our inner wisdom.

Bob, one of our study group comrades, had left New Jersey to explore and deepen his spiritual life. During that soul searching he not only found himself but also found the great power of Reiki, an ancient form of healing energy. He became a Reiki Master, and upon his return offered the group this new tool. I already knew that the power of the mind connected to Spirit could heal the body—I was living proof of that phenomenon—so I quickly signed up for the training. Joining me were Sondra, Vannee and Hildy—my new soulful friends.

We were hungry for knowledge and had been spending our evenings doing a simple form of energy work called laying on of hands; Reiki was the next logical step in our spiritual evolution. Bob told us that this Japanese/Tibetan form of healing had been practiced over 2,500 years ago and rediscovered in the late 1800's by Dr. Mikao Usui. He explained that Reiki brings the body into greater harmony so it can heal itself. In addition, it can bring the practitioner into deeper and higher states of awareness.

As Bob performed attunements, a method of passing the energy from teacher to student, he energetically opened our crown, third eye, heart and hands. We became channels for this Divine flow of ancient wisdom and healing touch. This simple yet powerful form of healing energy transported us into greater consciousness and sharpened our intuitive capabilities. Our ability to channel energy through our hands and across distances became more focused. We spent numerous nights sharing this energy of love with one another and then channeled it to our Earth Mother and all life upon her.

In my more solitary moments, distant memories began to emerge. I remembered the homesickness that invaded my soul at a tender young age. Gazing at the night sky twinkling with stars and rapturous beauty I would cry out, "Where have I come from? Where do I belong?"

In my youth I lived in a small, ocean town, a peninsula, just a few houses from the river. Nor'eastern storms often brought huge crashing waves over the sea wall. Tumultuous water rose from the river and joined with the rushing waves from the ocean just a few blocks away. The waters merged and flowed wildly into our small home. Town sirens screeched out the danger as rowboats came to carry us away from peril. Such mass evacuations were common in our tiny sea-side community.

To a small child, this all seemed a great adventure. As my father hoisted me up onto his shoulders, I would giggle, making it into a game. Clad in heavy fishermen's garb, with suspenders holding the huge plastic pants in place and long rubber cumbersome boots, he braved it through the chest-high waters, never failing to bring my mother and me to safer ground.

As a child I was very sensitive and somewhat otherworldly. When I was only four-years-old I began to have visions of severe floods with plummeting massive tidal waves. These were memories of a destruction far more deadly than the nor'eastern storms of Sea Bright, New Jersey. Certainly too young to comprehend, I must have placed the memory somewhere far down in my unconscious.

Later, in my twenties, after reading an article on the legend of Atlantis and her destruction, the memory returned, flooding me with questions. I devoured books on the subject in an attempt to understand. When Lucky and I met it further fueled my need to know since he too was fascinated with Atlantis, the ancient sites in Egypt and the Mayan ruins. As my spiritual life deepened after his death more visions came forth.

Gina Cerminara's book, *Many Mansions* based on the Edgar Cayce readings, answered my questions around reincarnation. She said that we were born again and again to complete unfinished business; that pain and suffering was a product of cause and effect. What we reaped in one life we would sow in another. Our continuous soul's journey was not a punishment from God, but a choice on our part to come back and do better.

Reincarnation, and the karma that drives it, are actually, Cerminara suggests, a great gift. Each lifetime has the potential to bring us closer to God and to remember those we had been with before. No wonder I was so attracted to Lucky the first time I laid eyes upon him. It wasn't merely love at first sight, but a deep and abiding memory of having been together so many times before.

Recalling our first night of love, I remembered his precious words.

"I have known you always. For time and all eternity we shall be together."

Our former lives surely went back to Atlantis. We both felt so connected to that period.

One night while reading, a strong and vivid image came to me. This time I saw myself with a young man. We were fleeing from a city's devastating destruction as crashing waters tumbled magnificent buildings to the ground and swept them away like sticks. Everywhere people were drowning and struggling desperately to hold to one another.

The young man and I ran stumbling up a hill, pulling one another along. We made it to the top only to witness the final annihilation of our precious city. As we watched, the water rose around us. Holding onto one another we wept, for our home, and for all those that we loved. The sea had claimed them forever. As the waters surged toward us, the image faded from my mind.

I was left in wonderment and confusion. What was this? Where was it? Could it have been Atlantis? And who was that young man? It didn't seem to be Lucky or anyone else that I had known.

Voraciously I read book after book hoping to acquire wisdom. All the while more and more past-life memories flooded me. There was a distinct and deep knowing that I had been with Christ during His life as Jesus. How did I know that? There were no words to explain it; I would feel His presence in my deepest meditations. The memory came from a place of certainty and profound love.

I began to realize that it was Christ who brought the Light to me, the Light that moved me through the cold and bleak casket room, and the Light that had carried me across the finish line of my five-mile race. He was with me and had always been. I knew Him as Jeshua.

The new spiritual and prayer life consumed me and soon I was traveling to the Association for Research and Enlightenment, the A.R.E., in Virginia Beach, Virginia for their summer conferences. I simply couldn't get enough of this new truth. The teachers spoke of Atlantis, Ancient Egypt, and the Essenes. As their words joined with my awareness, many memories and images came flowing forth. I had been in those places. I was sure of it. As songs were sung and ancient dances danced, I remembered them.

My consciousness expanded and held in its Light the present moment and also past moments that cradled far distant memories. In meditation I became aware of an energy link, much like a silver cord. The cord was attached to my body yet seemed to travel throughout eternity connecting me to other lifetimes where I had been a teacher and student of truth. An Essene life and my time with Jeshua were revealed. I recognized Edgar Cayce as Ra Ta, the high priest of Ancient Egypt. The cord went back to the Golden City of Atlantis, the home of my earliest childhood memories. Yet the question would always surface.

"Who am I to think that I have been with these holy ones?"

But I soon realized that this incredible group at the A.R.E. was my soul family. We had traveled together through many life sojourns, always returning in an attempt to live the Christ Ideal. Inscribed over the entrance door were the words, "*That we may make manifest the love of God and man.*" I understood those words. We were here to make sure that the destruction of Atlantis would not repeat itself in our time. Love could prevail; we could open our hearts and make a difference in the world. We could remember who we truly were. Confirmation after confirmation came to lock in place this new certainty.

On one of my first visits to the A.R.E., I boldly entered the office of the Director of Educational Development, Dr. Mark Thurston, and declared that I was a teacher for Spirit, that I had already taught the meditation course in my hometown, and that I had experienced a profound miracle of healing through the Edgar Cayce readings.

Mark must have thought, *Who is this presumptuous one?* As he quietly studied me, I continued.

"I am a high school teacher and I would love to continue teaching the A.R.E. material. I want to present a course of study at our adult school."

Mark told me that they were just then initiating a new national program.

"And," he said, smiling, "we need field instructors. Maybe you could represent New York and New Jersey. Why don't you send me your resume?"

Beaming, I agreed. *Oh my God,* I thought. *I'm home.* On the way out I had to pinch myself to prove it was real and not a dream. It's a wonder that I didn't let out a hoot and holler as I walked down the stairs.

On the A.R.E. grounds stood a room-sized pyramid built to the same proportions as the ancient Egyptian pyramid at Giza. When I entered the dark, sacred quiet of the meditation chamber, many loving energies began to envelop me.

"You *are* home," they spoke.

As the energy circled around my body, gratitude filled me. I knew in that moment that an old and forgotten, yet somehow remembered, ancient blessing was being bestowed upon me. I only wished that Lucky could be physically there to celebrate it with me.

"My life is in your hands dear Jeshua . . . Show me the way to make manifest the love of God and man. I am yours."

I was one of the first to be accepted into the Field Instructor program and soon received course outlines and slides to present my material. Filled with an inner force I never stopped to ponder what others would think of me; my enthusiasm was unbridled.

The adult school back in Matawan accepted my proposal and I began to teach courses on meditation, reincarnation, healing and the power of prayer. The disapproval of some did not affect me; I was just too excited. In 1979, I courageously took my place as a trendsetter and pioneer in awakening consciousness, solid in my beliefs.

Not long after climbing on board with the A.R.E., I received a call from Mark inviting me to do a retreat at Mount Freedom in New Jersey. He and Hugh Lynn Cayce would be speaking.

"Would you join us and do the past life reverie and meditations?"

"Edgar Cayce's son?" My heart skipped a beat. I was shocked and flabbergasted! "Would I? . . . Yes! Yes! . . . Yes! . . . I'll do it! . . . Wow! . . . I can't wait . . . When?"

Mark gave me the date and I quickly settled into preparations. My practice with the *Garden of Light* meditation had paid off. My voice had the ability to bring people into a deep state of peace and higher awareness. I created a past life reverie and chose prayers and meditations to enhance the program. Arriving at the retreat center I was excited and humbled to be with Mark and Hugh Lynn.

A chill of nervous energy ran through me. Here I was with two of the greatest teachers on the Edgar Cayce readings, ones that I looked up to and admired. I wanted to do a good job. Would I make the grade?

The first morning I opened the meditation with a shortened prayer.

"Not my will but Thine oh Lord, be done in me and through me. Let me ever be a channel of blessings . . . "

I left out, "Today, now, to those that I contact in every way. Let my going in, my coming out be in accord with that Thou would have me do, and as the call comes, Here am I, send me, use me."

My eyes were closed so I wasn't aware of the disapproval from my most beloved teacher Hugh Lynn. At the lunch break I joined him.

"Karla, in all of the years since my father brought us that prayer, no one has ever shortened it!"

I was mortified! I had done something terribly wrong, and I was being scolded. I felt like a little child, wanting to put my head down and retreat into a corner.

"I'm so sorry, Hugh Lynn, it won't happen again," I stammered.

As I spilled out those words, I had a sense of Edgar Cayce in the garb of the Egyptian priest Ra Ta. He was gently smiling at me; perhaps he didn't think it was so bad. In that moment I wished that he would communicate that to his son.

Okay, Karla, you can do it, I tried to ease myself. Since that prayer was the theme of the weekend I would have another opportunity. Happily, the past life reverie went without a hitch; it was apparent that the audience had great experiences and that knowledge buoyed my confidence.

The final morning I greeted the group and led them through the customary deep breaths and centering. Looking out I saw Hugh Lynn in the front row. He was watching me intently, as if to encourage me to do it the "right way."

Fixing my gaze on Hugh Lynn, I took a deep breath and began.

"Not ***Thy*** will, but ***mine*** oh Lord, be done in me and through me."

I saw Hugh Lynn's eyes widen and his mouth drop.

Stopping dead in my tracks, I muttered, "Oh no!" Then I sent up a silent prayer, *Oh Lord, please HELP!*

Hugh Lynn simply lifted up his hands in a gesture of disbelief and closed his eyes. Sitting next to him was Mark; it was evident that he was holding back his laughter.

Thank goodness everyone else's eyes remained closed; perhaps they were relaxed enough and intent on Spirit to not notice my huge blunder.

My inner dialogue began. *You can do it, you're a teacher for God, and you know this prayer like the back of your hand. Get it together Karla.* I continued with the prayer and repeated it in its entirety at the end.

*"Not **my** will but **Thine** oh Lord, be done in me and through me.*

Let me ever be a channel of blessings,

Today, now, to those that I contact in every way,

Let my going in and my coming out be in accord with that Thou would have me do.

And as the call comes, here am I, send me, use me."

Hugh Lynn smiled.

"Whew!"

My first official, very public and witnessed presentation and I had nearly flubbed it.

My disappointment was obvious as I approached Hugh Lynn to apologize once again. He greeted me like a tender father.

"It's okay, you were nervous, just don't do it again."

As he laughed the stress eased out of my body, perhaps Edgar *had* whispered in his ear. We spoke of his father's work, past lives, and the possibility of us having been together as student and teacher before. I hung on his every word. I adored him.

After that, I spent every vacation and long weekend in Virginia Beach. A new airline offered a one-way trip for $19.00. In one hour I was back at my spiritual mecca, devouring the readings and attending the conferences.

During a quiet evening while at home in New Jersey, I experienced a vision. I was getting off a plane, driving to the A.R.E. and then speaking from their podium. A large group was assembled to hear my words. As I taught I pointed to a chart. The chart contained a figure with chakras, their associated colors and the Lord's Prayer. Each line of the sacred prayer had the power to open one of the spiritual centers. It was a quick image, yet very exciting. I then remembered Cayce's words,

"Spirit is the life, mind is the builder and the physical is the result."

I had already experienced the power of the mind aligned with Spirit. Could *this* really manifest?

"If it is for my highest good oh Lord, then let Thy will be done."

It was the middle of the 1981-82 school year. Tommy was completing a very successful high school career and had been accepted into many colleges. His emphasis was physical therapy. He had spent a year volunteering at the local hospital in the physical therapy department. Tommy felt it was his calling to help others in pain. That awareness had come to him when he was a very small boy ministering to his handicapped grandmother's polio-stricken legs. With great seriousness and purpose he would run his tiny hands over her legs and then say,

"Okay, Mom Mom . . . get up . . . You can walk now . . . You can do it."

As I recalled my mother telling me this story my heart overflowed.

Filled with tears she had told me,

"I have been comfortable with this handicap for many years, but for the first time since I was a young girl, I wanted to get up on my feet and walk, just for Tommy. I told him that I was happy just the way I was, and when he grew up he would be a great healer. He would learn to help many others."

I was so proud of my little boy.

As Tommy and I visited colleges, I began to consider a move for myself. Feeling imprisoned by the high school curriculum, I knew I had to broaden my spiritual work and teaching. With great faith I asked for a leave of absence from the school. I had decided to move to Virginia Beach when Tommy left for college.

The end of the summer arrived. My home was rented to a good friend and Tom was on his way. I had no job and my Virginia Beach living arrangements fell through at the last minute. Still I was determined. On fire with a desire to learn and teach, I continued my forward quest.

On the day of departure a room opened up at the beach. I packed my little Toyota Starlet with the bare essentials. Joining me were a few clothes, lots of meditative music, my journals, teaching materials and incense. Traveling light felt great!

The ride to Virginia Beach was magnificent. As I drove over the long twenty-mile stretch of the Chesapeake Bay Bridge Tunnel, the sun was just setting. Surrounded by water I gazed at the glorious colors adorning the sky: deep purples, oranges, reds, golds and iridescent pinks. The sky kissed the water gently. It felt like the brilliant colors were laying themselves softly down upon the water, in an act of devotion. Seagulls flew overhead, their graceful flight silhouetting the deepening sky. Its exquisite beauty held me captive and breathless. Each time I had crossed that bridge I felt my heart leap for joy and my soul dance. Now it was welcoming me home.

My first stop was the A.R.E. I wanted to spend some time in the meditation room before traveling on to my new abode. No sooner had I arrived when Cathy, the conference coordinator, approached me.

"Karla, we're in a bind. Meredith Puryear, our primary teacher, is ill and can't teach the program on Spiritual Healing. Do you have any experience with that? Can you do it?"

Startled, yet excited by her request, I agreed to do the program. I had not done it before, but felt the many hours of listening to Meredith's great teaching had found its way into me, and I was after all a product of spiritual healing.

"Yes," I repeated, "I can do it."

There wasn't much time. Cathy gave me Meredith's outline and I quickly added my own personal stories to the presentation. The experiential segment of the program included the *Garden of Light* meditation and prayer circles. The large group was broken up into smaller circles. As they held hands and brought the Light of God within them, they passed it around the circle. One to the other, the Light poured in from Spirit, filling their minds and hearts. They then channeled that Light from their hands, their breath, and their awakened hearts. It went out into the world as a gesture of peace and healing to all those that they loved and to our dear Earth Mother.

I was in my element, guiding others into the sacred space. As soon as I closed my eyes and drew in the breath of peace, Spirit was with me, offering the images and the words to bring people to their inner divinity.

During that transpersonal state I opened my eyes and realized that someone had placed a chart right next to me. The chart of chakras, and colors, holding the words of the Lord's Prayer waited for my next presentation. The vision had manifested, just as it was revealed to me.

"Thank you Spirit, thank you."

I had been a screaming wild woman to some, a spiritual trendsetter to others, a victorious runner, a life guard's bikini-clad blonde, and a widowed young mother. Many of those characters that lived within me would share their miraculous stories in the two years that followed.

From tragedy to triumph, from crisis to Christ, life was incredibly delicious!

Chapter 9
The Way

No sooner had I completed the spiritual healing workshop when offers for a full time position came, one for the Study Group Department and the other as Prayer Services Coordinator. Prayer Services captured my heart, as it would give me the opportunity to share the wonders of prayer and healing through writing, ongoing lectures and workshops. I accepted the position as coordinator and staff teacher. Everything was falling into place.

It didn't take long to realize that employment and spiritual awakening were not the only reason I had moved to Virginia Beach. There was still much in me that needed to be healed. While attending one of the summer conferences I experienced a powerful inner journey. Carol Bush, the leading expert on The Bonny Method of Guided Imagery & Music (GIM), led the group through a music-centered imagery experience. She had prepared us well. During her lecture she discussed how the great masterworks of classical music enable us to get in touch with various levels of consciousness. She spoke of our spiritual journey here upon the earth, the challenges to be met and the inner wisdom available that could help us overcome life's obstacles.

Before beginning the music, Carol guided us into a state of focused relaxation. It was easy to let go, as Carol's voice was soothing and melodic. At the end of the relaxation, just before entering into the music, she said,

"As the music begins to play, allow it to take you to the source of your inner wisdom."

The coaxing, rich, majestic sound of Barber's *Adagio for Strings* filled the room and my senses. Immediately the inner imagery began. I found myself in a beautiful meadow lush with trees and wild flowers. Just off in the distance the peak of a large mountain loomed, silhouetted against the clear blue sky. The imagery was very much like a waking dream urging me forward. I made my way down a narrow path to the mountain. There was no doubt that I was to climb up; the music was inviting me to ascend. I was no longer cognizant of what was going on in the room as the rapturous beauty of the music and the wisdom of my inner knowing captivated me.

Without any strain I journeyed up and around the winding path. At each turn loved ones appeared encouraging me to travel on. As I climbed, I came upon my husband; his beautiful and smiling face communicated his deep love. He handed me a red rose, the symbol of our commitment. Weeping, I fell into his embrace, wanting so to stay in the comfort of his love. As I did, a deep sense of the unresolved grief began to emerge. As if feeling my thoughts, he said,

"No, you must keep going."

It was difficult to move away but I knew he was right and the music was lifting me, catapulting me higher. Journeying on I met others, many that I had helped in this life, and many that had helped me. I realized that they were all on the other side of the veil in the spirit state.

My father greeted me and I dissolved once again into tears. He had left home when I was a mere thirteen-years-old and then died suddenly when I was only sixteen. I had never fully grieved that loss. Many times in my youth I thought I felt him but was never really sure. In this state, though, there was no room for doubt. As with my husband, I wanted to stay with him, be held and comforted as when I was very little. But he too urged me on.

"You must continue forward. You will see why." The message was delivered to my heart; no literal words were passed to each other, just a knowing, and an ability to feel into one other. *This must be what it's like in heaven,* I thought.

Waiting for me close to the top of the mountain was a young man, perhaps in his early 20's, small in stature with dark hair and penetrating dark eyes. A knowing smile graced his face. He seemed strangely familiar but I couldn't quite place him; I wanted to get closer but as I moved toward him he mysteriously vanished.

Just as the music was reaching its brilliant crescendo I reached the summit. At that moment a magnificent Light appeared, the sky was ignited with its brilliance, it poured itself down upon me encircling my entire body. Emerging out of that Light directly in front of me was Christ. I was held breathless, captured in a transcendent moment. Never before had I envisioned Him with such clarity. In my earlier meditations it was always a sense or feeling of His presence. But here in this moment He was completely present with me, more real than anything I had ever known. He stretched His arms out, beckoning me to come closer. Like a small child I ran into Him, tears of joy and gratitude overflowing.

He cradled me in the most tender of all embraces. I heard over and over, *Be still and know that I Am God.*

Christ assured me that my path was straight and that I

would help many to awaken to the Light, yet there was trauma still embedded within that needed to be healed. As He gently held me, the all too familiar pain locked in my chest surfaced. I then heard His gentle words,

You need to heal this.

Held in His arms I agreed to do the work and the pain eased. The now gentle and supportive music came to a close and Carol brought our group slowly back to the awareness of the room.

When she asked for volunteers my hand shot up. I was visibly moved by the journey, so it was clear to Carol that I had had a very deep and powerful experience. She immediately called upon me. Without being too lengthy I shared the highlights of my experience with the group. Yet there was so much more to tell; feeling drawn to Carol, I pursued her after the workshop. Barely able to hold back the emotion I shared the tragedy that had catapulted me on a spiritual quest. She listened with genuine caring and compassion; tears were glistening in her eyes as I spoke of the suicide. Reaching out, she placed a hand gently on my arm and said,

"Perhaps you need to do some more work."

This connection would prove to be one of the most important of my life. Carol would not only help me retrieve a lost part of myself and put to rest the surfacing grief that was locked deep inside my cells, she would also set me on a course that would change my life professionally.

"Karla, I think you're a natural for this process."

Based on the experience, I decided to explore this powerful form of music and mind travel further.

"I'll call you soon Carol, when I am ready to do the work. I'm just amazed at how potent the music is and what it can do in that magnified state. I can't wait."

With my new staff position underway, I began preparing

workshops and classes. As I shared the wealth of the Cayce readings regarding prayer, spirituality and healing I also shared my journey from tragedy to triumph and developed meditations that helped others to tap into the deep inner wisdom to heal, forgive and release. During the presentations many tears flowed as hearts were opened and lightened. The inner journeys transported many to higher and deeper realms, places within that held the blueprint and promise of wholeness.

At each presentation that I gave, a long-stem red rose adorned the podium, as a tribute to my husband and the love that had brought me thus far. During a talk entitled, "Forgiveness – The Way Home," I spoke of the life and love of Christ, His journey of complete and total forgiveness, unconditional love made manifest in the world. I spoke of Jesus as the pattern of that love, as *the way* home that as each and every one of us awakened to His Will, His calling, we would come a little closer to peace. I wasn't speaking of the Jesus of structured, fundamental religion, but the Jesus Cayce spoke of, our Elder Brother who demonstrated the Christ pattern of Universal Love and Oneness. That pattern is inherent in all of the world's religions and can be awakened as we align our little will with God's Will.

This pattern of love was *the way*. Truly loving and forgiving would bring us home. No one could be kept out of our hearts, as all were already forgiven in the eyes of God. All were children of the Most High, no matter what name one chose to call it. Love one another, seek for the highest good in all brothers and sisters, forgive self and forgive others, for we are all on a journey back home to Spirit and we must go together. Whether our God is called Jesus, Buddha, Allah, Jehovah or Krishna, the message remains the same. No one can be exempt from our forgiveness.

In the workshop I shared Cayce's thoughts, that we are all one, all corpuscles in the body of the living God, nothing truly separating us only the fear thoughts and old conditioning of our minds. We are all joined, one to another and to God. Love and forgiveness is *the way,* the only way out of the illusion of separateness into higher truth.

Each program concluded with a guided meditation. Primed by the talk on forgiveness, I relaxed the group and then led them to a door within their inner awareness where someone was waiting, one that needed forgiveness. As they opened the door, parents, a spouse or old lover, a former teacher, even an aspect of themselves appeared. Many were freed that night from years of bondage. For as Cayce said, we are locked into one another as if by a ball and chain when anger, lack of forgiveness and resentments are held. As we forgive the other, we forgive and release ourselves. In our hearts we know *the way.*

By their sharing it was evident that the group was touched deeply. There were few dry eyes. As I was preparing to leave the dais a conferee approached. What she shared astounded me, yet made perfect and total sense.

She asked me how I pronounced my last name. Emphasizing the vowel sounds, I responded,

"La Voy."

Continuing, she said, "You see, I have the same last name as you, I am from Quebec." She then corrected me,

"The true sound and inflection of our name is *Love Wah.* Do you know what it means?"

"No," I admitted, feeling very curious as to where the conversation was going.

"Why you spoke of it continually during your workshop, your name means *The Way.*" I was taken aback, flabbergasted.

"What?"

She emphatically repeated, *"The Way."* A myriad of thoughts came flooding into my mind.

"Oh it all makes sense," I blurted out. "My husband gave me his name when we were married, but by his death I found

90

the way to God, to Christ and to Home."

A still small voice whispered from some place deep within me, *"I Am the Way the Truth and the Life."* Oh, dear Jeshua, dear Christ, my heart was at once overflowing; of course it is the work that I am to do to help others find their way out of darkness into Light. Tears had escaped and were flowing down my cheeks; it felt like God had graced me with an angel. I would never forget her. In her deep sensitivity she felt the expanding of my heart. We spontaneously embraced as she said,

"I just thought you would like to know."

We then parted never to meet again. A deep healing and awakening had occurred in that sweet moment. It was then that I changed the pronunciation of my name to the French version and declared to keep it always. A reminder of tragedy to triumph, crisis to Christ, the name was part of my passage and I would honor it.

More and more the A.R.E. became a place to serve and to apply what had been so freely given to me from Spirit. Work was incredibly fruitful, my monthly prayer messages were being published and distributed to thousands. I was teaching what I most believed as my avocation became my vocation.

Soon the call was made to Carol; it was time to do the inner work. It was hard to believe that there was still so much more. The former sleepless nights, the agonizing long suffering, the endless tears that had consumed so much of my life, how could there be more? Yet I knew that the time with Joe had been a distraction, a way to give myself a break from the enormity of the loss. He had given me a respite. There were still pockets of heavy emotion concretized in my body affecting me in ways I didn't fully comprehend.

Carol greeted me at the door. Her quiet strength assured me that I was safe and in the right place. She explained the GIM process. A relaxation would be suggested first to help me become inwardly focused and receptive to the music. She said that music had the ability to awaken feelings and emotional patterns that were in need of healing and release. We discussed a focus for my first journey. It was clear that I needed to work on the long-held grief and pain around my husband's death.

Carol explained, "Just before the music starts, the journey will be seeded with a simple statement that the music take you to the source of your pain. Much like a waking dream, images will begin to surface from your inner knowing. They are often related to the intention and will become more clear as we later discuss the journey. The imagery is not always visual but can be sensory, kinesthetic or emotional. All you have to do is share whatever you are experiencing. I will encourage you along and sometimes ask questions."

Becoming nervous, I found myself wondering if I really wanted to dredge up that miserable pain. But as I recalled the reassuring image with Christ on the mountain from Carol's first exercise, I was calmed. I remembered His words, "You need to heal this."

Tears just under the surface, I took a deep breath and said,

"Okay, let's do it, I'm ready."

Following her suggestions, I relaxed each body part. Her voice was soothing, almost mesmerizing. I found it easy to let go, to sink into the quiet and to trust her. The magnificent textured sounds of Debussy's *Danses Sacred & Profane*, began to play, inviting me to explore. The music coaxed me and urged me to travel, drawing me in.

The impressionistic quality of the music suggested a rich inner landscape. I became aware of myself in a lovely garden lined with beautiful trees and fragrant flowers. The music was creating a soundtrack for my inner world. The full sound of the violin strings and enticing harp along with Carol's guidance invited me to explore the garden. It wasn't a thinking process; the thinking analytical part of my mind had withdrawn. This imagery had an energy of its own, leading me into deeper and deeper recesses of my inner world.

As I described the scene, Carol asked what I felt drawn to and immediately a very large rock came into view. I moved toward it. Feeling the need to rest, I leaned my back against it and dropped into an even deeper state. No longer consciously aware of the music, just the coolness and strength of the rock as it supported the weight of my body, I let go. As I did, a wave of sorrow passed through me. I began to feel a deep loneliness—the old ripping away of my heart had returned. Carol gently and strategically asked,

"Can you allow yourself to go into that?"

I was transported back to the night of the suicide to find myself standing in the living room of my old house in New Jersey looking at a young woman frozen on the couch.

"Oh, my God, I'm still there," I cried.

At Carol's prompting I described what I saw, becoming aware that some part of me was still in that room.

Carol asked, "What is it like for her?"

Still shocked by what I was witnessing, I hesitated with my answer.

She looked so young. She was locked in time and terror. Suddenly I heard the gunshot and then her scream. It was all encompassing, as if imploding in her cells yet exploding throughout the room, echoing through the house. I was hardly aware that I was physically releasing the scream until Carol's voice said,

"Yes, let it out!"

My own body was wracked in convulsive sobs. It seemed endless, as if every part of my form was releasing its tight hold, its long held pockets of terror. Every fiber of my heart was in the scream, was the scream, and after what felt like an eternity it finally subsided. It was so very different from the scream of the "Wild Woman" from long ago; it came from an endless well of unimaginable fright and sorrow.

I felt exhausted yet freed. Carol asked where was I now? I noticed the young girl was still in a heap on the couch unable to move. The scream was silent now but she seemed dead and lifeless, still trapped in the endless moment. She couldn't move. The trauma had rendered her powerless.

Quietly Carol asked, "What does she need?"

Deep compassion arose from within as I approached my paralyzed self softly murmuring,

"It's okay."

She reminded me of a frightened animal huddled and curled into herself. As she looked up at me with blank eyes I whispered, "I'll help you."

She seemed so fragile, so small, a child in a young widow's body. Picking her up I felt the deadness in her limbs and then our eyes locked. I found myself looking deep inside her, inside myself. Speaking to her as though we were separate I assured her,

"Oh you poor child, I'm here and I love you so."

Carrying her to a rocking chair, I felt she was all but lifeless—her head arched back, her arms and legs dangling in a manner reminiscent of the Pieta. I supported her body, gently bringing her head up so it could rest upon my breast.

Slowly rocking I whispered, "I know what you went through, I know."

I held her close for what felt like a long time and then began to feel the rising and falling of my chest breathe life back into her. I murmured words of tenderness and support. As I held her Lucky appeared and said,

"I'm so sorry, please forgive me, I love you so much. Can you heal this now? "

He placed a hand on each of our backs, allowing his love to fill us, and as it moved in I felt my younger self begin to stir. Life was returning to her eyes, she looked up and then began to merge with me. Breathing deeply I absorbed her into my heart. This would be a safe place for her to rest and heal and I would take care of her. Then it was just Lucky cradling me in the rocking chair. I leaned back and let myself reside in his tender embrace. There was no need for words, just the gentle rocking. Carol's voice entered my awareness once again.

"Just allow yourself to take that in and when you feel ready you can return here."

In a few moments I emerged from the experience feeling peaceful but with many questions.

"Carol, what was that? Was I really on the couch all of those years, frozen in time?"

"An aspect of you was apparently still trapped there, you had lost a part of yourself. Although locked in the past, that pain was still affecting you, just waiting to be released. That frozen part of you could not move forward. There are many sides of you, Karla, that make up the totality of who you are. When you have a deep experience like this, you often bring up what is painful and unfinished, the wounded parts as well as the strengths. There are many sides that are wounded together with many strengths."

I shared with her my shenanigans as the screaming "Wild Woman."

"Ah, that too was a part of self that helped you through. That was your inner warrior. You pulled her up from the deep recesses of your unconscious in the same way you have been

95

in contact with the Divine Self."

"But that sounds like the three faces of Eve. Am I that split apart?"

"No, no," Carol assured me. "We are all a culmination of many aspects."

"But does that mean it is not really Christ in my meditations and journeys? Is He just a symbol of my imagination?"

"No, I believe He is real within you, guiding your every step. Today you have contacted a part of yourself that was lost. With this process you are on a journey toward wholeness where you can find all of the answers to life's questions. Music provides the carrying wave for your consciousness to open so you have a chance to release those bottled up emotions in order to be healed."

I felt graced, incredibly grateful and enriched. As hard as my pain had been, I knew that I could never have touched the deep, mystical, precious moments of life and my inner world without it. A doorway into the sacred had been revealed to me, an unconscious part of my mind that was not under the laws of time and space, a place where great healing and miracles could manifest.

"Wow! This is incredible."

She smiled as she said, "That's why it's called magnified states of consciousness."

"That's for sure!"

Leaving Carol, I felt fuller, yet at the same time lighter. How many other parts do I have floating around in time/no time? What an adventure!

Chapter 10
Feathers and Forgiveness

Work at the A.R.E. continued to flourish. I felt lighter and more joyous; I loved my job and at times could not even believe that I was teaching the Edgar Cayce readings. I felt a closeness with Edgar, strange as that may sound. Two events occurred confirming that I was just where I needed to be.

A new administrative director had been considering abolishing Prayer Services. I had fought tooth and nail to keep the program in existence: after all it was Edgar himself who had started that first prayer group. He deeply understood the power of prayer, the power of the mind and healing. There were still members left from that original group. The Glad Helpers, as they were called, prayed tirelessly for all those who sent in requests for prayer and healing. Those requests filtered through my office. Connected to the Prayer Services department, the group had been volunteering since 1931 in selfless service. I deeply respected and loved them. I also knew that

Meredith Puryear, the spiritual leader of the group and one of my most important teachers, who was then on a leave of absence, would be devastated if Prayer Services was cut.

Eleven Virginia Beach spiritual comrades and I had been studying Native American healing and ritual with a medicine man from New Mexico. In the powerful Native American sweat lodge we were taught how to connect with our living and breathing Earth Mother and how to release what no longer served us. Through sacred ritual we honored the four directions and then entered into the lodge. Dark and small, it was constructed with willow branches and adorned with tarps and animal skins to keep the elements out. We huddled close to one another, at times gasping for breath as water and sage were tossed onto hot lava rocks, creating steam so hot we sweat, wept and prayed all at once.

"May we become spiritual warriors willing to die to the old self in order to rise to our greatest heights."

I learned how to connect with my deep feminine, how to release the past and open more fully to the Oneness that permeates all of creation. Our prayers were sent to all our relations, all brothers and sisters, all life, even unto the very last blade of grass.

A block dance was shown. This was a dance performed by a native when an obstacle occurred on his or her path. It was a call to Great Spirit to abolish and release the block. Abolishing Prayer Services clearly called for a block dance.

Adorned in my Native American vest and with feathers in my hair I presented myself outside the conference room door just as the head honchos were gathering to decide the fate of Prayer Services. It had leaked out to the staff that I was up to something. By then they knew that I was not just the girl who had healed herself of a serious physical injury and emotional tragedy but a woman who also embodied a wild, determined, and spontaneous side. That part of me would not stop even if it meant looking foolish for a cause that was noble and needed. This in my mind was one such cause.

Nearly the entire staff showed up in a show of solidarity and support as I prepared to do my ritual dance. On the floor near the open door of the conference room where I would dance I placed a piece of wood. It represented the block to spirituality, healing and Edgar Cayce's vision for Prayer Services. Hardly caring what I looked like I proceeded to dance. I hopped over the stick then turned and hopped back, first on one foot then the other. The feathers in my hair bounced up and down and side to side in rhythm with the dance. A low guttural sound emanated from the back of my throat as I chanted to the Great Spirit. The staff didn't quite know what to make of it; there were grins, mouths hanging open in disbelief, and supportive nods. I knew that I appeared crazy but all of my letters and appeals for Prayer Services had been ignored. This would surely get their attention; they would recognize me now.

As I danced, an administrator came to the door. Glancing in I saw the wide-eyed, alarmed group staring back at me. The door slowly closed. Back and forth over the block I danced with a prayerful intent that the energy of love and commitment to truth would indeed abolish the obstacle. After a short time the administrators began to exit the room, clearly uncomfortable with my seemingly bizarre behavior. They kept their gaze down, away from mine, but there was one administrator who shot me an open smile and a thumbs-up. The crowd that had gathered opened a pathway to allow those in authority to pass and my dance came to its conclusion. Chuckling to myself, I reveled in the auspicious moment, at the same time wondering if I would be fired. I was not fired. With me at the wheel, Prayer Services remained intact, and flourishes still.

Just a few nights later while working late on my monthly prayer message I thought I heard something down the hall. Everyone had left. I was alone at the end of the long hall in my small, third-floor office, which was in what had once been the hospital built by Cayce and his supporters. An enormous white building at the top of a hill just behind the conference center, it contained the therapy rooms and the various offices of the fine staff who organized the conferences, prison projects and study groups all over the world. It was a place resonant with history and spiritual intensity.

Chills began to move through my body as I felt spirit energy approach. Taking a deep breath I reminded myself that God protected me, that only Light could be with me, so I waited. As I did, the block dance flashed into my mind.

Remembering this with amusement my attention was then drawn back to the energy that was approaching. It felt larger and closer. In fact, it felt huge. As I sat with my mouth hanging open and my eyes wide I knew at that moment that it was the spirit of Edgar Cayce coming to thank me—I can't explain how, I just knew.

I felt his spirit body enter into the room. I did not clearly see him but I felt his energy, and his abounding love. I could even feel him smile as a palpable wave of gratitude moved into me. His smile and presence felt gentle and kind much like a loving and approving grandfather. No sooner had his spirit come in than it departed, like mist rising off a lake. But in its wake my small office was filled with a warm and tangible feeling of that gratitude and love.

The memory of that glorious visitation stayed with me and I joyously spent my mornings at the office coordinating prayer requests from all over the world while afternoons and evenings provided an opportunity to teach. I began each day with prayers for direction, each noon I joined the staff for meditation, and then evenings were devoted to play, joy and gratitude.

I made many good friends and found much support among my co-workers at the A.R.E. One of my main cohorts was Edie, a robust, passionate and generous, redhead who had moved to the beach from New York City to further deepen her soul work. She came to every lecture and workshop I presented. Standing at the back of the conference room her brilliant presence encouraged and urged me on.

Nervousness always plagued me at the beginning of my programs but I knew that I could always count on Edie. No matter how busy she was she would find a way to support me. There were times when she would make a silly face in order to get me to lighten up. Gesturing a mood of gaiety in a sweeping motion of her full skirt she mouthed her favorite nickname for me, "Wa . . . Wa . . . Luv . . . Wa . . . "

Once I laughed I could let go of the fear and allow spirit to move through me. It's amazing that no one ever asked what I was laughing about. Edie was my anchor as well as an instigator and supporter of my shenanigans. I loved her with all of my heart.

Mary Lou was a different breed. A born volunteer, she would find a cause and give of herself fully and freely. She was like a mother to me, a confidant, teacher and friend, possessing an extraordinary sense of humor. For a spoof she taped a mock meditation guiding students through a journey suggesting that they had a five-pound crystal taped to their foreheads just above their third eye. The meditation began with her gentle and soft tone, those listening expecting a profound experience as she explained the importance of the crystal.

"Let yourself relax now," she said. "Breathe deeply and feel the Divine energy fill your body. Allow the crystal to bring you into higher dimensions. That's it, settle in."

Her serene voice led them through a full body relaxation. Then without forewarning a louder more shrill voice roared out.

"Look out, don't lose that crystal, balance it on your head, it's the only way to get to Spirit, you can do it!" She was nearly shrieking at this point.

As we listened to the tape, Edie, Mary Lou and I laughed uproariously. I am certain that our conservative and serious boss didn't know what to do with us. We were a dangerous threesome, each one of us having a bizarre and wild aspect to our personality. Laughter oozed out of our office while we spent countless moments hysterical over something yet at the same time we all had a deep desire to serve. Most importantly we had the ability to laugh at ourselves as we met the challenges of rich soul growth and living in "Karma City," as Virginia Beach was so fondly named. We knew it was no mere accident that we were placed together. Mary Lou's constant warning was,

"Now, Karla dear, you stay away from those sweat lodges. You're going to get in big trouble."

And of course I did. My dear friend, Mary Lou filled with the wisdom of the sage knew that I would be dredging up the unimaginable past, but all that happens in life is part of a greater plan. The emotions dredged up became the substance and focus of my deep inner work with Carol.

My GIM (Guided Imagery and Music) journeys with Carol continued with powerful exploration and release at each session. During one of those sessions I contacted my long-held guilt about the words I had spoken to my husband. The guilt bubbled up from yet another layer of trapped memory and pain. Carol was playing Marcello's *Oboe Concerto in D Minor* from the *Grieving Music Program*. The strings of the lonely solo oboe haunted me as they traveled deep into the recesses of the long-standing guilt. I felt a pain in my heart and stomach and then a memory began to emerge. I was recalling the night that my husband was horribly drunk and in gripping pain. In my long-spent frustration and exhaustion the words and heavy emotion poured out. The shameful and guilt-ridden words that I would never be able to call back rose to the surface, repeating over and over in my mind.

"You're killing yourself with this alcohol! Why don't you just blow your head off instead of this slow and agonizing death?"

I was fully back in that terrible moment. My body aching with pain, the words spilled forth gushing out between uncontrollable and wrenching sobs. How could one body hold so much shame and still function? But the words rang out, offering no rest; they were escaping from the hardened pockets of deep memory.

Looking at my crumbled husband in utter desperation I cried out, "I can't stand your agony." Then, at last, came the realization: "I can't do anything to help you."

"Yes," Carol encouraged, "Keep speaking to him."

I found myself softening as I spoke to my distraught husband. "It's just so hard to see you this way, I want you to be well, not to die. Please forgive me. I am so sorry for what I said, I didn't mean it."

I was holding him, caressing his face as I whispered. "You are my endless love."

He turned to me, no longer inebriated, and whispered back.

"Dearest Doris, my angel, this was in place long before your words were spoken. It was to be the way for us."

He was once again the healing force, the spirit that had been freed of the physical form.

"You didn't cause this. There is nothing to forgive."

As clearly as if I was fully awake, I saw him, heard him, felt him, his presence as solid as Carol's sitting next to me, somehow even more real than "reality." Holding me close, he continued to whisper, reassuring me with his loving words,

"Let it go now, you have much to do, know that I am fine as I have shown you, I am close and will remain close to you, to Tom, and my girls. There is great purpose in this, you know it."

As with the earlier out of body experiences, his words traveled into me, to be felt by my heart and absorbed. As they did, energy permeated throughout my entire body. I allowed myself to fully feel it.

I was utterly exhausted after the session. Realizing this, Carol suggested I see her friend Mary Elizabeth Marlow for some hands on healing and nurturing. Knowing the power of Reiki I was ready to take another step in my healing. I quickly made the appointment with Mary Elizabeth.

As I lay on her massage table while soft meditative music played, Mary Elizabeth placed her hands gently on my heart. I could feel a penetrable warmth sink in. Waves of energy flowed through my relaxed body. She worked at each chakra, flooding the area with Light and healing, removing blockages as she helped me to gently release emotion.

Often, fleeting memories would surface of precious love-filled moments—the birth of my son, his first baby steps, and the day his tiny, chubby hands cupped my cheeks. Moments of tender love with my husband returned to my awareness— the first time I saw his face and knew that he was my beloved.

The GIM work had opened the door of my heart, where so much excruciating pain had been stored, blocking me from the true richness of my earth existence. Now there was room to be fully present with the depth of love that I had been blessed with. How tender and sweet it was to feel it all again, my dearest child, my beautiful husband.

During one of our healing sessions a strange image emerged. I saw a woman that seemed to be me standing outside a burning building. As I looked up to the second story I saw a small child. He was hanging out of the window screaming, "Mommy, Mommy!"

The building was engulfed in flames. Terror came over me; I was viscerally feeling the emotion, my body contracting into itself. But it didn't make sense, this had never happened to me. Yet the imagery persisted, flames and smoke completely overtook the building, then the screams stopped and the child was gone. I was left with unexplainable guilt and grief. It was a mother's grief. This child, I felt, had been mine.

But how, where? It didn't seem to be my Tommy. Could he be the mysterious young man I had seen on my first GIM inner journey, the one with the dark, penetrating eyes?

I was perplexed, but felt certain of one thing: I would see him again.

Chapter 11
Ram Dass
Beloved Teacher

I was becoming more and more comfortable with the wisdom that surfaced from my inner knowing. I began to pray for the child and for the aspect of myself that had emerged from some far distant past.

GIM journeys and Reiki continued as needed. I felt all of the pieces of my life were coming together. My dream world was further activated and most of my important decisions were guided by that state. Visions and remembrances of other lifetimes continued to flow as my contemplative life deepened. Many new soul friends and I found ways to cherish life through song, sacred dance, Native American ritual and just plain fun. How wonderful life was!

One afternoon a flier arrived at my office announcing an upcoming weekend workshop in Chapel Hill, NC. Graced on the outside of the flier was a face that captivated me—Ram Dass, he was called, a spiritual teacher. *Conscious Living,*

Conscious Dying was the theme of the program. Planning to read through it later, I tacked it on the bulletin board near my desk and tried to return to work. I couldn't; I found myself glued to it. When I rested my gaze upon his face I felt myself deepen, my heart opening as I nearly sank into meditation.

How could a picture have such an effect? It was as if I had known him all of my life; the depth of his eyes pulled me in. *Oh it's you,* came to mind over and over. Quickly I called the number to register, hardly interested in the subject matter: he could have been teaching quilting for all I cared. I just had to go.

I did not gravitate to the guru/student relationship, preferring to learn from many masters and great teachers, but I was fixated on Ram Dass. By this point I was comfortable allowing my intuitive nature to guide me so I decided to trust my soul urgings. After all, here I was in Virginia Beach doing the work that had been revealed to me in the deep state.

Plans were made and soon Sharon and Carolyn, two of my new-found friends and I, headed west for Chapel Hill. I was attending a conference on death and dying and hardly knew why. I just had to be in the presence of Ram Dass.

The conference was held at a rustic retreat center. Entering the hall, I saw scores of people sitting, most of them on the floor. Big pillows were strewn about—very different from the straight-backed chairs and structured programs at the A.R.E. We found three spots up front in the center and settled in.

The dais was adorned with an Oriental rug, where flowers, eastern musical instruments, beautifully colored scarves and a picture of Ram Dass's guru Neem Karoli Baba were displayed. Incense wafted through the room filling one's nostrils with a sweet scent. An empty, soft, easy chair sat in the middle of the flowers, heightening our delicious anticipation. Ram Dass was coming. I had never heard of him before that flier came to my office yet my heart was overflowing at the thought of seeing him. *What on earth is this,* I wondered?

The group was silent. A stillness permeated the space, as all waited for the beloved teacher. The mood invited one to go within and many were already in deep meditation. As soon as Ram Dass entered I felt the familiar stirrings of my heart; tears were just under the surface. Dressed simply and casually he moved to the chair, assumed a lotus position and closed his eyes. Everyone followed suit; his mere presence transported all of us into another level of awareness. I, however, could not take my eyes off him. I felt a strong and mesmerizing sense of remembrance. His eyes opened and very slowly he scanned the room, as if drinking each and every one of us in. Many seemed to be in a blissful state, their eyes glistening with joyous tears. *So I am not alone, does everyone feel the way I do? What on earth is this?* Bringing his gaze back he centered and then focused on me.

An energy of love moved from his heart into mine. Feeling this love and his incredible clarity I began to feel my own mind become clearer than it had ever been. Every word he uttered to the group spoke truth to me. I felt as if I was falling deeply in love, but it was a love of another realm, not of this earth or of my physical form. I sat in the wondrous moment absorbing it. There were no conditions, no expectations, just love. How incredibly delicious!

Ram Dass told us of his guru, the intensity of love for him and how even now on the other side Baba was still a constant presence in his life, chiding him and laughing with him. He spoke of changing consciousness like changing television channels. He explained that most of the time we were operating from "channel two"— our concretized set of belief systems based on past history or future outcomes and filled with judgments and feelings of inadequacy.

What if we changed the channel to five or seven, or how about thirteen? Did we dare move out of the old paradigm? Instead of observing ourselves as an ego what if we were just a soul? What if we knew something much grander than what presented itself in front of our mortal eyes? Every concept he suggested aligned with my beliefs.

Yes ... yes ... I kept repeating within. *I know that too!*

He began to talk about death and the incredible privilege of being present with one who is dying; sitting not as a body but as a soul; listening with all of the senses; simply being with the one dying; offering a space where pure love could be present.

As he spoke his eyes fell upon me over and over again. His soft penetrating glance exposed me at the deepest recesses of my being. I was totally visible to his gaze. The Light in me, the darkness, the joy and the sorrow were all present. It was all right there rich in the moment; he knew me and completely accepted me. I wanted to curl up into him, to love and be loved by him in every way, spiritually, emotionally, mentally and physically. Numerous moments throughout the weekend I experienced this magnificent love connection as his gaze steadied with mine. As it did, my breath resonated with his until there was only one of us. I was being in-filled, deeply loved and made love to. Our spirits were silently dancing in the center of his words, a joyful and beautiful dance of love. All in his presence were offered this unconditional gift of love and acceptance. Ram Dass held a mirror that reflected our own beautiful and Light-filled souls.

This was 1982, and he spoke of the AIDS crisis: so many dying, so many abandoned and abused. He shared from personal experience, not afraid to reveal his own shortcomings and mistakes. Ram Dass used all of his life experiences as a way to learn and to teach.

As he brought us into the many meditations he gently spoke,

"It's all One, change the channel, embrace the pain, face it, become familiar, sit with it and let it speak to you. The pain will be the way out of the pain. Just observe and when anything comes up that seems less than whole be with it."

While he spoke, his hand was positioned just in front of his cheek, palm facing in. With a soft, flowing backward wave he moved his fingers, as if caressing the thoughts that emerged and the energy around him. All the while saying,

"Ah, and that too . . . and that too . . . is perfect . . . Whatever thought comes up, just be with it."

I realized that with complete acceptance of myself, of my seeming inadequacy and pain, I would be able to heal. That which was dark within me would no longer have power over me as long as I could sit with it. The intensity of my guilt, the shoulds, judgments and all of the words that meant "not good enough" melted in the light of my accepting presence. Ram Dass had witnessed my inner being and still loved me; now I could behold myself with that same kind of love.

I was transfixed. Of course I am not my body, that is just a form; we all are far greater than the body. We are formless, in a dance with God, a dance of remembering. We just happen to find ourselves in a body, and as we become clear we can dance the dance with God from the body sacred, the conduit for the soul. The more I listened to Ram Dass the more I understood. I loved him so much because he allowed all of us to dance with him. I saw the God in him and he saw the God in me. We were intertwined in the rapturous love of Spirit. Everything he said and did spoke waves of truth and called me to my greatest self.

The intimate group felt like a band of old friends hanging out with their elder brother, sprawled out on the floor, leaning on pillows quietly taking it all in. My thoughts went to Christ, Jeshua. It must have been just like this, hanging out together listening to our Elder Brother, laughing and singing with Him, His words lifting and penetrating our conscious awareness as He brought us to greater truth.

Ram Dass led us through chants, and though it seemed impossible we went still higher. Our channels were certainly changing each passing hour; channel two was long gone. He led us through *Jubilate Deo,* breaking us up into three groups and singing along with us, visibly delighted. Up into the wooden beams of that vibrating hall, our song echoed like the choirs of heaven.

I wanted to be just like Ram Dass. I already taught from my heart, shared my tragedies, my visions; helped others to change their consciousness. My desire was to be as real as he was, to absorb the group that came to hear me, taking them in one by one with my love, as he did. His every move, gesture and demeanor was imprinted upon me. He was my teacher.

I left that retreat feeling authenticated and empowered, determined to open more fully to love and to Spirit and to be a "way show-er" for others, in the style of Ram Dass. I had that opportunity as soon as we returned to the A.R.E.

The summer conferences were in full swing and I had the honor of working with the eminent physicians Gerry Jampolsky, Raymond Moody, and Bernie Siegel, and other great teachers. Even though I was representing great spiritual truth from the Edgar Cayce readings on reincarnation, meditation, prayer and healing, and soul development, and was sharing my own personal experiences, I still felt like a mere babe. I started each presentation nervously but as soon as I surrendered to God, I entered the flow of the moment. I remembered Ram Dass's words,

"Ah . . . this too is perfect."

I began to share the truth of my jitters with the audience. I was becoming more real and authentic and they loved my candor.

During one of my talks I decided to be more like Ram Dass. Instead of greeting the audience in my usual fashion I simply closed my eyes and breathed, fully expecting the large group to join me, as Ram Dass's devotees had done. Opening my eyes I proceeded to gaze, a Ram Dass gaze drinking each one in. Perhaps it was the straight-back chairs; this group was not melting with me as the Ram Dass group had done with him. Rather than taking the audience's lead, I persisted. Somehow I had lost my channel, fallen into ego and *tried* to make it happen. Uh-oh, channel two.

Moving closer to the edge of the dais I continued my gaze. The group must have wondered what on earth was I doing? I must have looked idiotic! Slowly walking back and forth on the edge of the podium, I caught my heel in the wires of the sound system. Before I knew what hit me I tripped on the wire and went flying off the stage, landing in a heap on the floor right in front of the first row of the audience.

Some kind and sympathetic soul helped me up; I brushed myself off and resumed my spiritual stance. *What a dope*, I thought. *Well the only way out of this one is to tell the truth.* I explained the channel selections and that I was a Ram Dass "wanna be" who had lost her channel. Laughter ensued; they loved it. For the remainder of the workshop, each time I would look at someone just a little too long laughter would break out. I felt like a cartoon, but even in my most embarrassing moment Ram Dass was teaching me

"Just embrace it all, let it teach you."

Ram Dass became my inner guide. When something was troubling me or a decision needed to be made he would appear in my dream state offering clues and symbols to assist me on my journey. I had been touched deeply by him. Without realizing it, I was being primed to turn down yet another new and exciting path.

Chapter 12
Here Am I Lord

My time on staff at the A.R.E. brought me innumerable gifts. My presentations became more polished and I felt increasingly serene as I spoke to audiences. Even though the straight–back chairs offered a more structured program than Ram Dass's, the audience clearly felt my heart and quickly aligned with me. With each presentation I gave, I felt more connected to and in love with the people in the audience.

One evening, Dr. Elisabeth Kübler-Ross came to lecture. The large conference hall filled to overflowing. She was a spitfire. Her tiny frame and huge presence held us all captive in the moment. Many sat in the adjacent small conference room and the upstairs meditation area, only able to hear her voice piped in through the intercom. Nevertheless, she held all spellbound. Her wisdom echoed through the A.R.E., bringing us into deep appreciation and awe for her work and her magnificent spirit.

Her stories touched me deeply. A pioneer in the field of

death and dying, Kübler-Ross had witnessed much. Her 1969 book *On Death and Dying*, a monumental contribution, had brought death out of the closet and into an arena of beauty and honor. Because of her research with near death experiences and her famous stages of dying, a new layer of knowledge had been birthed into the world. Unbeknownst to me at that time, I would soon be exploring this knowledge firsthand.

Elisabeth told a story from her childhood that pierced my heart. She had been an animal lover from an early age, creating a makeshift hospital where she cared for injured birds, frogs and snakes. She even nurtured an injured crow until it was able to fly once again. Animals instinctively trusted her. On her family property a dozen or more bunnies were housed in a hutch in the garden. Elisabeth's duties were to clean their cage, feed them and play with them. Occasionally her mother served rabbit stew. Elisabeth did not allow herself to think about how the rabbits got there nor could she eat the meat. But she knew that the bunnies only approached the gate for her.

Elizabeth was a triplet and caring for the rabbits offered her the separate identity she so needed; the bunnies were able to distinguish her from her sisters. She doted on them and loved them dearly. Then one day her very thrifty father decided the rabbits were multiplying too fast and began reducing their numbers. They ate only dandelions and grass and so cost nothing to feed. He was interested in the grocery money he would save by serving them for dinner.

One morning he instructed the very young Elisabeth to bring a bunny to the butcher on her way to school so her mother could make a rabbit roast that evening. He told her to bring it back at lunchtime so it would be ready for the evening meal. Her father was a strict father. She obeyed. For many months she repeated the trip to the butcher until, eventually, only Blackie, her favorite bunny, was left.

Blackie was a big ball of fluff that she cuddled and shared her deepest secrets with, for he was a great listener; she felt he was the only one who truly loved her unconditionally.

Then one horrid day her father ordered Elisabeth to take Blackie to the butcher. She was shaking and speechless as she ran out of the house to the hutch. Opening the gate she pleaded with Blackie to run away but her little bunny didn't budge. She scooped him up into her arms and tightly held on to him as she ran to the butcher, all the while crying frantically as both their hearts raced wildly. She quickly placed her beloved bunny into the hands of certain demise and ran off. At school she was unable to think of anything except Blackie. Did he know how much she loved him and how much she would miss him? She had been too distraught even to say goodbye.

Elisabeth was filled with regret and devastating pain, hating the feelings she was having and the horrible task that had been given to her. She adamantly blamed her father. As she arrived at the butcher's shop after school, he met her at the door with the small parcel in hand and said,

"What a pity that you had to bring this one, she was about to have bunnies."

Devastated, she realized her precious Blackie had been a little girl. Filled with despair Elisabeth dutifully carried the still warm bag home to her mother. That evening she watched stoically as her family ate her bunny. She never shed a tear, for she would not let her parents know how much they had wounded her. Feeling completely unloved, she decided that she would have to become tough in order to survive, for if she could make it through this she could make it through anything. Little did she know then that this crushing blow was molding her for the great work she would do much later.

As I heard this story, tears flowed down my cheeks; I thought my heart would break for her and her little bunny. As I looked around the room I saw that many others were weeping. I'm sure there was not a dry eye in the house.

Elisabeth then shared another story. During an Easter week she presented a workshop on death and dying in Hawaii. The organizer was a cheapskate. He had secured a horrible place for the conference, complaining all the while that too much food was being eaten, he even charged her for the paper and crayons used. The workshop was a success but Elisabeth was miserable. On the way home she stopped in California to visit some friends but was clearly out of sorts. She was so distraught that she couldn't even speak about the program. In an attempt to be humorous and break her black and heavy mood a friend said,

"Tell us about your Easter bunnies."

Little did they know what they had opened up. Elisabeth crumbled; uncontrollable sobs escaped as the anger and frustration spewed out from her previous week. This was clearly not normal behavior for her and that night while alone she attempted to understand why she had been so reactive.

The horrible memory of Blackie returned. All of the repressed emotions that had been held for forty years flooded out. Endless tears that had needed to be cried when she was a young child broke free. Elisabeth then came to a realization; she had developed what she called an allergic reaction to cheap men. She had always been affected by that kind of man, subconsciously reliving the death of her beloved bunny every time she was in contact with a stingy man. The experience with the Hawaiian penny pincher had pushed her over the brink.

She mentioned how our unfinished business creeps up and out at the most inopportune moments and that if we are angry for more than fifteen seconds it is our own stuff that has been triggered. The one we are angry at is holding a mirror for trapped emotions held inside.

Fifteen seconds, I thought. Whoa, I'm in trouble. How often in life had I held on to anger or resentment for far longer than fifteen seconds! This new wisdom put the burden of responsibility on me to become very conscious and explore my feelings whenever I experienced anger. That would surely take some work.

Elisabeth spoke of her Life, Death and Transition Training, in which participants could clear trauma that kept them stuck in the past. Trainings were held throughout the country enabling caregivers and dying patients to release long-held emotions and to clear the fear of death—a passage that we would all have to embark upon one day. She fascinated me and I hung on to her every word. She completed her story saying,

"It is impossible to live life at the highest level unless you get rid of your negativity, your unfinished business, your *black bunnies.*"

I was certain that I still had many black bunnies to release.

I shared many similarities with Elisabeth. I too had been an animal lover from my earliest memories, caring for hurt birds, communing with my pets as if they knew everything I was saying. Even saving all of the bugs I could from certain death, as an unenlightened person would attempt to crush them with heavy shoes or fly swatters.

Elisabeth had also mentioned sweeter moments with her family as they gathered in the music room to sing their favorite songs, one being *Always.* Many times I had joined my own musical family, as my mother sang her heart out and my father played piano. The song that I loved the most was *Always.*

After the lecture, I couldn't get Elisabeth out of my mind. Was this to be my new path? Was I to work with death and dying? Out of all the famous and influential teachers I had worked with and learned from, it was clearly Elisabeth and Ram Dass who had touched me the most. What the two had in common, I realized, was their involvement with the AIDS crisis. Elisabeth cared for AIDS babies and Ram Dass sat in "the sacred" with many AIDS sufferers as they were leaving the earth plane.

I was being called; I knew that, for I felt a stirring from deep within. That evening left me sleepless. I tossed and turned, dreaming of Elisabeth's bunny and her agonizing trip to the butcher. At least the little bunny had her deep and unconditional love just before it died. Realizing that my path was soon to change, I sent out a prayer to God,

"Here am I, Lord, send me, use me. Lead Thou the way. I commit my mind, my heart and my body to be one with Thee."

At that time, I was receiving invitations from all over the country to present workshops. I was intrigued and excited, but did this fit with what my new path was to be, and was it timely? The only way to know for sure was to go within.

I asked Carol Bush if we could go on a GIM journey to explore what my path should be. She assured me once again that all of the answers to life's questions were held in my inner knowing. Traveling into the deep music-centered state, I posed the question, "What is my purpose now?"

As the imagery journey unfolded, I saw myself speaking to many groups of people and, to my surprise, facilitating a group of predominantly men, all of them ill, some barely able to stand. It was clear that they were suffering and near death. It was a very disturbing scene. At the end of the session I shared my concern with Carol. She urged me to trust the process; if it was right it would fall into place. It was apparent in the imagery that I would be traveling and meeting new people.

Trusting the urgings of my restless spirit I placed some calls to A.R.E. regional representatives across the country. Were they serious about hosting me? Could a cross-country tour support me financially? The responses were more than favorable; all were delighted to have me visit and speak.

Wow! I guess it is time. I fasted for a number of days, spending most of my free moments in meditation and sacred retreat. Leaving my staff position, especially Prayer Services, was no small matter. I loved the work, yet knew something else was calling. Giving a month's notice gave me time to orchestrate a four-month speaking tour across the country and prepare myself mentally. To my amazement I was asked by the Conference Director to present workshops while traveling through California and Washington State. There would even be a program for me at the Virginia Beach headquarters when I returned home the following August.

The Edgar Cayce readings and the A.R.E. had supported me from my initial days while suffering with severe injury and trauma, and they were supporting me still on this next exciting exploration. I felt incredibly blessed. Soon I would be off on a new and exciting journey.

John and Carolyn, my housemates and partners in shamanic study offered to rent my room to an A.R.E. visitor while I was away. All was falling easily into place. And before I had time to catch my breath off I went, my little brown Toyota Starlet packed with some clothes, music and workshop material—just the bare essentials.

Often throughout the journey I had to pinch myself to believe it was real. At every stop my hosts showered me with graciousness, ushering me to sacred sites and points of interest. But the most powerful moments were the ones experienced in solitude. I felt one with nature, with all of my surroundings; the trees swayed for me, the ground rose up to meet my feet, the air gently caressed my body. All of life tenderly filled my senses and enveloped me as I traveled west across this great land. New acquaintances who felt more like ancient long-lost friends welcomed me with open arms and blessed my path.

I had the great privilege of visiting Elisabeth at her farm in Headwaters, Virginia. It was tucked away in a rural area, a sprawling, peaceful piece of land. It was home for animals of all kinds and beautiful gardens. A welcome sign held the imprint of the sacred butterfly, her personal symbol, representing the beauty of life, death, and transformation. We sat on her terrace overlooking the lovely gardens eating a leisurely lunch as we celebrated her 60th birthday.

Pinch me, pinch me, I thought. Here I am with a woman who changed the face of our mortal earth journey and on her birthday no less. She was an icon to me yet I found her easy to be with, down to earth and very funny. How grateful I felt. We talked like young girls about all facets of life, from the ordinary to the mystical. She then asked,

"Do you believe in spooks?"

I dissolved into laughter. Our conversation rapidly turned to the personal and fascinating psychic phenomena that we had both experienced. We chuckled like young schoolgirls. At the end of our meeting Elisabeth urged me to attend her Life, Death and Transition Training, letting me know which ones she would be teaching herself. She sent me off with her famous Swiss chocolates, a small picture of Jesus, a replica of one that I had admired over her fireplace mantle, and an overflowing heart.

Munching sweet chocolate, I slowly meandered down the long gravel road leading out of her farm. Suddenly I was transfixed. My heart leapt into my throat and my breath ceased. Directly in front of my car only a few feet away stood an eagle with a huge and magnificent wingspan. It gazed at me for what seemed like an eternity but surely was just a moment. As our eyes locked, it communicated its wordless wisdom then majestically took flight.

I couldn't move. Feeling suspended in time, I sat in my car in the middle of the gravel road allowing the eagle's blessing and all of the miracles and magical moments with Elisabeth to sink in. Through my Native American study I had come to understand that all of life spoke to us if we would but listen and that there was no blessing greater than the eagle's. It was clear that I was on the right path. Yet even more would come that would speak to the Divine providence of my upcoming choices.

During a rest stop, I returned to find that a butterfly had flown into my car and was sitting on the driver's seat as if waiting for my return. *What is this*, I pondered? Its little wings gently pulsing, I cupped it carefully in my hands and brought it close to my heart.

"Hello little winged being, so you too are gracing me."

It nestled in the folds of my shirt right at my heart and remained there as I drove over four-hundred miles. When I stopped at a motel for rest it too joined me, resting on a soft T-shirt near the bed. I felt that it was coming to the end of its short life and had chosen to honor me with its passing. I thanked it over and over again, all the while in wonderment of God's sacred creations. All of life was making itself known to me, and this beautiful little being was clearly the message that represented my new work with life, death and transitions.

Although I had been given the medicine name Deer Tracks when I completed my Native American study, I now heard an inner voice speak a new name. It said,

"You are, Woman of the Butterfly."

My dearest little winged friend gave up its form and returned home to Spirit. This was clearly the richest time of my life. As I traveled to each new state I wondered where I would settle. Northern California called to me as well as the beautiful Blue Ridge Mountains of Virginia and of course I still loved Virginia Beach. The workshops I delivered were powerful and inspiring for both the participants and me. My presentations were more eclectic, including a little bit of Ram Dass, Edgar Cayce, Elisabeth Kübler-Ross, music and imagery journeys, and Native American ritual. I couldn't have been happier.

Not only were there numerous programs in many states but fun-filled and exhilarating side trips. My travels took me to Hopkinsville, Kentucky where I visited with D.D. Cayce, Edgar's nephew. D.D. shared family stories as we leisurely walked the grounds where young Edgar had lived. I felt an incredible kinship with Edgar and his wonderful family.

Later, in California, my dear friend Douglas and I took a very long excursion, slowly driving up the glorious California coast highway to San Francisco—in my opinion the most beautiful drive in the world.

Then on we went to the Grand Canyon and Yosemite State Park. All of it held me spellbound. The country had opened itself and lavished me with its indescribable and immense beauty.

On the way home I went to the Southern Ute Sun Dance in Colorado. I witnessed the undying and courageous spirit of many medicine men as they performed a ritual dance that had been practiced for many centuries. They danced without food for three days and three nights in honor of Spirit and all of creation. It was a dance of peace, one that would go out to awaken compassion and consciousness in all hearts and minds that were open to receive. Those of us invited entered into the circle, silently offering our healing thoughts, energy and prayer to the holy men who danced the dance of life and oneness.

Will I ever be the same? I wondered as I traveled east along the vast and open highway of the heartland. I felt expanded in a way that was not possible to express. While soaking in the beauty of the Blue Ridge Mountains and the Shenandoah Valley on my way back to Virginia Beach, a shattering and uninvited thought invaded my peace. I clearly heard,

"You are going back to New Jersey."

What? . . . That *can't* be! . . . It was unthinkable. I needed to be in open spaces where I could commune with nature and further grow. New Jersey felt tight, constricted, and not spiritually mature.

Well that's just crazy. My plan was to buy a piece of property, somewhere new where I could settle with enough room for Tom if he chose to live with me after college and a place for my mom. As wonderful as the Jersey Shore had been to me, it just didn't feel like my nesting place anymore. But then my thoughts returned to a conversation that I had with a spiritual teacher while visiting my deep soul sister Sherry, near Seattle, Washington. We spoke of places to live that would offer growth and spiritual community. When I brought up my aversion to New Jersey he simply said,

"Well, Karla, someone has to go to the outpost."

Was it already in place then? Oh no, this just can't be, but the thought persisted. Perplexed, I drove the remaining miles to my home in Virginia Beach, all the while trying to get the unwanted and disturbing thought out of my mind.

Carolyn and John greeted me with open arms.

"Welcome home, your space is ready and waiting for you."

I loved them dearly; we had all grown in our shamanic work, supporting each other through numerous ups and downs.

Just as I entered the living room, plopping my bags on the floor, Carolyn said,

"This just came today. It's a certified letter, looks like it's from a courthouse in New Jersey. I knew you would be coming home today so I signed for it. I hope nothing's wrong."

"What on earth is this?" Then my thoughts raced to Tom. He had left Virginia Commonwealth University to return to Rutgers in New Jersey. For a time he stayed with Trina, a former student and her husband Eugene who were renting our home. He then convinced me that he was mature enough to stay in the house without them. Tom said he would rent a room to a local teacher so I wouldn't need to worry, as there would be an adult present in the house.

Tom was in his second year of college and had always been trustworthy and levelheaded, a really good boy, so after many conversations and much contemplation I had agreed.

However, after he moved in on more than one occasion an image popped into my head of wild parties. When I confronted him he denied it vehemently.

"Mom, no way!"

Until one night I called and said.

"Tom, you're having a wild party right now, I can see it."

"How do you do that?" he questioned.

"I can't explain, Tom, it just happens when I least expect it."

"Okay," he responded. "It won't happen again. I'll keep it down, Mom, I promise."

Poor kid, it must have been challenging for him having such an intuitive mom, but it was a plus for me.

"Uh-oh," I said to John and Carolyn as I looked at the mail. "This doesn't look good."

They waited for the ripping of the envelope with obvious anticipation. Still standing in the living room, bags strewn around my feet I opened the letter.

"Dear Mrs. LaVoie:

There is not now nor has there ever been a zoning ordinance for a "mud wrestling pit" on your property. A court appearance is scheduled for September 20, 1984 at 9am. You must appear."

Don't ask why but my first response was not anger, it was laughter. That little stinker, he had asked me if he could take down the above ground pool and I had said no. He had obviously done it anyway. That had to be it. A big hole in the ground was now a "mud-wrestling pit."

Before contacting Tom, I called a close friend in New Jersey who lived down the street from my house.

"Candy, have you been by the house lately? Is there anything strange going on?" She broke up in hysterical laughter.

"Tommy is having a great time. The other night I passed by and saw that there were cars lined up and down both sides of the street and music blaring from the backyard. I heard through my daughters that he is announcing mud-wrestling games at the beach. He brings fliers; I think it costs five dollars a head to get in."

"What?" I exclaimed.

She continued, "Yup, and he made bleachers out of cement blocks, put them all around the pit."

"Candy, why didn't you call me?"

"I thought about it, but knew you were traveling. It really

127

is funny, Karla, and I know Tommy wouldn't do anything terribly wrong."

"Well," I responded, "He certainly is an enterprising little cuss."

We were both laughing at the image of people rolling around covered in mud in my backyard.

"Oh, and it's co-ed," Candy added.

"Oh jeez."

"You know your neighbor across the street is the zoning officer," she added. "He probably got tired of the noise."

I tried to get serious once off the phone with Candy, but to no avail. As I shared with John and Carolyn, we laughed uproariously. It really was funny.

The call was made to Tom; I read the letter verbatim. With strong conviction he emphatically denied the accusation.

"Mom, what mud-wrestling pit?"

It was an outrageous and ridiculous effort to save himself, but the handwriting was on the wall.

"Tom, I'm coming home."

A softer, more pensive response followed, barely audible.

"Okay, Mom."

I was spinning. What am I going to do? I had resigned from my high school position a year earlier. Private practice would not fly in New Jersey, at least not at this point. The area hadn't opened its arms to the innovative holistic and new age thought.

I paced back and forth. Maybe just a visit will do, but I knew deep down that Tom needed me home. Surely the parties were going on strong while I was traveling. I feared that his grades would suffer or he would get into serious trouble. I loved my son dearly. Too much of his life had been spent fending for himself as I merely survived during the first violent marriage to his father and then the consuming years spent caring for Lucky.

Even after Lucky's death, I wasn't a fit mom. We both needed help then but I was too caught up in my own pain and suffering to realize it. Life had robbed him of the nurturing mother he deserved; yet it was clear that he needed me now. I was far more mature and balanced and wanted desperately to be there for him even if that meant straightening his butt out. It was the last week of August. I was scheduled to do a three-day program for the A.R.E., and then what? I put the request for guidance and direction into the hands of Spirit.

"Show me the way, Lord."

I knew that there was power in surrendering the situation to God for three days. Asking for a sign to mark the way, I prayed and meditated and asked counsel from my closest friends, Carol Bush, Carolyn and John.

When the Universe moves to change your life it moves quickly. Two nights later the phone rang; it had to be past midnight. Carolyn got to it first afraid of a family emergency.

"Karla, Karla," I heard. "It's a Dr. Hall for you. He says it's important."

Dr. Hall was Superintendent of the Matawan School District. Why would he be ringing me in the middle of the night?

"Karla, I'm so sorry to call this late, but we have a problem and need your help."

"What is it?" I asked.

"I've just come out of a grueling board meeting, Karla. Look, we need you to come back to work. I know you've resigned, but we will do anything to secure your return. Your vocational program is not doing well, and we haven't found a highly qualified person to teach this year. I would hate to see the program dropped; I know how hard you worked to create it. Even if it is only for six months that will give us time to find someone. And if you return I believe you can reinstate your pension."

Wow! I had written my resignation letter while sitting under a beautiful cypress tree on the Monterey coast of California. A deer had grazed close by as I looked out at the magnificent ocean, never imagining that I would return to the high school. Now I was being called back. This was wild.

Fully cognizant that it was the right move, I still asked,

"Can I think about it?"

"Karla, I hate to press you but I need to inform the board. What do you think?"

"Okay, I'll do it, but just for six months. I have a whole new life now."

"Thank you, Karla, we'll see you on Tuesday, good bye."

"Tuesday, oh my God," I screamed to Carolyn.

"It's already Friday morning, I have a three day workshop, I have to pack, I'm going home. How am I going to do this?"

"You'll do it," Carolyn calmly responded.

The next few days were a whirlwind. In between presentations I raced back to the house to pack. I felt terrible for my friends, knowing that they would be affected financially by my unexpected move.

"John and Carolyn, I am so sorry that I'm leaving you in a lurch. I can't believe it, I just got back."

"Don't worry." John said, "The Universe will provide."

"Thank you, John, I guess that is really an understatement, I am always provided for, I must stay focused on that. You will be too."

On Monday morning I loaded up my final belongings and tearfully bid goodbye to my dearest friends and their beautiful daughter, Lynara.

"Rent my room, but I'll be back." John just nodded as I sadly pulled out of the driveway. We were all in tears.

The ride across the Chesapeake Bay Bridge Tunnel was as captivating as always yet my heart was heavy. Two years earlier it had welcomed me with its spectacular beauty, now I was bidding it and my beloved Virginia Beach farewell.

Returning to my roots, I was different, forever changed in a way that was not describable. Having been immersed in deep spiritual and emotional growth, shamanic studies, and a whole new way of being, would I be able to adapt once again to the more mainstream world? I was leaving my mecca. The work with death and dying now seemed very remote. As I made my way down the long stretch of ocean highway I cried out.

"Here am I, Lord, lead Thou the way. I commit my mind, my heart and my body to be one with Thee."

Chapter 13
Great Awakening

Pulling into the driveway of my New Jersey home I was consumed with a myriad of feelings. How would my old school chums react to my return? I was no longer the fast-stepping high-heeled blonde that had left over two years before. So much had changed in that short time, even the way I moved. Much slower now, I was more present in the moment, absorbing all around me. Gone were the heels and fancy clothes. The look was certainly softer and new age, with long flowing skirts and sandals, my hair no longer blonde but long and dark with many silver streaks. Very different from the girl who once was, I didn't think I could even walk in those high-stepping shoes anymore.

Quickly I made my way into the house. It was already late in the evening and there wasn't much time to unpack, find work clothes and brace myself for the next day at school. Although a bit pensive, Tom was glad to see me. He tentatively embraced me.

"Welcome home, Mom, I'm sorry about all this."

"It's okay, Tom, I'm happy to be here, everything will work out."

As I looked around my home it was more than inviting. Tom had everything spotless and shiny. The initial shock of my return had worn off during the seven-hour drive and I was ready for the next step in my passage.

At 5:30 the following morning the alarm rang, certainly not what I had become accustomed to in the past two years. Good grief, it was still dark out. How, I wondered, had I done that early rise for ten years? Barely awake, I hopped into the shower, letting the warm stream of rushing water rinse off the dreams and soul travel of the previous night. At this crazy hour there would be no time for meditation and dream recording, at least not this first morning. I had all I could do to get myself out of the house on time. A light breakfast, cup of coffee and out the door I sped with not a moment to spare.

None of the teachers knew of my return so there was much excitement and surprise. All welcomed me with open arms and overflowing hearts. This too was a soul family, different from my Virginia Beach friends but nonetheless endearing to me. I realized how much I had missed them as well as my other friends and family.

It didn't take long to get back into the swing. That first day was set aside for department meetings and class preparation. The rest of the week flowed easily. I had always loved teaching cosmetology and personal development to my high school students; they loved the visualization, breath and meditation techniques I incorporated into my classes. It offered them a way to relax and imagine their future successes from passing tests to career choices. This is good I thought, standing in front of a class again: I can do this and with joy.

Living with Tom again was a pleasure. He had grown into a fine young man, tall, amazingly handsome, with dark hair and deep brown eyes. He had developed his body into a work of art from exercise and weight lifting. Gregarious and fun-loving, with an extraordinary sense of humor, he had many friends who adored him. Even though he had disobeyed me with the mud-wrestling pit, I was still very proud of him. He had always been a model child. Perhaps he had to be, for I had been so distracted. We discussed his future plans and decided he would attend the pre-chiropractic program at Bloomfield College the next semester to prepare for his new career as a Doctor of Chiropractic medicine. Wow, my little boy a doctor! Proud was an understatement.

Our unlikely and tense first excursion together was to the Municipal Court. Thank goodness he only received a small fine and a reprimand from the judge for the mud pit. It was covered up with dirt in no time flat and he paid for that fine with his mud-wrestling earnings. It was a very good lesson for my enterprising young son.

What happens now? I wondered. I remembered how Carol had urged me to train in the Bonny Method of Guided Imagery and Music and of course the Life, Death and Transitions Training with Elisabeth Kübler-Ross still called to me. Perhaps I could do the training programs during school breaks. *Just do it*, I thought. My inner wisdom had never betrayed me. Calling Carol, I made the commitment to start my GIM training. I knew how powerful the method was through what it had done for me and I was excited about becoming a facilitator for others. That coupled with Reiki could help many travel within to explore, release and heal their past. I had discovered a way to transform obstacles into stepping-stones and I needed to share it. The training would provide something else as well; it would help me stay connected with my spiritual life as I attempted to find my place in the mainstream world I had landed in. And now there would be time for Tom and me to heal our past.

There was tremendous tension between us. I wanted desperately to be closer to my son but a wall had been erected to keep me out. No matter how hard I tried to reach him he kept himself shielded. I couldn't blame him; he had to take care of himself as I tended to Lucky. That part of my life had been all too consuming. From the time of his entry into the world I was consumed. First the crazy years with his aberrant father, the long hours away working to keep a roof over our heads after I left Pat, and then Lucky's drama. And to make matters worse, my escape with Joe had followed. Finally I was grounded, focused and more whole but Tom had taken the blow, a big hit.

There were too many nights eating alone at the dinner table while I was glued to my husband's side. I had often tried to be closer to Tom during his younger years but the walls were already in place. He didn't want me to attend his base-ball games. I had to hide behind the bleachers just to get a glimpse of him. My heart broke as I thought of the sadness he must have endured. I had become his suppressor and I was supposed to be his nurturer. *How cruel,* I thought. As a young girl I had wanted many children. The most joyous time of my life was carrying him in my womb.

While his father was away from the house I would spend countless hours holding my belly and speaking to his precious soul. If only he knew how devastated I was at not being able to be a better mom. I wish he had made more noise to get my attention, to pull me out of my consuming distractions. But he didn't. He was just a good baby and a good boy. Rarely did he do anything wrong. We were separated far too much as he was farmed out to relatives and baby-sitters while I worked those long, grueling hours, a single mother before single motherhood was fashionable.

I understood that as souls we choose our parents and our life experiences to further our soul growth. Certainly I had chosen a tumultuous path as well but that knowledge didn't make it okay. Tom was my greatest joy. He had always been in spite of my early aberrations. Tom held a place in my heart that no one could ever fill. He was my precious child, my good boy. I wanted more than anything in the world to reach beyond his armor and touch his heart. Tom was unable to speak openly about the traumas of our past or the love he felt for me, but he gave me many cards at Christmas, birthdays and Mother's Day that expressed his feelings. Tom's love for me was great. I knew that but his heart remained shielded.

At night I spoke to his Higher Self, asking forgiveness and encouraging him to open, to allow me to show my love even if that meant him speaking his truth about our journey, for he had never uttered a word about his pain.

My prayers were soon answered. We had gone out to dinner at a nearby restaurant. After some initial small talk he looked me squarely in the eye and said,

"You were never there for me."

Finally here it was: what I had prayed for, an opening in the armor, but the pain was horrific.

"I know, Tom, I wanted to be but . . . "

His anger exploded. "You were wrapped up in Lucky and I was alone, alone eating, alone in my room. You didn't even know I existed. And then after he died you were gone. You were with Joe and other men. Everyone was more important than me."

It all spilled out. I wanted to respond, to try and make him understand how devastated I had been, how thoroughly unaware. But it was not the time. My son needed this moment and I would not take it away from him by reasons or excuses. He was right. I had neglected him. All I could say was,

"I'm so sorry, I love you so much. More than anything or anybody, more than you could ever know. I'm just so sorry."

He wasn't ready to hear it and stormed out of the restaurant, leaving me alone at the table.

I couldn't move. My world felt like it was tumbling in and all around me. My throat was burning from the constricted muscles that fought to hold back sobs. Placing a hand on my forehead I leaned down in an attempt to cover my face as I tried to disappear into the teacup in front of me. It was hard to stay in my body; the heartache was so great. But it was what I had asked for, a major breakthrough, a start. I hadn't denied my responsibility or tried to justify it, although there were so many conditions that had set up the pattern. Guilt, remorse and unbelievable maternal grief gripped me as I slowly walked home. I felt like a zombie moving stoically numb through the dark night.

"Lord," I prayed. "Please bless us, hold my dearest child close to your heart, whisper in his ear of my love for him, help him to heal, and help me to heal. Bring us closer to one another. This is my greatest pain and you know he is my greatest joy."

For the next few months, until he left for college, Tom and I made small strides. The wall was there but a crack had opened. I made every attempt to be fully present for him, making his favorite dinners, placing a hand gently on his back or reaching across the table to lovingly touch him. All the while praying that we could heal. Over and over I heard, "It's never too late." *"It's never too late."*

Thoughts of my own childhood emerged. I too had been isolated and abandoned. My mother, stricken with polio at the age of three, had been raised in a home for handicapped children and had no idea how to be a mom. She had not been taught the basics. Oftentimes I felt more like the parent, having to take on huge responsibilities at an early age because she just couldn't.

Trouble ensued for my parents as I approached my adolescence. Daddy, a crane engineer, had suffered a job accident. Steel grating had flown into his eyes and he was rendered partially blind. With him unable to work, the pressures on the family mounted. My mother was the dominant of the two, my father distant and aloof. As the stress built up there were many fights. Unable to communicate and to cope with the distress, my father would leave the house and head for the local pub. Little did Mom know at that time that he was seeking refuge elsewhere, and with a friend of hers no less.

My father left us on the day of my 13th birthday. As I sat with friends eating cake, he offered a feeble goodbye, never to return. That abandonment would haunt me all of my days; no birthday would ever be the same.

In the early years it was a love/hate relationship I experienced with my mother. I knew she loved me and I knew that she was the most courageous woman I had ever known. She had beaten all the odds. Told she would not walk in her youth she victoriously mastered canes, her vibrant personality and beautiful looks winning her many friends and suitors and capturing the heart of my father. He was a six-foot tall, dark-haired, good-looking man who was artistic, incredibly sensitive with a natural musical genius. Together they joined in song; he played the piano, as her operatic voice sang out *Indian Love Call* and *Always*. Through music they expressed their love. In the beginning they were passionately mad about one another. Adoringly, this big strong man would lift the 4'10" pipsqueak up onto his shoulders and off they would go to play.

But all hell broke loose after my father left. Having been known to drink a bit, my mother now drowned her sorrows. She was inconsolable and alone. Mom had to find a way to escape reality, if not through alcohol then through an out of body state. She referred to that state as her *bubble*. When she went there I couldn't reach her. As I thought about it I realized that from my earliest memories she had gone away into that bubble. It must have started when she was first diagnosed with polio and sent away to a home for handicapped children. Twenty-six major operations followed. She left for her bubble when Lucky died just when I needed her most. The pain had been just too great for her.

A tiny little girl, my mother spent months in a full body cast then gleefully moved to braces and canes, living her life bravely and joyfully. But as she aged her worst fear was realized: she was confined to a wheelchair. Thinking of her, many emotions came up. Like Tom, I had been angry with my mother. The pattern was all too similar. I remembered feeling alone and isolated with too much responsibility, and then the men my mother dated invaded my memory. She was preoccupied, trying to keep from drowning, trying to survive as our world crumbled.

Three years after he left, my father died of a massive heart attack. Mom desperately tried to hang on to the house, and many nights there was little to eat. At times we shared a single potato. But she couldn't hold it together and we were forced to separate. We lost everything. My sister Sharlene and I went to our maternal grandfather's home and Mom rented a tiny room in a horrible building. She drank most of the time.

I had heard from my uncle, Dad's youngest brother, that he was going to ask my mother to take him back, but it was too late and the news offered little comfort. Mom was devastated, for even though he had hurt her he was the love of her life. I too was deeply wounded, as was my little sister.

In my youth I blamed Mom for my pain and my horrible choices. She just didn't know what was going on with me. I was lost and out of body myself most of the time, either escaping reality with incredible fantasies, pretending I was someone else or otherwise preoccupied. As so many do in the face of raising children, I came to realize that I was very much my mother. I was my mother's daughter.

Other memories of my mom flooded my awareness. Told she would never have children due to the damage done to her misaligned internal organs from polio, she defied the doctors and put her own life at risk. Having faith in God to support her decision she brought two healthy girls into the world. I marveled at the incredible sacrifices she had made in her life.

I was who I was because of her. I had inherited some of her shortcomings but had also inherited her courage and her outrageous spirit. We were psychically attuned, probably because we both had spent so much time in that out of body state. Many times when I was on my cross-country tour driving in the car I would hear her summoning voice. It would break through any other thought that was in my mind.

"Karla, . . . call me!"

That communication always made me laugh and just as soon as I could find a phone I placed the call, inevitably to hear her say,

"Well, what took you so long?"

Through my mother I realized what "all minds are joined" meant. It was the power of love that kept us connected and attuned; we were never truly separated from one another.

But there were downsides to that sensitivity. Mom was so sensitive and high-strung that I could never yell or disagree with her. I had to keep much bottled up. Then one afternoon, as an adult, I let it all come storming out. It was difficult for her but for the first time she really listened to my grievances. She truly heard me. We became even closer after that outburst and my anger dissipated.

The work with GIM had helped me to see deeply into her and to realize that she had played an enormous part in my spiritual evolution. I came to understand that she was indeed a very high soul. I forgave us both and prayed that as he matured Tommy would be able to reach that same level of forgiveness. I longed for him to realize how much I loved him and to know that he and only he was my brightest star, no matter what our early life had looked like. I realized that

Sharlene and I were my mother's greatest joys despite the family pain and dysfunction. I wished the same for my son. In my adult life, Mom became my biggest fan, supporting every move and reveling in every adventure. Finally I loved and respected her with all of my heart, for all of who she was— the bad, the best, and the sublime. She was clearly my hero.

I began composing letters to Tom to help widen this new opening. The first step had been taken and I knew that time would heal our wounds. After all, my mother had been patient with me. I would be patient with my dear son.

I was back in the groove and the school year flew. Soon it was spring and I made my first trip back to Virginia Beach. The GIM Training was held in a remote area of Virginia Beach called Sand Bridge. This lovely town was tucked away in a rural area a good distance from the now-bustling Virginia Beach proper. The southern-most part of the state, this beautiful area bordered the outer banks of North Carolina and was home to a National Wildlife Preserve. Houses lined the ocean where wildlife of all kinds gathered. Dolphins passed by each day, traveling early in the morning to the north as they fed and then back again in the later afternoon. Quiet and in-filling, this magical place fed my soul.

If I thought I worked hard on my personal process with Carol, the training proved to be more intense, invigorating and powerful. As the students gathered with the masterful teachers we learned how classical music could affect consciousness and how to artfully guide a person into the deep state. We had many opportunities to individually travel and guide as well as many group experiences. Screams echoed through the waterfront home along with the booming and tumultuous music as many released pent-up anger and pain from their past. Glorious moments were spent in high transpersonal states as the awe-inspiring sounds of Vivaldi, Wagner and Mozart transported us into peak experience.

I loved guiding. I was becoming a midwife, creating a safe container where others could tap into what still needed release as they claimed new life. And how blessed I felt to be able to hold that sacred space as they touched the Divine.

During my own personal sessions I released more of my past pain. As the early wounds cleared I became more effective at guiding others, for I had confronted the dark place within myself and no longer feared it. Eagerly I looked forward to becoming a facilitator of this powerful method. Many books were to be read related to expanding consciousness and music and many documented sessions were needed to complete the levels of training. Surprisingly, a few of my high school buddies offered to take part in the practice sessions and over the next year I was able to guide many into the deep state. They were far more avant-garde than I had given them credit for. I felt privileged to share something that was so precious to me and honored to be part of their inner world.

I spent every school break and long weekend traveling back to the beach for training and personal time with Carol. During one of our group storytelling sessions I shared one of my amazing encounters. I had experienced a powerful dolphin connection while at a five-day dolphin-human interspecies workshop in Key Largo, Florida some time earlier. The initial purpose of the week was to connect with the dolphins at a spiritual level, to deepen our breath capacity, and to become accustomed to the communication and echo sounds of the mammals in preparation for a swim with them.

The small group accomplished this through meditation, guided imagery journeys, and a form of breath work—a gentle and rhythmic process that along with special music helped us explore the dolphins' oceanic world. During the week in preparation for the actual encounter, we experienced an incredible imagery and music journey. We spread out on the floor, our heads centered in the middle of the room, slightly touching, while the rest of our bodies stretched out in a full circle. As we gently breathed in unison, we were guided through a calming induction, relaxing each body part. Ocean sounds and a low and deeply penetrating synthesizer accompanied the calls of whales and dolphins. The haunting sounds echoed through the dimly lit room, filling our senses. Our group facilitator expertly guided us, suggesting we imagine ourselves submerged in the ocean swimming along with the great water beings. She then remained quiet, allowing our creative imagination and the music to take us on a journey to our inner knowing and the oceanic realm of the dolphins.

Finding my own pace I breathed deeply and rhythmically to the sounds, entering more fully into the experience. I was able to hold my breath for longer and longer periods, reaching an ease in my body as I did so. Dropping further into that deep state the images and sensations heightened and I began to feel like I had taken on the form of a dolphin. It was a luscious sensation—the feeling of freedom was unlike anything I had yet experienced. Joy filled me as I flowed through the water alongside the great beings, part of their pod.

The dolphins took me to a temple nestled deep on the ocean floor, a mystical place of wisdom and healing. Indescribable, angelic beings graced this ocean underworld, offering their blessings as we moved through. Light from the sun above showered its rays down, penetrating the water and creating a luminescent glow upon the temple's stone structure. In and out we swam, around ancient pillars decorated with the carvings of wise elders. This was a holy place. I wondered if I was being shown remnants of the lost continent of Atlantis, a place that I felt to be part of my soul. I didn't want the inner journey to end but the music had closed and the group was being called back.

My aquatic comrades and I gathered into a sitting circle to share our experiences. We were amazed to discover that we had similar imagery; each one of us had taken on the mammals' form and each one was moved to tears as we felt a penetrating love and energy fill our bodies. Some even experienced the ancient underground world. Our consciousness had been linked, one to another's and to the dolphins'. It was at that moment that we all realized something incredible was going to happen when we made our real swim.

After a few days of traveling in the altered state it was time to find our comfort zone in the actual water. Laden with snorkel gear, wet suits and flippers, we entered the crystal blue sea to practice our new breath techniques. Our arms were positioned behind our backs, hands clasped in a pose that mirrored the graceful body of the dolphin. My own body felt sleek and fluid in the water and I was able to dive in deep, holding my breath for very long periods—all in preparation to meet the great creatures and enter into their ocean world.

The time for our great adventure came. The small, excited group arrived at the Dolphin's Plus Research Center, where we learned of the dolphin's life, evolution and present service to humankind. The Center was conducting research with the mammals, placing handicapped and autistic children into the water to swim with them. Many children showed improvement and studies were being performed to determine if the dolphins' echo system, the radar sounds that vibrated through the water, had any healing affect.

Our guide told us how playful the dolphins could be and how once you had an encounter with them they would always remember you, as evidenced by swimmers who had returned to meet an ecstatic and loving old friend. These amazing dolphins even seemed to anticipate the visit before the actual arrival. *Unbelievable*, I thought.

We were then instructed on how to enter into the water.

"Let them come to you," the guide said. "They have ways of communicating. If one brushes up against you, it is a hello. One may come in very close to look at you. Remember to keep your arms clasped behind your back and stay calm. Keep in mind they do not have arms like you do, so stay respectful. You may be very lucky, one may want to play with you or even offer you a fin. If that occurs, it is okay to touch, just hold on tight and take a deep breath because you will be taken down into deeper water."

I was so excited, I thought I would burst, but I quickly centered myself, hoping to align my spirit with the dolphins' as I had done during the imagery journeys. Truly in my glory, I prayed that I would have a very close encounter, then quickly surrendered the expectation.

"Let it be Your will Lord, not mine."

Entering the water face down with hands behind my back, I breathed through the snorkel gear. I was not to be disappointed. Only a moment passed before a dolphin came up and brushed along the side of my body. It was exhilarating. I was soooo excited! It was a hello. I sent a mental message.

Hello beautiful being, I am so happy to be here in your world. As if hearing me, it then brushed against my opposite side. It was unbelievable.

Our group of eight tightly linked arms together, the person at each end holding one hand behind their back in a gesture of deep respect. The group had become a pod slowly making its way across the water. Our dolphin friends joined together too, a number of them swimming just under us, mimicking our movements. Back and forth we moved across the large ocean-water filled tank. We were swimming directly above them. It was outrageous! With each action and play they communicated with us. There was no need for words.

Later, while I was off swimming by myself, I began to actually feel the radar echo sounds, a clicking sound that moved through the water. It felt like powerful healing energy as a tingly feeling came into my neck. *Wow, how did they know that my neck had been stiff and sore?* It was the only place in my body where I actually felt the vibration. The energy was focused directly on the point of pain. As the vibration moved through the area my neck muscles relaxed and the pain and stiffness vanished. I was amazed.

Even more was to come; while off alone on one side of the tank a dolphin came up directly in front of me. I was submerged in the water as the being approached within a few inches of my face. It slowly turned its head so only one eye was looking at me. Then methodically it rolled over so the other eye could focus on me. This new friend was taking me into its world and consciousness, reading me, understanding me and making deep contact. Overjoyed, I barely managed to stay still as I transmitted my love to the great being. It wasn't easy; tears were flowing down my cheeks and fogging the tight glass mask. I had all I could do to just contain myself and not flail about in the water. More than anything I wanted to reach out and touch the great being yet knew I had to keep my arms behind my back.

But soon I would get my wish. Our group leader was actually playing with a dolphin. As I began to swim toward her a young female dolphin approached me. I was above water at that time treading to stay afloat. Just as she reached me her head and upper body rose out of the water. She looked directly at me with that wonderful dolphin smile on her face. This dear one must have read my thoughts, knowing I had wanted to reach out to express my love. She allowed me to gently caress her cool, smooth skin. This beautiful female, Ilya, then nestled her head into my heart. It felt like she knew me, as if she could feel the grief that I had suffered in this earthly life. Ilya gently and slowly moved me across the water, rubbing her sweet face back and forth on my chest as I cradled the top of her head. It was a deep and sensual encounter, she was loving me and I was loving her, truly an indescribable moment. We were joined in a timeless moment of love as she brought healing into my heart and blessed me. What wondrous gratitude I felt for her, for her love and her great sacrifice for humankind. For Ilya was willing to live out her life in an ocean cage just to be of service to us. My heart could barely contain the admiration and respect I felt for my new friend.

And if all of that wasn't enough, as I was preparing to leave the water, an adult female named Jeannie offered me her fin. I climbed on and down we went. What an incredible rush! Her body moved fluidly through the water, up and down—a flowing, gentle yet fast movement. We moved easily, coming up for air as the need arose. Because of my excitement I was having difficulty with the snorkel gear. In hindsight I wish I had just pulled it off, for I was able to hold my breath for very long periods. Jeannie felt the shift in my body and immediately brought me up for air, coming to a full and abrupt stop. It was spectacular. I wanted to go down again without the gear but the whistle blew. It was time to leave. I kissed my dear friend as I said goodbye. This was an encounter that I would never forget and I believed that she too would not forget nor would Ilya, for she and I had connected deeply. Ilya knew of my suffering and wanted to heal it. She and the others would remain in my heart always, for it is said that when you experience a connection with this angelic life form you are forever aligned with their collective spirit. I found that out the next time I traveled to Sand Bridge just three months later.

It was the end of the GIM training and I was in a high state from the many imagery journeys and healing sessions. In order to bring the week-long experience to a close and offer my final goodbyes and gratitude to the glorious wildlife and pristine beauty of Sand Bridge, I went to the ocean for a walk. It was late in the morning and I had missed the early run of the dolphins. The sea was calm and inviting so I went out into the water to just above my waist. Placing my arms behind my back as I had done when swimming with the magnificent creatures, I began to chant. It was a sound that needed no forethought; it had an energy of its own coming up from deep within, a call to the beloved water beings and a song of gratitude. While chanting, I imagined myself in the ocean water swimming alongside my dear friends. Projecting the song as energy flowing through the ocean water, as the dolphins' echo/radar sounds do, I dropped into a very deep meditative state. Enraptured in the moment, I completely lost track of time; it felt very long but then something prompted me to open my eyes. To my surprise and incredible delight, two dolphins swam in front of me about twenty feet out.

Playfully they moved back and forth in opposite directions, passing each other then turning again to repeat their play. Then an amazing thing occurred. As I continued my song of gratitude to them they made their way toward shore. A "V" was formed with me at the apex, and each dolphin swam in toward me on an angle. I was mesmerized and overjoyed. It was clear that they had heard my call; they knew me.

The dolphins approached, just two feet from me. With heads up and out of the water they looked directly at me. Then as quickly as they had come in they turned back. Swimming to their original play area they faced one another and leaped into mid air. They were side by side in a gentle, beautiful and perfectly timed arch. The sun's rays bounced off the water, causing their skin to glisten and shine. The spectacular scene was reminiscent of a brilliant Gilbert Williams painting, but this was real and it was just for me. Astonished and amazed, I could not contain the overflowing joyous emotion. More than anything, I wanted to swim out to them and lose myself in the wondrous moment, but I wasn't an expert swimmer and I had no gear. Just as that thought surfaced I felt them say,

No. Stay where you are, that is why we came to you.

Realizing the great blessing that had been offered I bowed my head to them, for I knew it was an acknowledgement of the love and connection made over a year before in the altered state and in the ocean tanks. I was joined with their collective spirit; we were part of one another. The encounter with Ilya flooded my mind and heart and I was sure that through them she too had heard my song of gratitude. Too emotional to chant, the words *thank you, thank you*, repeated over and over in my mind. I knew that they heard me.

What a gift they had bestowed upon me. Clearly I understood that all life was connected, that there is but one consciousness and that consciousness flows through all. We are joined from the tiniest to the greatest and our vehicle of expression is our expanded hearts. Many times throughout my existence I had felt more connected with the animal kingdom than the human, for I had received so many unconditional and mystical gifts from them.

That was the key—unconditional love. Thanking God for the immense blessings that had been bestowed upon me I clearly understood that the shattering I had endured with Lucky's death had opened me to the higher realms of creation in all of its wondrous ways. I felt that Eden still existed if we could but transcend our conscious awareness from the mundane, from the domain of the ego, judgment and separation to the higher knowing of Spirit where just love exists and where all life is One. Words from *A Course in Miracles* entered into my awareness.

"The journey to God is merely the reawakening of the knowledge of where you are always and what you are forever."

I got it! We are on a journey of awakening, awakening to the truth of who we really are and to the remembrance of a place that we never truly left. This earth experience is a dream, an illusion; the real truth and reality is captured in moments of sublime love and forgiveness. That was it. That is how we experience miracles, that is how we awaken. I

prayed that all of humankind would soon rememb
open their hearts and minds to the love that could trans
all hatred, separation and war.

Heaven is now. The knowing penetrated my every cell. I
felt such joy. Unable to leave the water, I reveled in the
moment for a very long time.

er and
end

Chapter 14
Rude Awakenings

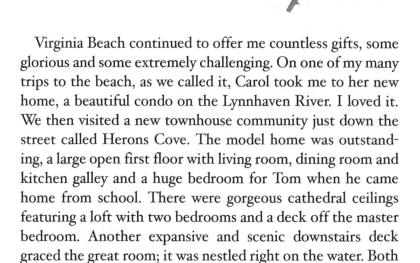

Virginia Beach continued to offer me countless gifts, some glorious and some extremely challenging. On one of my many trips to the beach, as we called it, Carol took me to her new home, a beautiful condo on the Lynnhaven River. I loved it. We then visited a new townhouse community just down the street called Herons Cove. The model home was outstanding, a large open first floor with living room, dining room and kitchen galley and a huge bedroom for Tom when he came home from school. There were gorgeous cathedral ceilings featuring a loft with two bedrooms and a deck off the master bedroom. Another expansive and scenic downstairs deck graced the great room; it was nestled right on the water. Both decks offered spectacular views.

My thoughts began to race. I missed Virginia Beach living, the A.R.E. and my soul friends. Tom was safely settled in at school and I had already completed a full year at Matawan: why not move back? I was unable to share most of the mystical and high consciousness experiences that God had gifted me with my school chums, family and other more mainstream friends. Knowing it was too much for them I kept most of the extraordinary experiences to myself, feeling that I would be thought delusional, crazy or just plain weird. In that regard life was a little lonely.

The idea of moving filled me with excitement. *I'm going back home to my spiritual mecca,* I thought, *it's where I belong.* Impulsiveness captured me and I placed a deposit with the manager for an end unit identical to the model that was being built right on the water, contingent on the sale of my New Jersey house.

Returning to Keyport, I placed my home on the market with the full intent of moving back to the beach. Within a week the house sold. Rushing headfirst into the decision I hadn't gone into meditation for guidance. Since my home sold so quickly I thought Virginia Beach was the right decision. I was very wrong.

Closing came just a few months later during summer break. Tom, his friends and I packed up the truck with all of my furniture and belongings. Off I went again, but this time I was in for a rude awakening. As Tom and I took a tour of the new house a very negative feeling came over me. It had been broken into; there was evidence of that damage everywhere. Paralyzed and unable to move I felt like I had walked into a brick wall.

Standing in the living room I realized that I had made the wrong decision. *What's going on Lord?* I inwardly questioned, knowing something was terribly amiss. I knew that I couldn't move forward but didn't know how to move back. It was clearly not where I was supposed to be and closing was the very next day. Quickly I sent a prayer out to Spirit.

"Show me the way Lord." Immediately the word, *"Call"* moved into my awareness. Rushing out of the house, I found the first phone and called the builder.

I told him of my aversion, mentioning the damage and the many defects. The worst was that my end unit had been constructed in a way that the water view was partially obscured by the adjacent home. To my amazement he released me from the contract. I am sure he had a new buyer ready to take over the house and I am equally certain that Spirit was intervening for me.

The value had gone up considerably in just a few short months. The builder would not be out money; he even returned my deposit. That would teach me not to rely on my own impulsive thoughts but to go within for answers to important decisions. It was a very close call. Thank God I had not handed in my resignation. Many prayers and thanks went out in that moment.

The furniture and larger belongings found a resting place in the garage of a friend, and I solemnly made my way back to New Jersey while Tom returned to college. I was without a place to live but as always the Universe provided. After staying with my sister Sharlene for a few days, I was rescued by my colleague Aileen Meares, who was looking for someone to share her house with. I lucked out. Not only was Aileen a fellow teacher but a comrade in spiritual growth and an A.R.E. member. Her grown children Tommy and Jennie were musicians. I would have a warm, comfortable and musical place to live with great people until I knew where I was to go next. These words kept moving into my awareness.

"Someone has to go to the outpost." I tried to ignore them.

Turning my thoughts inward I prayed and meditated until the guidance came. It was time to do the Life, Death and Transition Training. As the summer of 1986 rolled around I made my way to Seattle, Washington to study with Elisabeth Kübler-Ross and take care of my black bunnies—the shadows that still lived inside of me. This without a doubt was the most intense training week of my life.

Much of the program, which was attended by terminal

patients, counselors and spiritual teachers from throughout the U.S., touched upon Elisabeth's five stages of dying. She spoke about the anger still locked within most of us and how those diagnosed with life-threatening disease and impending death had no avenue to clear their frustration, shock and rage. Her dream was to have rooms set aside in hospitals where patients and staff could release their heavy emotions through appropriate means. Elisabeth and her expert staff introduced us to many processes. First we were taught how to interpret drawings. During a centering meditative experience we were instructed to create a picture of how we were feeling at that moment. Elisabeth then taught us how to read the picture. The drawings were folded twice to indicate four quadrants. Each one related to a segment of life: the present, the past, the immediate future and the distant future. Pairing up we practiced with each other. We were able to determine what was present in a person's experience, what needed to be addressed, and their overall health. Everything had meaning, all the colors, symbols and placements. I had also studied mandala drawing (the circle of the soul) with Carol and between the two techniques now had a powerful tool to help me assess where individuals were in their life process.

Then the big guns were introduced. Thick telephone books and rubber hoses were brought out.

"What's that?" I groaned, getting a little nervous.

The staff explained that it was a way to release long-held anger. We were to pound the books with the hoses. Each participant was scheduled throughout the intensive week to work individually with a staff member. *Oh I'm clear,* I thought, *this is going to be a breeze. My earlier meditations and exercises have brought much to light and I've already done tons of powerful work. There won't be much to release. It will be a snap.* The angels that watch over me must have been laughing for I was in for another rude awakening.

My turn came. Little did I know how much anger and rage

still lived inside of me. Miss Spiritual was about to meet her rageful inner shadow. Black bunnies was an understatement. Kneeling in front of the large book, rubber hose held tightly in my hand, I let the facilitator expertly guide me back in time searching for trauma that still fired within.

"Let the anger come up," he said.

Stonewalling, I felt myself break into a sweat, not wanting to bare my soul in that way. I had already released much with the GIM work but that process was different. An altered state had been achieved through the music, my eyes had been closed and shielded, and I was able to yell and flail about with my guide close by attending to my needs and coaxing me on. Because of the eye shields I had felt invisible and safe. But there were no shields or music here, just myself and a stranger kneeling two feet away from me in a very bright and bare room. Two people looking at each other, a phone book and eighteen inches of rubber hose, and I was expected to perform.

Petrified, I stared at the facilitator. As my body shook and rocked I knew that there was something huge hammering at me. Desperately I tried to keep it down but couldn't. Startling and horrible memories of sexual abuse by my uncle when I was very little were bursting to get out. All I could say was,

"It's my uncle, oh God, it's the abuser. It's him."

My chest constricted and nausea gnawed at my belly. I thought I was going to throw up. Wanting to run away and hide as I had done when I was a small child, I looked for a way out. But I wasn't going anywhere. It felt as if venom was burning my throat and setting all of my insides and skin on fire. I had to confront it.

"That's your uncle," the facilitator urged, pointing to the phone book.

It felt like a stand-off but then, after long moments of painful resistance, I drew the hose up and with a thundering blow hit the thick, unyielding book. Years of pent-up rage roared out.

Again and again I struck the book; pages flew wildly as I nearly demolished the phone book. All the while profanities that I did not know myself capable of spewed forth.

Other horrible moments throughout life emerged. The callous mistreatment Lucky and I had experienced came up. Anger at the courts, the insurance doctors who had belittled us, and the lack of proper medical care roared out of me. Then the horrible violence inflicted upon me by my first husband released with a deafening blow. It was enormous. Finally the loss of time with Tommy that I suffered from my early, consuming and unstable life erupted. That deep pain and remorse felt like it would annihilate me. I screamed at all of the choices, circumstances, and people who had robbed me of that loving time with my son. By now, there was almost nothing left of the phonebook and I was in a heap, exhausted, yet freed of the long-held pockets of rage and pain that had lived within my body and mind for so long.

Elisabeth's training was expertly orchestrated to include rest, meditation, healing and music to help us integrate what had been so vigorously released. But I was extremely tired, my arms ached and I began to question if I could facilitate this kind of process for another.

Earlier in the week I had made arrangements with a man from the Gay Men's Health Center in New York City to get involved with the AIDS crisis. But now it felt too big, with too many dying, and just too much pain. *Perhaps I'm not cut out for this work,* I thought. At the end of the week I felt like I needed to be rolled out in a wheelbarrow.

Thank God it was summer; I could rest and recover from the intense yet releasing experience. Once home I discovered a winter rental in the newspaper, a very small riverfront apartment in Sea Bright, New Jersey, the place where I had grown up. The second floor apartment offered a terrace overlooking the river, so close that with a good throw you could toss a stone into the water. The ocean was directly across the street. This place, although tiny, would offer the peace and quiet that I so needed. I had loved living with Aileen and Jennie but solitude and the water called to me. The winter rental offered the time needed to determine my next move. Would I be staying in New Jersey or would I make my way back to Virginia Beach?

Again the words repeated, as they had done so often,

"Someone has to go to the outpost."

In early September, I moved in. I could barely turn around in the kitchen and the living room could only hold a chair, small couch and coffee table. The tiny bedroom felt like a womb that I crawled into each night. But I loved the place. I woke to the sounds of the ocean every morning and each evening took my breath away as I gazed upon the most glorious sunsets I had ever seen. Colors sparkled on the water as boats lazily cruised by, slowly making their way under an old granite bridge. An historic 1700's stone church sat directly across the narrow river; its bells rang out gloriously, declaring throughout the day the rare beauty of this place.

Even the nor'eastern storms that frequently descended upon the small peninsula town enraptured me, reminding me of my childhood days. *I could stay here forever,* I thought. But of course that was not to be. I had wanted to begin a private practice with Reiki and guided imagery and music, and there just wasn't enough room.

A call came one evening from the man I had met from the Gay Men's Health Center.

"Are you interested in volunteering?" he asked. "Maybe touch-therapy for dying patients or a workshop for AIDS patients and their caregivers? You could bring in Reiki, music and imagery, even what you learned from Elisabeth's course."

The intensity of the Life, Death and Transition Training flooded my mind. "No, not just yet, but maybe later," I begged off. "I'm not quite ready but I'll get back to you."

159

It was clear that I was still processing my own experience and my thoughts around death. Feeling disturbed, I had a conversation with God that night. Or perhaps I should call it a screaming proclamation. I yelled out.

"God, I don't want to do this work with death and dying. I've changed my mind. I have had enough death in my own life. It's too intense. I won't do it! My life has been too tumultuous. No, I won't do it! I'm tired."

Sitting in the middle of my bed I was adamant. "No! I won't call the Gay Men's Health Center; I won't seek out this work. Find someone else. It's not for me."

I was emphatically declaring my decision as I shouted. Then realizing how insolent I was being, I spoke more softly,

"If you want me to do this, Lord, You will have to set it up. I won't do anything to move in this direction. It's just too hard."

Falling off to sleep, I murmured, "I am sorry, Lord, I just don't want to, I can't, please forgive me, it's too big."

That night I dreamt of Ram Dass. I saw him sitting quietly with one who was ill and dying. Oh jeez, I thought as I awakened, is it already in place?

Only a few days had passed when another call came. Christine DeVizia, a former student of mine, greeted me on the phone,

"Hi, Karla, I heard you studied with Dr. Elisabeth Kübler-Ross and now you're working with AIDS patients."

Before I had a chance to protest, she continued,

"My brother Anthony has the disease. I want to give him a gift certificate. Will you help him?"

I was flabbergasted, but then remembered something Elisabeth had said about her own journey.

"I was destined to work with dying patients. I had no choice when I encountered my first AIDS patient."

In that moment I clearly understood what she meant. My response to Christine flew out without censor,

"Yes, Christine, I will see him."

"Great," she responded, "I'll have him call."

The path had been put in place. It was my destiny. How foolish I was to think I had any choice in the matter. I should have known when I dreamt of Ram Dass that the decision had already been made, at least by my Higher Self. However, my ego still protested vehemently.

Anthony called the following day and we scheduled the appointment.

Part Two
Love Never Dies

Chapter 15
Love Never Dies

Still at odds I ruminated, as I got ready for Anthony's arrival. How have I gotten myself into this? My tiny matchbox apartment could barely house my few belongings and me. Where would I set up a massage table? Could I even move around it? I wasn't ready to start private practice and I didn't want to do this kind of work. The resistance surging within me was enormous; I knew, however, that it was out of my hands. I was being called to do the work.

The doorbell rang and I was transported out of my internal, compulsive chattering. Opening the door my heart leaped into my throat.

Standing directly in front of me was Anthony. But all I could see was the child of my earlier vision. I knew this was the one. He was being returned to me just as the vision had prophesized. There was not a shred of doubt. Looking at him I stammered a feeble hello and at the same time the memory of the burning building from my healing session years earlier filled my mind. The child was hanging out the window of the second story building, his blood curdling screams piercing through the night, calling to me over and over again,

"Mommy, mommy," until the flames overtook him.

Barely able to breathe I held onto the door in an attempt to keep my knees from folding.

Karla, get a grip, clear your head. Afraid he would feel what I was experiencing I quickly gathered my composure.

"You must be Anthony, Christine's brother. It's very nice to meet you, come on in."

Holy jeez! kept running through my mind.

"Sorry if I seemed a bit taken back. You see I remember you from high school; you played Mordred in the production of *Camelot.* I hadn't made the connection between you and Christine until just now. You were great in that play. It's really good to see you."

"Thanks," Anthony responded. "That feels like an eternity ago."

In front of me was the young man who had captured my attention at the high school nine years before. There were many talented students but this one stood out. He had been an extraordinary talent.

When I saw Anthony in *Camelot,* I felt certain that he would make his mark in the world as an accomplished actor. No wonder I had asked his drama coach Margo of his whereabouts. I didn't know him personally but followed his career through her. Now I realized that it wasn't just his acting abilities that had intrigued me but a connection that was distant and far removed from the life of a high school teacher and an aspiring young actor.

Twenty-seven now, Anthony was small in frame with dark hair and deep dark-brown eyes that were piercing yet sparkled with light. His energy and essence were far greater than his stature. As we sat at the small kitchen table I began to gather the pertinent information. When had he been diagnosed, how was he feeling, what medications was he on and what were his expectations in coming to see me?

"Christine says you're doing this Reiki stuff, and that it can heal me. I've heard about it, can it help? I don't want to die."

He was choking back tears and I could feel the near-panic rise up in him as he spoke of death.

It was more than challenging to hold my focus; I certainly couldn't blurt out what I was experiencing, that I was reliving a mother/child connection from long ago. Instead I explained the possibilities.

"Anthony, Reiki can bring your body to a state of ease so that it can better heal itself. I don't do it, I'm merely a channel for the energy, it flows into me and then into you. The wisdom of the Reiki energy and your own innate intelligence know just what you need, and I believe that healing always happens no matter what form it seems to take. The healing can be physical, and often it is mental or spiritual. Energetically Reiki can bring your body into greater balance and harmony. It can even help with the release of emotional pain."

"Oh I could use that. I'm carrying so much pain, so much guilt, especially about being gay and making stupid, horrible mistakes. I took some terrible risks. I just didn't know, didn't realize how devastating it was, what it could do."

His now solemn voice trailed off, becoming nearly inaudible as he whispered,

"I just wish I could take it all back."

Anthony's words felt more like a prayer to God than an admission of sorrow to me. Reaching across the table I gently touched his hand, lingering for a while in a gesture of support and understanding.

"You didn't know, Anthony, no one realized the horrors of this disease, many people made mistakes."

He then opened up and with great candor shared many of his hopes and dreams as well as the hardships that he had endured trying to make it as an actor in New York City.

Guilt and remorse had found a dwelling place within him. I explained the GIM process and how I might incorporate that along with Reiki if he chose to return. He released a deep sigh and nodded,

"Recently I saw a therapist in the city, but we just talked. Maybe I need to do some deeper work."

Wearing my counselor hat, I was amazingly centered and focused on the professional work, yet the voice of my inner knowing was repeating over and over,

"This one has been yours, you are to help him on his journey."

And still another voice, one much more in touch with my present earthly sojourn, was yelling,

Holy jeez! Many channels were operating at the same time.

As Anthony signed the customary release form I had the opportunity to take a deep breath and marvel at what was happening.

He hopped up on the massage table and as soft music played easily relaxed. To enter into my state of surrender I silently prayed,

Not my will but Thine, Oh Lord, be done in me and through me. Let me ever be a channel of blessings for this dear one. Please keep my ego out of the way.

I took in a centering breath and visualized the Light of Reiki pouring into me and was instantly filled with peace. Gently I placed my hands at his crown chakra and allowed the energy to flow into his mind to clear blockages and bring greater clarity. It was obvious that Anthony was dropping into an altered state. As they often did when I administered Reiki, deep feelings of love rose up from within me. Along with this Divine love came something far more personal—an abiding maternal love.

As I channeled the energy flow I returned to the prayer *Not my will, but Thine* to keep my mind still. Then I moved my hands to Anthony's heart chakra. *What a dear and beautiful heart,* I thought, feeling his capacity for love; but it was clear as well that a deep wound resided there. Tears began to stream down his face as his heart opened more fully. It appeared that he was clearing out some of the pain held there. Trusting the Reiki flow to do what was needed, I lingered until he calmed then proceeded slowly down the rest of his body.

After thirty minutes I completed the Reiki flow on the front of Anthony's body and then proceeded to help him turn over onto his belly. Just as he was turning a deep sob escaped. He cried for a few moments, the release of energy evident as his body softened and surrendered even more to the power-ful yet gentle flow.

I knew that the Universal wisdom held within Reiki and the blueprint of wholeness held within Anthony knew far more than I. He was clearing. I didn't need to intervene; the energy had flowed into him, helping the emotions that had hardened in his heart to release. My primary job was to stay out of the way.

I remained quiet as I completed his back, ending at his heart chakra. He appeared very relaxed and at ease. Softly I spoke.

"As we close now, allow a sense or a thought or an image of yourself whole, perfect, and healthy to come to mind. And when you have a sense of that take a very deep and slow breath."

While Anthony breathed, I anchored the session with the suggestion that every cell in his body and mind receive the healthy image. His eyes opened slowly and with a blissful look on his face he dreamily said,

"Whoa, I feel like I'm high, like from drugs. What was that?"

"Reiki state. It can bring you into magnified and very deep states of consciousness where you can heal. It is a perfect natural high. Opiates, natural hormones that place the body into a state of greater harmony are flowing through you. Reiki actually brings in a Divine energy, a little bit of heaven."

"Wow," he exclaimed again. "It's awesome, I'll be back."

"Use that image of yourself whole and healthy every day, at least three times a day. With a prayer of gratitude breathe into it as if it is already complete."

He emphatically replied, "Done!"

We chose a date in two weeks and just as he was leaving, hand on the door, he swung around and with a brilliant smile gave me a great big hug. As I watched him make his way down the stairs I felt as if I had known him all my life. Which wasn't exactly true; I had known him longer.

All that day I remained in an elevated state. I was astonished at the turn of events. But then a voice from the past came into my awareness shouting, *You must be crazy!* So I attempted to reason away my strong feeling of connection to Anthony as a product of my very creative imagination.

It was impossible. My inner guidance would not let me get away with that; instead it met those negative thoughts with,

This is your child returned, you will see.

Gratitude began to wash over me. I felt that I had been prepared for a long time to meet Anthony. Each step along the way—oh there it was again *the way*, the meaning of my name—had been a step toward him so that I could help him along *his way*. My thoughts went to those steps: Lucky's death, the A.R.E., Ram Dass, Elisabeth Kübler-Ross, the visions of the child, and the young men with AIDS—all was in perfect timing and order. I would just need to completely trust the process—not always an easy task. I was human.

Could the healing power of Reiki fully heal him? This was my child from the burning building. I couldn't save him then, but maybe I could now. *Careful, Karla,* I told myself, *just trust the process.*

Two weeks passed and I found myself anticipating Anthony's arrival. At the door, he seemed tense and pensive. There was a tightness around his mouth and his jaw was clenched.

"Hi, come on in, how are you doing?"

"Fair," he responded. "A lot's come up since I last saw you, around abandonment. I've been feeling so angry!"

"Do you want to work with that today?"

"Yes, I am angry with everyone, my mother, my entire family, my father who died when I was too young, and this ugly disease. Why me? The words keep repeating over and over in my mind but I'm angry with myself for those bad choices. I hate being a victim! I hate it!"

His voice was escalating; it was clear that his long-held anger and emotion were about to pop. I grabbed my Elisabeth Kübler-Ross tools, the huge phone book and the rubber hose. Escorting him to an open area on the floor I placed the phone book directly in front of him and showed him the long piece of garden hose.

"There, Anthony, the phone book is the disease or whoever or whatever you need it to be."

I struck the phone book hard with the hose, letting out a deep belly grunt. No sooner did I hand it to Anthony than he began to pound the thick phone book, screaming,

"Why me? Why me? I hate you."

He was down on his knees annihilating the book, and as it slid across the floor I quickly and carefully pushed it back so there would be no pause in his remarkable release. The ripped pages were flying everywhere as the hose hit the book again and again, creating an enormous, nearly deafening thud.

"Give it a sound, Anthony," I urged.

He held the hose in both hands, lifting it up and back over his head then down with a mighty force as he screamed at the top of his lungs.

"No! No! No!" Then deep guttural sounds roared forth.

"That's it!" I continued to urge him on, "Let it out!"

One last attack and it was over. There was nothing left of the phonebook, just ripped pages strewn all over the place. He let go of the hose. Tears were pouring down his reddened face and his clothes were disheveled, soaked in sweat. Clearly spent, Anthony collapsed onto the floor; I gave him a pillow to rest his head on then cleared the space of the shattered and thoroughly demolished phone book.

"That was all of it, all the anger from my whole life."

"You did great, Anthony. That took courage, good job."

As he closed his eyes to rest, I placed my hands on his heart and abdomen, allowing Reiki to further clear and restore balance within his body. Just as I turned him over onto his side to reach his back the familiar deep sob returned, the same sob from his first Reiki session.

"What's that?" I asked. He didn't respond.

The sobs quieted and were replaced with soft weeping. After a few minutes he turned back to me and professed,

"Remember when I began to cry on the Reiki table last time?"

"Yes, I remember. It was just as I turned you over, just like now."

"A strange vision or memory or something, I'm not sure what it was, came to me. I was in a field and there were soldiers pulling us apart, away from one another. I was very little, I tried so hard to hold on. One of them grabbed me out of your arms."

"Me?" I gasped.

"Yes, you. I kept yelling 'Mama, Mama.' You were kicking and screaming as they dragged you away, hitting the soldiers hard as you called out to me in some foreign language. But then they held your mouth closed and dragged you out of sight. That's all I saw. I don't know where they took you but I know you were my mother. I don't understand it, but I know."

How often had I heard myself say those same words, "I just know."

Time stopped. Everything felt expanded: the room, my body, my heart. Here in this moment I was looking into the eyes of my long-lost child. It was not the lifetime that I had remembered with the burning building but he was confirming what I had known when I opened the door two weeks before. He was my child.

"I know, Anthony, I feel it too."

Our eyes were truly the windows of the soul as we gazed into one another. *How many times, how many lives have we shared,* I wondered as I looked deeply into him.

He moved into my arms. Cradling him I rocked back and forth as if he was a very small child, my child. Quietly we wept. A door to the knowing had opened. It was a door to love; there was no doubt that we had been together before.

I continued to soothe him as tears rolled down my own cheeks. Anthony and I were fully present in the moment as a distraught mother from some long-distant past and her child were reunited. In that moment all of us were healed.

"I'm here, Anthony, I will never leave you again . . . I'm here."

And then I got it. "You won't be *turned over* to anyone ever again. There is nothing to fear."

The image of the burning building filled my awareness once again. Yes, this is the same child. There have been many lives together; I knew it, yet I chose not to share it with him. This moment was enough in itself. God was giving us both a rare and precious gift. I now knew that love and remembrance were eternal. We come together over and over again to love, to help one another, to complete unfinished business, often changing roles as we do so. Love never dies, love is a whisper, a calling, a gentle urging through many levels of awareness to remember who we are and to realize that there is truly nothing but love, all else is illusion. It is love that propels us, joins us and guides our path.

And once again I murmured, "I'll never leave you, Anthony, I remember you."

While I stroked his hair as I would a child's, he looked up and with arms tightly wrapped around me questioned,

"What now? What do we do with this? Would anyone believe us? Oh I can't tell my mother, she'll never understand. I'm afraid she'll be jealous."

"Anthony, no one needs to know. We know who we are to one another, let's walk this path together, your journey is now mine."

Collecting himself he shoved his soaked and disheveled shirttail back into his pants and then went for his checkbook.

"Oh no, Anthony, I can't take that."

"You have to," he responded. "This is your work."

"But you're mine, you're my child, how can I take your money?"

In spite of my protest, he tossed the check on the table and said,

"Please, you have to, I need you to take it."

Our relationship was obviously far more than couselor/client and as our journey unfolded we discovered other phenomena that had prepared us both for this healing earth sojourn. We fought about the money at every visit, until he finally relented and allowed me to care for him, a maternal caring that knew no bounds. It came from the depth of my heart and an undying devotion to him.

I made a decision not to speak about the burning building since I wanted to stay as clear as possible and not subject him to any of my personal visions. There was enough to digest and process right in our present experience.

"When can I return? Can I call you?"

"Come back this time next week and call me any time."

He was beaming; his entire body seemed lighter and I felt alive, more alive than I had felt in a long time. My consciousness had expanded beyond my highest channel by quantum leaps. *Wow, this is just so amazing, thank you, God, thank you.*

With Anthony's confirmation of my mystical life, much was solidified within me. I sent out a prayer of gratitude to Spirit for all of the visions and all of the sacred moments I had been gifted with. Life on the other side was real—I knew that, I always felt it, but now I realized that there was just a very thin veil separating us from truth and remembrance. Lucky's love felt even closer, and I joyously reveled in his embrace and in the wonderful, familiar feeling of having one foot here and another on the other side. The side that I knew as Home was deliciously present.

Ten years earlier, after Lucky's suicide, I experienced profound mystical moments and the incredible grace of God, but at that time I was scrambling to stay afloat through my grief. Now I was focused, grounded, and pruned in the work of Spirit. I knew that I could totally trust whatever was to happen with Anthony. Our journey was Providential. We would be *way show-ers* for one another.

Chapter 16
Unwelcome Mandala

During the week I had time to marvel at what was happening. My normal routine felt quite mundane, not as important as what was occurring in my spiritual life. Often I had to pinch myself in order to stay present in the moment, tend to my students, and other daily activities and chores. It was a wonder that I didn't have a body full of pinch bruises from all of the many miracles that had occurred in my life.

I had all I could do not to run down the high school corridor to Margo's office, Anthony's friend and former drama teacher, and tell her of my meeting with her star student. So often I had questioned her about the incredibly talented young actor. Now I understood why. I had a hunch that Margo might be open to such things but the concern over my mystical life being exposed stopped me in my tracks. As I thought about it there really was no way I could share it with anyone. It was a deeply private and transpersonal moment.

That moment of oneness and love that Anthony and I experienced captivated me throughout the day. It was a glorious moment that would forever stay etched in my memory and my heart. I asked God to guide my time with him, to help me remain open to the miracles that were manifesting, and to keep my emotions in check so I could be a clear channel of healing and a solid counselor for him.

As the week flew by I was exhilarated at the thought of his return. But when I least expected it the image of the child from the burning building would permeate my thoughts. Each time tears rose up and I felt my heart ache. Should I tell him? Repeatedly the same answer from my inner wisdom surfaced,

"No, stay present, Karla, stay grounded." Thank God, meditation helped me to stay focused as I surrendered to the present moment.

Anthony came from a large Italian family, one of ten children. He had been raised predominantly by his mother, a powerhouse of a woman. Josephine was a true matriarch, the epitome of the classic Italian mother. Though only five feet tall, she seemed to tower over most people, with a beautiful face that lifted when she smiled and lovely olive skin capped by short, raven black, wavy hair. Seeing her face, even in worry and sorrow, was like seeing the sun break through clouds. She had endured the death of her husband at the tender age of thirty-one. A fierce and sudden heart attack had stolen the life of her thirty-six year old husband, Charles, leaving her the sole support of her huge family.

It was a time when Anthony desperately needed his father. He was just twelve-years-old and was searching for answers to his sexuality as he tried to find a place in the world where he could fit in. Anthony was indeed different; small in frame and very sensitive, he was not inclined to play sports or go hunting with his Dad. He couldn't stand the thought of killing an innocent animal and couldn't bear to witness it. During a session he confessed that when he tried out for baseball, he was afraid of the pitch. He could never hit the ball or catch it when it was thrown to him. Often he ducked or ran away. For this he was laughed at and ridiculed. When he shared this with me he softly murmured,

"They go by so fast."

Those horrible moments filled him with shame and embarrassment.

When his father died, Anthony cried for weeks. A dark and inconsolable grief enveloped him. He did not understand the horrid intensity of his emotions since he and his Dad had not been extremely close. His father was macho and conservative, not at all like himself. But he did know that the masculine figure in his life was gone, never to be seen again, and he missed him. Feelings of abandonment consumed his tender years.

Josephine rose above the tragedy and managed to raise all of the kids and keep a roof over their heads. Even though she later married Ron, a fine man, Josephine was without a doubt the dominant force and center of the DeVizia clan. Three of Anthony's sisters had been my students at the high school. Linda, Josie and Christine were spectacular girls, incredibly creative, beautiful and intelligent. It was evident that Josephine had done a great job.

I came to understand that Anthony was her pride and joy. From when he was little he stood out, he was different. Even as a youngster he was amazingly creative, sensitive, kind and endearing, always wanting the best for his mother and his siblings. Anthony's sisters and younger brother Billy gravitated to him for support and encouragement. He was indeed special, an accolade he had great difficulty accepting.

Anthony arrived right on time for his next session and greeted me with a warm hug, exclaiming that he was ready to do the deep inner work. I asked him to draw a mandala, a circular depiction of how he was feeling in that moment. I knew the mandala, a coded message from the inner self, could reveal what his inner wisdom already knew. But I had no idea what I was in for.

After leading him through a short relaxation exercise, I suggested he open his eyes and allow himself to be drawn to colors, to not think about it but to allow the colors to choose him. Spread out on the floor with crayons all around him and white drawing paper with a large circle waiting for his mark, he eagerly and with a sense of delight started to draw. Before my eyes Anthony became a giggling little child completely engaged in the moment as he playfully created his picture. His melodic laugh could make my heart swell. Wanting to give him some space I offered to make us tea and with gleeful anticipation of what was to come moved into the kitchen.

Just as the teapot whistled, Anthony's excited voice beckoned to me from the living room.

"I'm finished."

"I can't wait to see," I responded as I poured the boiling water into the teacups.

My heart leapt into my throat as he handed me the mandala drawing. *Oh no,* I thought, *this is not good.* Fear moved through me like a runaway freight train. I felt nausea come up from my belly and fought to hold my emotions at bay.

Steadying myself, I sat down next to him and said,

"Wow, look at that."

The focal point of the drawing held a rich brown cross that topped a bird feeder where two black birds were feeding. Two other black birds were in flight, one very close to the feeder and the other a short distance away, as if it had just taken off. Gray clouds hung low in the sky, dark portent of an approaching storm. Beneath the cross grew nine flowers. Seven were lovely pink orchids with rich green leaves and two were rose-red chrysanthemums.

What felt most disturbing to me was the absence of earth

beneath the flowers. There was no dirt, no ground, nothing. The flowers were actually suspended in air. My mind began to race. *Oh dear God, there's nothing holding the flowers here. Has his soul already made the decision to leave this earthly plane? Do the two birds feeding under the cross mean he will be fed and nourished by Christ? Two birds are leaving. But who are the two?*

Training with Carol Bush in Mandala Assessment had taught me about color choices. In that system, dark rose red was suggestive of old wounds, old pain. I knew Anthony had not fully grieved the loss of his father and I surmised that there was a great deal of pain still locked up in his heart from that loss and from other traumas. The nine flowers were significant as well. Elisabeth Kübler-Ross had suggested that the number of similar symbols in a drawing created by an ill patient could determine how much time might be left on the earth before passing over. Did nine flowers mean nine years, nine months? More than anything I wanted there to be ground under those flowers. But there was none.

Concerned and confused, I did not want to acknowledge what I was seeing and feeling, neither to Anthony nor to myself. But the drawing was in my hands, and it felt like the handwriting was on the wall.

Scrambling, I said,

"So how does this feel to you?" Anthony's response was as always intuitive and precise.

"I like it," he proudly responded. "See the cross and the feeder? That's Christ, He will nourish me through this. And I pray that He will forgive me, for I have felt so separated from Him and ashamed of some of the things that I have done. Maybe the birds flying through the dark clouds signify the work I will do here, exploring the sad parts of my life. The flowers mean growth to me, and see the two birds in the feeder? That's you and my Mom. You both nurture and feed me with your love."

He was beaming as he shared his interpretation, and I was deeply touched.

"Anthony, that's great. And I know that Christ already loves and forgives you. In fact there is really nothing to forgive. You are His."

"Oh, Karla, I hope you're right."

"I am, Anthony, I am."

Eyes glistening with tender tears he reached out and gently touched my hand.

There was nothing more for me to say. He was quite comfortable with his drawing and ready to do some deep soul searching. Inwardly my heart was full, full of love for this beautiful soul and full of sadness for what might be. All I could do was surrender it to God. Anthony had come to me to heal. It was clear that this was to be a spiritual journey and very clear that we had been brought together for a reason. There was no doubt in my mind that our meeting was pre-ordained.

I would counsel Anthony based on where he was in each moment. We would go for the gold each day, and perhaps, I prayed, the experts were wrong in how drawings were to be interpreted. At least this time.

Anthony took the mandala home, and for that I was very grateful, as I did not want to have it as a reminder of what could be. Instead I decided to be joyful for the gifts that were being given to us.

"Lord, lead Thou the way," I prayed. "I will trust this process and let You show me how best to care for him. We are in Your hands."

The sessions with Anthony intensified with every visit. He spoke of his guilt over being gay, and the terrible choices that he had made while trying to make it as an actor in New York City. For he knew that one of those poor choices had filled his body with the dreaded virus.

Over and over I told him, "Anthony, you just didn't know, nobody knew. It's not your fault."

It was hard for him to accept that.

Anthony's heart broke for his mother Josephine since he knew the anguish and fear his disease was causing her. He adored his mother; his greatest desire was to become a successful actor and to accumulate wealth so he could buy his mom a new house and be a greater support to his siblings. Now he was dreading the thought of having to move back home only to become a burden to her. Life had little meaning and Anthony felt like a failure.

He had many fears. The worst one was that he would develop Kaposi's Sarcoma and its red sores would then make his desperately guarded secret visible. He would become like a leper with sores on his body for the world to see and judge. His shame and fear were at times immobilizing. Continually I suggested that he stay in the moment.

Wearing numerous hats I was able to be his counselor, spiritual mentor, and friend, guiding him through many GIM journeys and Reiki healing sessions. All the while at the core of my very being was the voice of remembrance.

"This is your child from the burning building."

Little did I know then that Anthony would become my greatest teacher, for together we would travel through ancient visions and dual memories as the sacred path of our aligned souls made itself known.

Elisabeth Kübler-Ross's teachings became invaluable. She had suggested that as counselors we could determine where a person was in their life process by the stage they were exhibiting: denial, anger, bargaining, depression or acceptance. Anthony and I would travel back and forth between stages. I realized how important it was to hold the vision of healing in whatever form that meant for him. For how many people diagnosed with catastrophic, life-threatening illness succumbed to depression due to believing the time-line given them by physicians and the horrors suggested by the media?

Yes, we would claim life in every moment; we would go for the gold. The Edgar Cayce readings had taught me well too. "Spirit is the life force, mind is the builder, and the physical is the result." I knew that from my own miraculous healing journey. I would meet Anthony where he was. His desire was to become closer to Christ, heal his physical body and his emotions. And it was clearly time for him to forgive himself, to know himself as God knew him, a perfect innocent Divine child. Of that I was very certain.

Chapter 17
Going for the Gold

As he journeyed with me into his inner world, Anthony was a model client. Each session carried him into the deep recesses of his creative imagination and past memories. His remarkable ability to travel quickly into the non-ordinary states of consciousness amazed me. As a singer, dancer and actor he had a natural affinity and love for music and was easily transported by it.

In fact, when not doing theatre or his spellbinding one-man shows, Anthony's career brought him to the Saint, a popular nightclub in New York City that was in some ways the epicenter of the developing AIDS crisis. He was an extraordinary and popular DJ there, and he was more than that. Anthony felt deeply the power of music, and intuited its emotional impact. In a sense, as his brother Billy told me once, Anthony didn't play music, he played emotions.

During each session, after the initial relaxation, a question was posed to his inner wisdom. The music was then introduced and his creative imagination took over.

Albert Einstein was certainly "on the pulse" when he said,

"Imagination is more important than knowledge," and "We can't solve problems by using the same kind of thinking we used when we created them." Those problems need to be brought to a higher level of consciousness and music-evoked imagery did just that.

Anthony's inner symbology took many forms. Often butterflies were present, suggestive of his transformative life journey. Even a rabbit appeared during a session and suggested that he eat nuts. Other wildlife often appeared as well telling him how he could live a healthier and more joyous life.

Our first long journey revealed what seemed to be a past life in France. As a priest in that lifetime, Anthony had experienced a sexual relationship with another of the cloth and was found out. He cried as feelings of shame engulfed him, but then he heard an internal voice saying that God still loved him despite his choices, for there was only love. I was delighted and encouraged that the promise of healing his deep, ever present shame appeared so early in our work.

As he returned from the music-evoked imagery journey, he exclaimed,

"I have always felt like I have had lifetimes as a monk or priest and have been fascinated by Gothic architecture. I so love being in a great church, when I am there I feel like I am home. Karla, I even wanted to be a priest when I was a little boy. I was committed to God in that French life, and that is what I need to do now. Maybe He does really love me. It's just so hard for me to accept that."

"I know, Anthony. It will just take a little time. Be patient with yourself."

Anthony traversed many life experiences, times of feeling inadequate with horrid moments of self-loathing as well as the excruciating feeling of being different and alone in the world. After each release of agonizing sorrow the soothing inner voice would return, gently easing his pain. Anthony continually heard,

"There is only love."

Yet repeatedly he would question,

"Where is that voice coming from? Whose is it?"

"Anthony, you are so deeply loved, rest easy. All will be revealed in time and know that there is a place within you where God resides, ever guiding and always loving you."

Throughout our sessions he bounced back and forth between self-acceptance and self-hatred.

One of Anthony's most potent journeys focused on his long-held grief. As the heart-rending and haunting sounds of Marcello's *Oboe Concerto in D Minor* played, the imagery opened with the appearance of his deceased paternal grandfather. When I asked Anthony if he could speak to him he dissolved into tears. Tenderly he told his grandfather how much he loved and missed him, then whispered,

"I can feel how much my grandfather loved my Dad, that love is flowing right through me . . . "

The next scene revealed people looking at him in judgment and ridicule. Yet each time a shameful or ridiculing image or feeling surfaced his inner wisdom would respond with something more tender and supportive.

During one such journey Anthony's deceased Aunt Jennie came telling him to be patient. As she held him she whispered that she was watching over him. She told him that there was no secret recipe. His body as well as his mind responded to the images. Returning to the death of his father, Anthony's chest actually felt torn apart as if nothing was holding it together. Gripping his chest, he wept long and hard, allowing the intense grief to release from the tight and painful pockets of his heart.

Anthony came to realize that as a child he had often become ill in an attempt to stay out of school and receive the attention he so craved. Since he felt himself to be a misfit, school was unbearably hard. He remembered his father visiting him in the hospital when he was in fifth grade. In the imagery he thanked his father repeatedly for being with him at that time, for bringing pizza and a model for him to play with.

In nearly each session his mother would appear, and he would revel in the love Josephine so compassionately showered upon him. She was his rock and, past-life memories indicated, his mother many times. They were joined and for this Anthony was exceedingly grateful.

Many shadow aspects of his personality emerged. As he encountered his living grandmother he was swept with emotion, for his love for her was enormous. Anthony saw her as a positive and endearing force in his life. She was growing older and her mind was failing. He worried that the ravages of his disease would begin to take his memory. With that thought, he became aware of himself standing next to her. He described the image of himself as negative, complaining, and crotchety.

"Oh, God, I'm bitchy," he exclaimed.

His grandmother then spoke to him saying quite simply,

"Eat ice-cream."

Anthony's charming giggle rose up as he said,

"I've got it! She wants me to have fun. Be more positive." Overjoyed he added,

"I see myself eating that ice-cream. It's good for me."

Then new images surfaced, one quickly following the other.

"I see myself, I'm healthy, smiling, laughing with people. No more closing doors."

"Doors?" I questioned.

"Yes, I see many doors; each one is opening for me, one after the other. As I open each one it becomes brighter, such wonderful light. I'm going through them. Here's my friend Tony. I shut the door on him a long time ago fearing my illness was a drag. We love the opera. I haven't been in so long. I will call him."

"Can you communicate with him now?" I asked.

With that his friend Tony shared how much he admired and respected Anthony.

"Oh he likes me for the same reasons I like him, but it's so hard for me to believe that."

"Can you take that caring in?" I questioned.

Anthony softened, "Yes it feels warm and comforting . . . Now I see Bruce, my partner. I have shut him out. He really does love me. I will try to absorb that too."

Anthony was taking in deep and full breaths, allowing each moment of love and caring to fill him.

"Oh here's another door. It's my Mom. She's getting into her mother thing, doting on me. I hate it! I can't be an invalid, can't be treated like a sick child."

"Is that familiar?"

"Yes, it's too familiar and comfortable. I like that attention but I will not stop doing things for myself."

"Can you speak to her?"

"No, it will hurt her feelings . . . Whoa . . . I've just lifted up; I'm on top of a room hovering there. There's sunshine and I'm eating ice-cream and my grandmother is here. She says, 'Live simply.' She tells me that I will find the things I want to make me happy . . . joy and simplicity. Oh, there's New Jersey Summer Theatre. I can do that. Margo's here and I'm directing, adjusting the lights as we laugh together. I do love Margo . . . "

"And here's Mom again. I'll tell her how much I love her but need her to let me do things for myself. Yes, I can do that. I will tell her."

As the flood of images ceased Anthony became very quiet.

Softly I said, "The music is about to end. Be with what has been most significant for you as you slowly return here."

With tears streaming down his face he responded,

"I have been so hard on myself. Perhaps I even drew this illness to me, for I wanted to die. I have felt so out of place here. I've criticized and punished myself. I need to forgive myself. I have an image of hugging myself and I'm making a deal. It will be easier. I will relax more. If I can't get things done they won't be done. I'm making a promise to love myself more and to eat ice-cream."

Anthony returned from the altered state with a new and beautiful peace radiating from him. His face was soft and he appeared to be glowing.

"Anthony, here's your homework. Keep in your awareness the image of hugging yourself and just as soon as you feel ready, speak to your mother. I know she will understand. She is just doing what any mother would do."

"Yes, I will. If I don't beat this disease and get worse, I'll need her comfort and help. Karla, I just have to do things for myself!"

After a warm hug, Anthony left with renewed hope and a greater sense of self-love. I was overjoyed to not only guide him but to also be a witness to his remarkable healing. More and more I realized that healing happens at many levels; the inner wisdom knows just what needs to be addressed. I needed to do very little as Anthony worked through the trauma and pain of his past. A gift had been given to me. I was watching an extraordinary young man heal his emotions and his soul and find ways to live more fully and joyously in his body.

He was going for the gold. In awe and deeply moved, I thanked God for the treasure in my life.

This brave young man continued with his deep work, at each session releasing the old wounds and further enhancing his will to live joyously. Outside sessions, we enjoyed walks together and music, our bond deepening. Though we did not speak of it, we knew we had shared an ancient and love-filled past.

Anthony arrived one afternoon feeling agitated and angry but unsure of what was trying to surface. I decided to use some tumultuous music in an attempt to explore and work through his heated emotions.

As the strong and evocative music of Holst's *Mars* played, Anthony returned to moments of turmoil. He recalled a fight with his older brother Charlie over baseball. Releasing monumental anger, Anthony yelled at Charlie and then his Dad for making him play the game he despised. Just as soon as that anger dissipated, images of his childhood hospital stay surfaced. Anthony imagined ripping up the cards from the school kids as he shouted out loud,

"You didn't like me, this card means nothing. The teacher made you send it."

Crying, he continued, "I just didn't fit in. I kept trying. People always said I was so special, so talented. But I wish I wasn't. Why couldn't I be plain?"

And then the huge rage erupted like a volcano spewing forth pent-up fire. The person who gave him AIDS was standing right in front of him.

"NO!!!!" . . . bellowed out.

Thrashing about the couch and violently punching a pillow,

he screamed as he remembered the moment he contracted the deadly virus.

"That's it," I urged. "Let it out."

Anthony continued to scream and rage, then, wet with sweat and tears, his body went limp, appearing almost lifeless. Slowly his beautiful smile appeared, softening and transforming his delicate face. He seemed to be in a moment of deep and profound peace.

In a whisper I asked, "What are you with?"

"I'm telling him it was not his fault. We are hugging. He too is very sick, much worse than I am. It feels so good to let this go."

"Oh here's my father again. I'm telling him how much I love him and I ask him to watch over me. He's holding me and . . ."

Engulfed in deep emotion, he was unable to go on. In a whisper I said,

"Take your time; just be with your father."

"He says he loves me and that I am a good boy."

With that recognition tears of bliss again enveloped him. As we closed, Anthony said,

"I must find a way to make good white blood cells. I can see light pouring through my body cleansing me and making those new cells."

"Work with that Anthony, be with that image every day and know that your father is with you every step of the way. You are not alone through this. Many are watching over you."

Embracing me he left, overjoyed, with a new feeling of clarity and possibility.

In just five intense sessions Anthony broke through layers upon layers of shame, worthlessness, anger and grief. He made a decision to seek out more holistic and alternative ways to heal. Perhaps that is what his Aunt Jennie was referring to when she said, "There are no secret recipes." He would discover his own special recipe, his own way.

He refused AZT, the standard treatment for AIDS then, because of the side effects. At that time his worst symptoms were fatigue and diarrhea, and Reiki was able to relieve much of that.

Anthony began to join me each week at my *Course in Miracles* meeting. The Course was teaching him that he was not just his body, but also a Light in this world, that fear was an illusion and only love was real. He began to understand that he was part of God's Sonship, as we all are—all souls making our way back to the One. Those of us who studied the Course knew that nothing could separate us from God's love.

We ended all of our meetings with song and celebration. Anthony was making new friends and was feeling closer than ever to Christ, although a small remnant of his shame persisted.

"Are you sure He forgives me?" he would ask.

"Yes, Anthony, I am sure. There is nothing to forgive."

My journey with Anthony included more than just counseling. Even though I knew I needed to surrender all outcomes, I did want him to heal; after all he was my child from the burning building. I felt responsible for his death in that lifetime even though I didn't know how or why. How could I not want him to live? It was part of my human condition. Although I knew there was really no death, just a change in form, I was compelled to do all I could to secure a physical healing for him as well as help with his incredible emotional and spiritual transformation.

AL721 was an AIDS remedy that included digesting a mixture of egg yolks. Since the FDA had not yet approved it, the Gay Men's Health Crisis organization in New York City was dispersing it as part of an underground movement. After a call to Israel to the physician who had discovered it, we made our way into the city. Like thieves in the night we scurried into the large hall where many stricken with the disease waited in line for the new and promising medicine.

Many were barely able to stand; their disease had progressed so viciously. To Anthony's horror some were covered with the angry hot and red sores of Kaposi's Sarcoma, a severe skin cancer that visibly marked one as an AIDS patient. Kaposi's Sarcoma was Anthony's greatest fear. It was very hard for him to witness the others branded by the mark so he backed away in an attempt to disappear behind me. Yet there was humor too. As he clung behind my full skirt I chuckled,

"Hey, lighten up, when's the last time you got to bootleg egg yolks?" We laughed uproariously at the insanity of it all and on the way home sang *Awakening*, a Michael Stillwater *Course in Miracles* song at the top of our lungs. Playfully we sang the verses,

Take the time to love yourself. You are beautiful
Take the time to heal yourself. You are beautiful

Beautiful like the sun on the water
Beautiful like the clouds in the sky

Beautiful you are, you are
You are beautiful, you are

In spite of the harsh realities we had great moments of joy, and for a number of months life was good. Anthony grew strong and we were having fun. He was following his new health regimen and diet, with of course the exception of the ice-cream he so relished.

I was becoming more a member of the family. I loved the DeVizia clan and most especially loved Josephine. It was clear that I was not just working with Anthony but all in the family who needed support and comfort.

Many times as Anthony rested upstairs after a Reiki treatment Josephine would share her worst fears. I urged her to be authentic, to share her feelings no matter what they were and to also live life fully each moment, to stay present to joy. For joy was walking hand in hand with sorrow.

"When you are afraid, Josephine, breathe and allow God's love to enfold you and hold a vision of Anthony happy and healthy."

Often she would respond with,

"I'll try, Karla, but sometimes it's just too hard. I pray over and over, 'Dear God, please don't take my son, please take this away.' But then I think even Christ asked His Father to take His pain away. But did He? No. I guess I need to remember, God's will be done, and try to live one day at a time."

Her breath caught in her throat as she repeated the words.

"Karla, it's just so hard."

We held on to one another and wept.

"I know, Jo, I know. I am so sorry you have to go through this unbearable fear and pain. I wish I could make it all go away."

The journey was agonizing for her but she rose to each crisis as a solid force for love. Josephine was a living symbol of that love and of enduring faith.

"Karla," she once said, "I know something good is happening. Anthony seems utterly exhausted yet after you do Reiki he always bounces down the stairs with renewed energy and famished for food."

"Oh I'm so glad, Jo, hold onto that image."

"And you know, Karla, you always yawn when you are finished with the treatment. There's an old Italian belief that says when you yawn like that around a sick person, you have taken the devil out of him, the bad stuff. Just like in the old days when someone gave you the *evil eye*. Sometimes the Italians from the old country would look you straight in the eye and say good things about you but they would really wish you evil. When you weren't looking they would point two fingers at you, the pinky and the pointer and sometimes they did it right in your face. Bad things would then happen. But you could send that *evil eye* right back at them."

"How, Jo?"

"If you thought someone had attacked you, prayers would be said as four drops of oil were put into a dish of water. If the oil stayed in one big blob you were safe, if it broke into smaller blobs then you had gotten *the eyes*. You were in big trouble. At least my ancestors believed that. But they could send it back, give them the *evil eye* by pointing fingers right back at them."

"Yowsa . . . Jo, that's scary! I think I better stick with Reiki and leave *the eyes* to the ancestors. That Italian stuff is definitely out of my league."

The idea made us both laugh and pulled us out of our sorrowful feelings.

I met seventeen-year-old Billy, Anthony's youngest sibling. Billy idolized his big brother, wanting to be creative and talented just like him. He had become the drum major in the high school marching band, as Anthony had been years earlier. To honor his brother, Billy resurrected Anthony's award winning and very funky march. Even while feeling ill and tired,

Anthony gave Billy pointers as they practiced the march to the music of *Land of Make Believe* in the bedroom. Anthony adored his little brother and was incredibly proud of him.

Billy was dear and we bonded instantly. I began to feel that I had not only been with Anthony in former lives but with many in this family. They all gathered around their brother wishing to support and buoy him. But there were times when many tears fell and fear surfaced. For the harsh reality was ever present. It was 1987. Nearly 50,000 had died of AIDS and many people believed it could be transmitted through any body fluid. This of course we knew wasn't true. Direct contact with blood or semen was the only way it could be contracted but many were afraid, not believing they were safe. This remarkable family held their heads up high, never faltering. They were proud of their brother and honored to be part of his journey, however painful it was. Or was going to be.

In February, with no warning, a tidal wave crashed down upon our optimism. Anthony developed pneumocystis pneumonia and was rushed to a North Jersey hospital. We were stunned, most especially Josephine, who had been see-sawing between hope and the unimaginable—that her child might die.

Here it was and we were all riveted to the gruesome reality. Anthony might leave us. Things didn't look good. Rapidly failing, he was ravaged with a fever and his lungs filled with fluid. After days of medicine our worst fears were realized. Anthony was not responding.

I was in disbelief. *No, God, this can't be, it's much too soon.* All of his imagery journeys had suggested he was on top of the illness. Passionately I prayed that he be held by angels, that healing come to his physical form as it had to his heart and gentle spirit. "Thank you, God," I repeated over and over. "Thank you that healing has already manifested."

During my visits to the hospital I closed the curtain around his bed and requested privacy from the nurses. This was not a time when Reiki and other complimentary modalities were accepted or approved of, but the medicine was not touching the pneumonia. We couldn't wait. Occasionally a nurse would peek in and give me a weird look, but I was not deterred. Placing my hands on his laboring chest I felt the warmth of Reiki begin to fill his body. Gently guiding him through a relaxation I then placed my mouth on his chest and blew my own breath, aligned with the Light of Spirit, deep into his lungs. This was a Native American medicine custom called the *breath of life*. As I released the long, slow and sustained breath I felt a quickening in Anthony's frail body, as if the Light and healing had been received.

Paled cheeks began to pink up and his eyes became clearer. In that moment a wave of welcome relief washed over me.

"Just rest now, Anthony. I'll be right here."

"Okay, Karlina," he weakly responded as a sweet smile graced his lips. He then slipped off into a deep and peaceful sleep.

Josephine arrived and we sat for hours next to his bed in prayer and unguarded hope. When Anthony awakened feeling somewhat better, able to sip a little water and speak to us, we were greatly relieved. Feeling he was, at least for the moment, safe I returned home with some hope renewed, but I knew he was still in a very precarious state. Most of my waking moments were spent in prayer and thanksgiving. "Your will be done Lord, but if it is right and perfect then let him live. I give thanks to You, that this is already done."

As I was drifting off to sleep that night a voice came to me.

"Bring your music tomorrow and drawing paper."

I questioned that, saying,

"But he's not up to an imagery journey."

Again the voice instructed me,

"Bring your music tomorrow and drawing paper."

Murmuring, "Okay," I succumbed to a peaceful sleep.

The next school day seemed excruciatingly long. I couldn't help watching the clock; the minutes and hours seemed so much slower than usual. Thank goodness my students were self-motivated and my lack of concentration was not terribly apparent. I was blessed to have such good kids and as I moved to gratitude the day traveled by far more quickly.

The last bell rang and out I flew, my therapy tools, stereo, music, and art supplies close at hand. *How am I going to pull this off? An imagery journey in the hospital? Well there is a first time for everything,* I thought. Upon reaching his floor I introduced myself at the nurse's station as his minister and counselor.

Without too much explanation I asked if I could have some private time to work with some soothing music and prayer.

"All right," said the charge nurse, "but first let me see if he needs anything."

She thumbed through his chart and said,

"Nope, he's okay with his medicine until dinner. Take all the time you need."

Wow, that was easy, I thought. With my boom box in one hand and a bag heavy with music and art supplies over my shoulder, I made my way down the long and murky green corridor. Anthony was awake and greeted me with,

"Hi, Karlina," the melodious-sounding nickname rolled off his tongue with such sweet endearment.

"Hi, Antonio, how are you doing?"

"I'm better than yesterday. The Reiki really helped me feel a little better. They're going to do some more blood work later to see if the medicine is working. I don't know, Karla.

Do you think I'm going to go home? This is scary. I don't feel ready to die. What can I do?"

Then he pointed to the paraphernalia I had carried in.

"What's all that?"

"Well, my sweet one, last night a little voice whispered in my ear. It said that we should do a journey. Do you think you are up for it?"

"Here?" He gasped.

"Why not? I spoke to the nurses. I told them I'm your minister and asked for some privacy."

"That's right. You are a minister, I forgot that. I feel really weak but I am willing to try."

"That's great."

Fortunately, no one was in the adjacent bed to question or be disturbed by our rather odd behavior.

Hooking up the stereo I got my paper ready to record his session and closed the curtains.

"What should I bring into the music?" he inquired. "What question should I ask?"

"Just let the music lead you," I responded. "Whatever needs to be revealed will come. I trust your inner wisdom Anthony, just share with me as you have feelings or imagery. Okay? Here are some eye shields to block out the light."

Anthony put them on and said,

"Oh that's so nice. I hate looking at all of this medical stuff, the IV's and all. It's so depressing."

I sent out a prayer,

"Thank you, God, that Divine timing and order is in our lives now. Let no one enter into our sacred space."

Leading him through a calming relaxation I suggested that each body part soften. When he was visibly relaxed I turned on the stereo and suggested that the soothing music take him wherever he needed to go.

In no time at all Anthony began to share with me.

"I'm at a pond on my knees scooping up handfuls of cool clear water. A deer is nearby and asks how am I doing? I say very well."

My hope heightened. "What else do you notice?"

"Charlie my older brother is across the pond. He's coming around to see me. We embrace and he tells me how much he's been thinking of me and how sorry he is that we haven't been close, that he hasn't been a better brother. I tell him how much I love him and how he has always been my brother. It feels so good to be with him."

"Now I see my sister Josie, I tell her to be happier. We're hugging."

"What else are you aware of?"

"I'm ice-skating. I have so much energy. I'm jumping and spinning, enjoying everything. It's all white and clean and cool. Now I'm skating towards a white house. I sit on the porch and take off my skates. It is so beautiful and peaceful here. I'm focusing on the sky as if I'm pulling layers of clouds away. There is a dark hole behind the clouds. I'm going up into that space."

"How is that for you?" I asked.

"Uncomfortable."

I began to feel concerned that this might be indicating his leaving, but kept my voice soft and relaxed.

"Can you stay with this?"

"Yes, Ann Marie, my little sister is here; she is off in a corner and she's so sad. I pick her up, kiss her and push her out of the hole."

"What's happening now?"

"I'm sitting on a log in a forest, my father is next to me and we're talking. He tells me to enjoy the simple beauty of nature. He tells me to love myself. But I feel like I'm falling into a sleep. What is it that I don't want to know or see?" Anthony's lips pursed as he shared his discomfort.

"What is that?" I gently questioned.

"I don't want to see the truth about myself, afraid I won't be able to live up to it. Afraid there is a way I'll have to be, a way I can't be . . . Now my mother is here, I'm giving her a kiss telling her that I have to move on but I'm not leaving her behind. I feel like I am walking above everything."

My heart again sank. "How does that feel?"

"Feels like I'm alone, there aren't too many people walking on this level. I can't see anymore, I'm lying on my back; I know I have to turn over. I'll be able to see things."

"Can you do that?" I asked as the familiar and poignant words *turn over* grabbed me.

"I'm afraid to turn over. I'll have to speak. I won't know what to say. There are just too many people underneath me. They are waiting to hear me say something."

Knowing how aligned Anthony was with the music I asked,

"Can the music help you here?"

The uplifting and beautiful sounds of Tomas Luis de Victoria's *O Magnum Mysterium* filled the room as he whispered,

"Oh it's Mary, the Blessed Mother. She loves me so much. I can feel it. She says,

'You are to serve people. You will be shown.' "

"How? I don't know how and she is fading. I can't get her back."

"Take a full and easy breath, Anthony, and slowly return here."

Anthony returned to full conscious awareness, perplexed and uneasy.

"What was that? What am I to do? It feels too big and scary."

"Anthony, I don't believe you are going to die in this hospital. There is work yet for you to do. Remember what the Divine Mother said. You will be shown and you don't have to worry things will fall into place. Do you think you could draw a mandala?"

"Okay," he said, appearing calmer. "I do feel much better and energized."

Anthony placed into the circle an image resembling a fetus resting in utero. It appeared to be swirling in the safety of the circle, clearly a symbol of new life and new hope.

"Anthony, this looks like birth. I think you are going to go for the gold. Rest now and gather your strength."

Anthony's fever waned as the day progressed and new life filled his cells. The pneumonia had passed and the terrifying crisis was over.

Just a few days later Anthony's twenty-year-old sister Linda visited. Cuddling up in the hospital bed together they enjoyed the delicious lunch she had prepared. Linda then played Paul Simon's *Graceland*, and to her enormous surprise and delight Anthony, his energy renewed, hopped up and danced right on the bed. They laughed uproariously for the first time in many weeks. Upon hearing this good news we all took a deep and welcome sigh of relief.

Chapter 18
Remembrance

Anthony left the hospital believing he had received a miracle, *a stay*, though for how long none of us could be certain. The pneumonia had come like a thief in the night. Who knew what might be next? This had been the first real battle; up to that point fatigue and diarrhea were the major complaints. During a Reiki session Anthony questioned,

"What do you think, Karlina? What am I supposed to do? The Blessed Mother said I was to serve, but how?"

"Anthony, I don't know, but I do know that what you need will be given to you. Let's use this time to revel in the beauty of life. Look, it's spring, a time for rebirth, just like your mandala suggested. Let's get some ice-cream and go to the park. We'll have fun."

"Let's," Anthony responded. And off we went.

Our lazy days were luscious, filled with the beauty of nature, our deep connection and Reiki. And we spent many evenings with our *Course in Miracles* group enjoying inspiring meditations and song. But this day as we walked through the swaying tall reeds of Sandy Hook State Park Anthony broke our contemplative mood.

"Karla, something else is coming. I can feel it, there's pain in my belly and the diarrhea is getting much worse. Maybe it's the AL721, all those eggs, you know. It always feels better after Reiki but it's there. I can't imagine another hospital stay."

"Have you told the doctor?" I asked.

"No, not yet, as long as it subsides with Reiki I think I'll wait a bit."

"Well not too long if it keeps up," I urged. He nodded. Feeling he had taken my advice I dropped the subject and we returned to our lazy walk. But I was yanked out of my bliss at the thought of another hospital stay. I too felt uneasy, as if the other shoe was about to drop. *Stay in the moment*, I reminded myself, as I had so often coached Anthony. Oh isn't it true that teachers teach what they need to learn? All that I spoke to my dearest one was really a message to me.

Let us not be fooled into thinking that it is the speaker at the podium, or the author of the book who is the wise one. It is the one who stands before you and questions. That one is the true teacher. That one invites you to go deep within yourself to the place of innate wisdom. Those dear ones that grace our path teach us, and I have come to realize that the most difficult relationships are oftentimes the ones that are the most blessed. For each and every relationship that we encounter throughout our lives is giving us an opportunity to reach deep inside and grow, through greater understanding, compassion, and forgiveness.

As you read these words know that your life is a teaching/learning journey and that the ultimate destiny of all our relationships is to be made holy in the sight of God. If not in this earth experience then in the next one, wherever that may lead us. It was clear to me that Anthony and I had traversed through many other times and dimensions. This felt to be our grace life, a life where we truly knew who we were and recognized our greatest purpose was to love one another.

My thoughts continued, yes something is coming. I can feel it too. Silently I spoke to God. *Dear Lord, I know we are already blessed in so many ways. This journey is filled with Your love. It is indeed a walk with You. There is really no need to ask for help, so I shall remain grateful. My prayers to You shall not be of supplication but of gratitude for all that is given.*

I then put my concerns away and Anthony and I enjoyed the rest of our lazy day.

Late one afternoon the following week, as I was preparing lesson plans at home, the phone beckoned. Anthony's agonizing sobs on the other end pulled me into acute alertness.

"What are you saying? I can't understand. Did I hear Kaposi's Sarcoma?"

"Oh, Karla, there is a red mark on my body," he cried. "Oh my God, I know it's Kaposi's. Oh, God, I can't do this. Please help me."

Anthony's greatest fear had been realized. The shoe had dropped, landing more like a bomb. Thundering and booming it threatened to annihilate us.

"Oh no, Anthony, I'm so sorry. Hang in there, I'm on my way."

I fled out the door, his terror ringing in my ears, absorbed by my cells, as if the horrid sound had found a familiar niche in me. *Oh yes, that's it,* I thought. *The scream that used to live in me. I understand, Lord, I know where he is right now. I know that blinding and debilitating terror. And I know You will give me the words, the Light, to work with him and to help him.*

When I arrived, Josephine met me at the door. Horror and fear in her eyes, she held her composure.

"He's waiting for you," she motioned upstairs.

"Thanks, Jo."

Standing at the bottom stair I squeezed the railing, as if gripping the very hand of Christ for support. Taking a full deep breath I went up the stairs into the room that harbored the son of an aching mother, the returned child of my ancient soul's path, the creative, talented actor and music man. Surrounded by his music, crystal stones, and pictures of Christ lay my dearest soul friend. He was curled up in a ball so tight that he looked even smaller than his mere five-foot-five frame. Anthony appeared so little in that moment that it took my breath away.

"Hey, baby," I whispered, "I know this is the worst."

Anthony slowly looked up with eyes swollen, face tear stained. As I placed my hand upon him he whispered,

"Look, it's here on my chest and my leg and there seems to be a spot starting on my nose."

He then cried, "I just can't do this, everyone will know I have this disease, like I'm a leper. What heartache and shame this will cause my family."

As always his thoughts were for others.

"You are so loved, Anthony. Remember what the Madonna said. There's something special for you, a way you are to help others. Maybe this is part of it. I don't know for sure, my love, but I do know that whatever you need will be given. You will not walk this path alone. Anthony, you have all of us and I know there are many on the other side walking with you: your father, Aunt Jennie, your grandfather and, Anthony, the Blessed Mother Herself."

Tears subsiding, he murmured,

"Oh, Karlina, I've known from the beginning that I was going to get this horrible cancer. It's all part of it. But I'm feeling so tired. I don't know if I will have what it takes to do whatever the Blessed Mother wants of me."

"All you need to do right now is rest, let's take one moment at a time. Can I do some Reiki for you?"

"Did you bring your table?" he asked. "I just hate the thought of you lugging that thing up these stairs."

"No, it's not here and I really don't mind, it keeps me in shape. Tell you what; you don't even have to move. I can work with you right here on the bed. Can I cuddle up with you?"

"Oh yes, Karlina, could you hold me?"

I crawled into the bed with him. As Anthony lay on his side I pulled him close and whispered,

"It will be all right. We'll get through this."

Like spoons we lay, my arms wrapped around his small form filling him with gentle Reiki until he drifted off to sleep.

Even before the loud screaming-red marks exposed him, word got out that Anthony had AIDS. A chiropractor refused to see him and people backed away in the grocery store. Billy was being hassled in school and Ron's haircutting business was dwindling. I wondered what the future had in store for this outstanding family.

Just a few days later the noble DeVizia clan gathered around the dining room table that nourished the bodies and souls of this extraordinary family and the decision was made. They would not hide behind the disease. They would stand up for their son and brother and also for who they were. This loving family would take a powerful stand for love and compassion.

Josephine had been a model citizen, respected and admired by many for her undaunting work in the community. A year prior she had organized and produced the town's greatest event—The Tri-Centennial Parade. Robert Shuey, the town mayor and former chairman of that committee, had recently approached Jo. She repeated his words verbatim.

"Karla," he said, 'Jo, you and Anthony have been such a powerful and creative force in this town. You have helped so many and Anthony is so well known and loved for his masterful performances in the high school plays not to mention the award-winning marching band. You have done so much for us and I would like to help you and Anthony now.' "

As Josephine shared his words she said, "Oh, Karlina, I was dumbfounded and said to him, 'What do you mean?' " Clearly moved she continued,

"He wants to get the Tri-Centennial committee together again to begin fund raising, to help us cover the costs of this disease. Bob said he would stand by us."

"Wow, that's great, Jo."

Josephine was filled with emotion and many questions. Would they really support her and Anthony? People in the town were afraid and in the news AIDS was grim. The papers were filled with horrific and frightening stories. The community of Acadia, Florida had run a young family out of town by burning down their house in an attempt to keep their three hemophiliac sons out of elementary school. What would they think of her gay son? Jo agonized over the gruesome possibilities.

People were lining up in separate camps. Fear, blame and outrage heralded the loudest camp.

"It's a gay disease," was the ear-splitting cry of many.

And, "We are all in danger, just by being next to the infected person. We're all going to die."

Then the horrid next line up: "They deserve it. Cart them all away."

That was one of the most despicable threats, a horrible reminder of other victims not so long ago who had been outcast, judged and eventually gassed. *Would we ever get it,* I wondered? *Would we ever learn?*

Was AIDS here to give humanity another chance, a chance to embrace each other and not condemn? My thoughts went to Lucky. He had been a champion for the downtrodden, for those ridiculed and abused. If he were still alive he would be at the forefront of this outrageous dilemma, probably admonishing those who were the accusers and abusers. My path however was different. It was subtler.

The thoughts and questions in my mind offered no rest. Were those suffering taking this on as a gift to us? I believed that many, if not all, were high souls who had chosen the gruesome path. It was a path of suffering and death, yet a path of possibility. In each town and community a loud cry was heard that disrupted the population's apathy, that confronted fear, which called each one to be his or her greatest self. I recalled the words of the Master, *"Love one another as I have loved you,"* and then thought of Him walking fearlessly among the lepers, touching and loving, holding a space for deep compassion. Yes, that's it. This is a disease that knocks on the door of compassion, a door that is within everyone's heart.

Let us wake up, I fervently prayed.

I knew there was another camp. I had seen it with the incredible Hyacinth organization, whose dedicated volunteers sat tirelessly at the bedside of those dying and did everything in their power to educate the fearful public. And of course my wonderful *Course in Miracles* group displayed no fear, only love, as they rallied to Anthony's side with unbridled caring and support. Now this brave and loyal DeVizia family prepared to stand in their power, and as they did others began to rally as well.

A week later Jo and I drove to the town meeting filled with concern and hope. Would they really support us? The community gathered and found their seats. I sat on the stage next to Josephine as Robert Shuey applauded her and said,

"Josephine is a friend. She did so much for us and she practically did it alone, with no reward. She knew then that Anthony had AIDS and she organized the parade anyway. It's time to do something for her. It's such a shame that Anthony, a friend, is one of the first AIDS cases in our area."

Josephine, looking out at the small group that had gathered, sat with courage and dignity as plans were made for a fundraiser brunch. The brunch was scheduled for May 3rd. As Jo heard the date she leaned into Bob, telling him that it was just days after Anthony's 29th birthday.

"Then it will be turned into a birthday party," Bob said. "Where speakers can educate the group about AIDS. We'll have fun too, lots of music, good food and entertainment."

Before we knew it, a long-time family friend, Robert Huntington, stepped forward saying he would walk from Atlantic City to Matawan to raise money for Anthony. Charlie Burke, a high school teacher, announced plans to air a panel discussion on the school's local cable television channel to further benefit the fund. Josephine was startled and I was blown away.

The imagery journey Anthony had experienced in the hospital was fast falling into place. The Blessed Mother had spoken truth; there was work for Anthony to do. This was no longer just about him, the family, and the disease. It was a statement about *Truth, Love, and Dignity*.

Sitting next to my brave and wonderful friend Jo, my heart swelled with gratitude for I knew that I was part of a grace-filled moment. Bob turned the meeting over to Jo.

"I hope I can do this," she said. "I'm going to try."

I placed a supportive hand at Jo's side as she then read her statement to the group.

"After the parade I thought about the nine months of work. Wow, it was great, wasn't it? But I didn't do it by myself. There were three-thousand people in the parade, and people who jumped in at the last minute to help me, the road department and letter writers. I won't forget the person who got me into the borough hall in the middle of the night or the people who lined the streets, the floats, and costumes. It was a great community effort."

"Most importantly, it was a loving, sharing day. That's how

we look back on it. Yes, there were times I felt that I took on too much, but I did it . . . didn't I? Yes, we did it!"

"Now six months later, again I'm faced with a task to fulfill. As you know, my son, Anthony, has Acquired Immune Deficiency Syndrome, otherwise and more popularly known as AIDS. Anthony has had a bout with pneumonia and has developed a skin cancer called Kaposi's Sarcoma, which, by the way, cannot be transmitted. Yes, you can shake hands with him."

"It is tough to face up to this illness. I've often wondered what people will think. But now knowing you are here in this room brings good thoughts to my mind, the comments of Matawan, made up of people like you here tonight tells me that the Christmas message lives all year long: love, peace, forgiveness, sharing and giving. God bless you all for that. For you are here tonight to give my family strength, love and support, and the gifts of friendship. What more could I want or ask for? No matter what we face, I can feel strength through your presence tonight. I am a blessed person to have the gift of a caring community."

The group broke into loud applause as I dried the tears from my eyes. And so it began. What had been prophesized in Anthony's guided imagery journey by the Blessed Mother was in full swing. At the end of the meeting, the press swarmed us.

"How is Anthony doing?" they inquired. "When can we speak to him?"

I shared Anthony's positive spirit and hope with them and Jo said she would ask Anthony if he wished to be interviewed. We were delighted, and once in my car we looked at one another, beaming from ear to ear, and in tandem, said,

"WOW!"

Before we had time to catch our breath, Anthony made a statement to the press. He admitted to being gay and to having the disease. The news article read,

"I have never been ashamed of my lifestyle and being gay has never been an issue for me. I'd have to say that at first I was skeptical about fundraising. Not everyone feels the same way about homosexuality and there is potential for backlash. I don't mind that all this is publicized, as long as it is done with dignity. I'd really like to promote a more positive attitude, how to live with this disease and not look at it so much as a death sentence. I have to live in this town, and I don't want to be trapped in my own house."

"I look at this as an opportunity to make a statement that people with AIDS are still human beings. I'd like to educate the public on this. Let them know that AIDS is something that can be knocking on their door, and it doesn't have to be the plague people have talked about if we show compassion. I think that compassion would make people a lot more comfortable with themselves in the long run. When we conquer this, they will be able to look at themselves and not be ashamed that they did nothing. Even before I got sick, I saw this as an opportunity to get people together."

"I know there is no cure, but I am aware of people who have had the disease go into remission. I've been blessed with a very loving family that has been supportive since before day one, when they knew I was being tested. I believe these things help and that I am going to live. Remission is not out of the realm of possibilities. I have to remain positive. It's important to do that to function as a human being."

As I read Anthony's words in the Sunday morning press, I was filled with pride and emotion. I couldn't wait to see him. I rushed to the phone and quickly dialed his number.

"I'm coming over to hug you," I blurted out before he had time to finish his hello.

"Oh, Karlina, can you believe all of this? Robert Huntington is going to do a 100-mile walk from Atlantic City to Matawan. The Italian American Club is hosting a benefit cocktail party, churches are doing fundraisers and townspeople and friends are sending us checks. It's a little embarrassing."

"But it's good, Anthony, you're making a difference in the lives of so many, just like the Blessed Mother said. You are doing *The Work*."

"I know, it's incredible, and I do feel blessed; yet there are lots of mixed feelings. I'm so exposed." Chuckling he added. "I would have rather had celebrity status for my acting."

"Oh you have that too, dear one," I said. "Can I come over and maybe do some Reiki?"

"Sure, that would be great."

Once at his house, I was greeted by his beaming family. Josephine had a twinkle in her eye, Billy was delighted, and Linda, the youngest sister, was gushing with hugs. It was as if the powers that be had turned a key. The dreaded anticipation of community rejection had vanished. The town had opened its arms, at least most of it had. We would find out later that fear still held many in its grip. But in this moment, we were ecstatic. Although the funds would certainly help with the skyrocketing costs, the greatest reward was the compassion flowing now from the community like a fountain that watered the family's courage and dignity.

I ran up the stairs and found Anthony listening to music and looking out the window.

"Hey, sweetie," I greeted. "How are you feeling?"

"Oh my spirit feels good, but this body is tired, and you know I really do hate these red spots. My face is getting covered. I look like a leopard."

"You're gorgeous," I teased. "Shall we do some Reiki?"

"That would be great. I could sure use it."

My massage table now sat in the corner of his room, no longer did I have to lug it back and forth. In a snap, it was up. As gentle music played, I let the healing power fill his body.

Anthony relaxed, and as my hands rested upon his heart space, I entered into the dreamy, heavenly state of Reiki.

When I held Anthony's feet, I suddenly became aware of Christ washing the feet of His disciples. Then an image of Mary Magdalene came to mind. She was washing her Beloved's feet with her hair. Humbled in the moment, I realized that this is how it is meant to be. Each one we meet on the path holds the Spirit of the Christ. We are to humble ourselves, awaken to that Spirit, and serve one another. We are to wash the feet. In the room in that moment I felt the presence of my Elder Brother Christ Jeshua filling me with pure and unconditional love. *This is it,* I thought. *If only the entire world could feel it, to remember who they really are and why we are here, to understand that we are all one body, as Edgar Cayce had said, "Each soul is a corpuscle in the body of God."*

Heaven was resting itself upon me, once again filling me with indescribable joy and peace. I was in rapture. As I was about to complete the session, I placed my hands gently on Anthony's heart again and as I did his eyes slowly opened. Lovingly he looked at me and said,

"Oh, Karlina, you look like a goddess. Just how long have I known you?"

There we were, held in another timeless moment, where illusion fell away and just truth, just love remained.

"Forever, my friend," I said, kissing his cheek gently. Deep feelings were stirred as we gazed at one another. We wanted to kiss. It was so clear that we had been many things to each other, and lovers was clearly one of those, in some distant lifetime. But our providential and deep soul journey was far greater than what we could ever hope to experience as romantic partners. We both knew it. We were aware of all of the feelings. There was no need for words. I held the unrealized kiss within my heart, as did Anthony.

The Reiki session complete, he crawled into his bed,

"Karlina, come rest with me awhile. Let's hold each other."

I moved into the bed next to him and quietly we lay together. Both of us on our backs, holding hands, as an energy of deep and unconditional love bonded us even further. For a long time, we silently rested next to one another while the soft music of the new-age artist Enya played in the background. Then Anthony's astonishing words drew me out of my peaceful reverie.

"Karlina, do you remember when we were running up the mountain to get away from the devastation and the floods?"

The vision of destruction given to me years before appeared in my consciousness as clearly as a scene from a movie. Then I remembered my first guided imagery and music experience, the one with the mysterious and smiling young man who met me near the top of the mountain. *Oh my God, it was Anthony.*

In the early vision we were holding hands as we helped each other up the rocky terrain in an attempt to escape the rushing water that violently surged beneath us.

"Yes, Anthony, it was Atlantis, you remember? That memory came to me in a vision long ago. I even had images of floods when I was a very little girl."

"Me too," he answered.

We gazed at each other first in amazement and then in deep knowing as I said,

"We died at the top, you know, but we were together."

"Yes, I know," he responded.

Anthony and I moved in closer to one another, holding on as if we were once again back in that ancient time. We were entwined within the knowing. A force far greater than we had brought us together. That force had whispered in our ears, opened our eyes to greater awareness and paved the way for the work we would do together. In that transcendent moment we became two hearts beating as one.

"I love you so much, Anthony. I am so grateful to be with you again."

"I love you, too, Karlina. I don't understand any of this, but I know you, and I love you."

Suddenly we were yanked back to this earth's reality. Billy had thrown open the bedroom door.

"Oops, sorry," he said, and quickly shut it.

"Oh jeez, your family's going to think we're having sex up here," I said. "Should we tell them what's really going on?"

"But wait," he answered. *Do we really know?*

We laughed and slipped back into our quiet time, perfectly content to be in the silence together. As Anthony and I rested, the image of the burning building flooded my awareness. We were in a moment so rich and deep within itself, there was no need to bring it up. I am so glad now that I didn't.

My dearest soul friend had days filled with joy and days filled with extreme pain and suffering. The diarrhea was his worst enemy, at times leaving him immobilized. Stomach pain would grip him and often he spent long hours in the basement on a cot, isolating himself from the questions of others and the sorrowful look in his mother's eyes. The basement was cool and dark and he could curl up in a ball, allowing the coolness to take the heat out of his burning belly.

"Anthony, tell the doctor," I pleaded, but his response remained the same.

"No! It's from the chemotherapy, there's nothing they can do."

I had learned to recognize that tone, his curt and very direct *"No."* When Anthony said no in that manner I knew he was adamant, so I backed off.

Chapter 19
Camp of Fear

Anthony, Jo and I were birthed into a powerful and pur-
poseful mission. Sometimes it felt like we were little chicks
just coming out of the cracked egg with not a clue where to
go or what to do. But we didn't have to worry, the plan was in
place. We were but players in God's Divine script and we
were being guided.

Anthony's journey was featured in every local paper, even
some from a distance away. At that time two-thirds of New
Jersey's AIDS cases were from drug use, yet the backlash hit
the gay community with violent force. By coming out pub-
licly, he began to change minds and open hearts.

"Be compassionate, this could be your brother or sister,"
was his constant appeal.

Josephine and Anthony regularly attended a Hyacinth
Support Group for PWA's (People With Aids) and I had
begun volunteering for others with AIDS, offering healing
retreats for PWA's and their buddies, who spent grueling long

hours sitting at the bedside of the ones dying. During the workshop retreats we laughed and cried together. Many had healing, powerful moments, as I guided the receptive group into music-evoked imagery states.

At one such event, the memory of a former imagery journey of my own came into awareness—the one where I was presenting to patients with AIDS. I felt incredibly grateful to know that God had been preparing me, probably all of my life, to do this rich and deep work. The visions and guided imagery journeys had been a compass guiding my way.

We were in a whirlwind of hope and excitement. Anthony and Jo were educating others, reaching out to those that had no one, and making a difference at a personal, local, and even greater level. They were changing consciousness. The press bombarded us all. Our pictures were on the front pages of the local newspapers along with our pleas for greater understanding and hope. Radio and television stations invited me to speak about the AIDS crisis and my innovative, holistic approach. A powerful force had set all of this in motion and we were catapulted into the mainstream, our deepest feelings, convictions and spiritual beliefs an open book to be read by all.

Anthony was quoted repeatedly by the reporters. Two words boldly stood out in all of the newspapers. COURAGE, which Anthony asked of others, and COMPASSION, for he asked us to love one another. Those words captured the sentiment of the public and the news media.

We never know the true value of our good actions when we are busily trekking through the mud. The recognition comes later, when we are tired and need a rest and maybe when we're hurting and cranky. That's what happened for Anthony. One afternoon when he was having a bad day an envelope arrived in the mail with a check in it for him. As he opened it a note dropped out; it read.

"Dear Anthony,

After reading your courageous words in last week's paper, I felt I had to write you of my admiration for your gallant spirit. How selfless it is of you to bare your soul in order to help and inspire others."

Then just a few days later another letter arrived.

"Dear Anthony,

I read the article in the Press. You are a strong person to own up to your destiny and are helping others like myself to be courageous. I salute you."

Humbled, he was as always moved to tears. It was hard for him to accept the love and most especially the money that was so freely given. Thousands of dollars poured in from friends and neighbors, even strangers. The camp of compassion was growing. Anthony, with the red lesions now spreading all over his body, and—his worst nightmare—to his face, still held his head high. He moved about his home town, living his life as normally as was possible for one battling the pain and ravages of AIDS.

Until one incident shook him to the bone. One day when he was at the supermarket a woman furiously glared at him. Branded with the tell-tale red spots, Anthony stood near her in the produce aisle, feeling the peaches. Their eyes locked. Her face showed horror, as if somehow he had contaminated the peaches.

Telling me about it, Anthony recalled a similar encounter.

"Karla, it reminded me of that horrible lab technician in the city. Remember when we went for the blood tests?"

"Yes, I remember. You were devastated."

"He tied the rubber tourniquet around my arm and when I said it was hurting completely ignored me, like I wasn't even there. Then he turns his back on me to prepare the syringe, with my arm turning purple. I thought it was going to burst. And such hate in his eyes when he plunged that needle into my vein and popped off the tubing, as if in victory. I've never felt such hatred. I wanted to disappear. I wanted to die. I really felt like a leper."

"I remember, Anthony, you sobbed all the way home curled up in a ball against the car door. My heart broke for you that day."

"Well, when that woman glared at me I was in that horrid moment all over again."

"What did you do?" I questioned.

"This time instead of falling apart I took a deep breath and I actually felt myself getting taller. I'm sorry to admit this, but in my snippiest tone I said,

'Lovely peaches today.' I didn't take my gaze away from hers. I then put that peach which was severely bruised and punctured from my tight clench right on top of the peach pile.

'Have one, sweetie,' I said, then I walked off."

"Wow, Antonio."

As he told me the story he had conflicting feelings.

"I feel bad that I did that to her. I doubt that's what the Blessed Mother was suggesting. But Karlina, I can't hide, I can't slink around. You know I can't contaminate anyone. I'm glad I did it."

"Good for you, I'm sure you freaked her out, but that's okay. You have to stand up for yourself and it may not always be pretty."

Laughing, he said, "Oh this wasn't pretty, Karlina. But it felt good. I'm not a leper and I can't be made into an outcast!"

"Nope, you're my spotted sweetie—cutie pie," I teased as I pinched his side.

"Uuuuugggghhhh, shut up."

Even with that one incident at the store we still felt confident, relatively assured that the majority of the community was behind us, until one unfortunate and grave afternoon not long after.

While engrossed in my work with students at the high school, I didn't notice that Josephine and Anthony were standing in the lobby just outside my large classroom window.

"Ms. LaVoie," a student called, "Look, it's Anthony DeVizia."

A number of the kids ran to the window to get a closer look and wave. As I waved, Josephine and Anthony made their way to my door. Anthony, with a glorious smile and his usual chuckle said,

"I'm feeling great today, so I thought we'd come to see you and Margo. When is your lunch period?"

"In about ten minutes," I responded. "I'll meet you in the cafeteria at the next bell. We can go into the teacher's lounge."

"Great! Margo will be there, too. It feels wonderful to be embraced by these walls, so much good has happened here for me."

With that, Jo piped in,

"Did you see all the plays, Karla? Anthony was in *Camelot, Hello Dolly,* and *The King and I*, and you know he was the award-winning drum major," she said with pride.

"Cut it out, Mom," Anthony chided, appearing visibly embarrassed.

"Of course I know, Jo. I saw many of the plays and many times I asked Margo about him. I always said, 'He must be a star by now.'"

Anthony jumped in, "Okay, that's enough. Let's get out of here."

Face reddened, he gave me a peck on the cheek and the two—proud mother and courageous, talented son—walked down the corridor toward the cafeteria.

"Okay, kids," I said, returning my attention to my students, "let's start cleaning up. You can finish your projects tomorrow."

One of the girls approached and said,

"Gee, Anthony looks really bad. He's so thin. Do those red spots hurt him?"

"No, honey, they just look awful. He's really doing quite fine."

"Well," she replied, "he's doing a great thing talking about AIDS, trying to educate people like he is. I think he's a hero."

"That he certainly is," I replied. "You know he was a real star here."

"Yup, I know. My parents went to all the plays. I was too little."

With that, the bell rang. "Okay, everyone," I shouted over the clattering and clanging of lockers being opened and shut while girls' voices shrieked.

"See you tomorrow."

I needed to spend a few more moments cleaning up the room to prepare it for the next class. The noise in the hall-way lessened as students found their way to the next forty minutes of their education. Putting the books and tools away I suddenly became aware of a commotion in the lobby out-side my window. The vice-principal and a male teacher seemed to be having a very heated discussion.

"You can't do that!" I heard the teacher yell. I wondered what was going on.

Ignoring the teacher, the vice-principal hastened down the corridor toward the cafeteria and out of my view. My stom-ach rolled. *Oh, God, what's this?* For a moment I felt frozen in my tracks. Intuitively I knew it had to do with Anthony. I fled out of my room. Everything happened so fast that by the time I arrived at the cafeteria doors Anthony and Josephine had been escorted out of the school through the back door.

Chaos ensued. Teachers were yelling at each other, clearly setting up their separate camps. I soon found out that a paranoid teacher had panicked and called the front office as Jo and Anthony approached the teachers' lounge. Was it the same one, I wondered, who had spewed out all of the cruel and heartless jokes over lunch when Rock Hudson had died? Oh it didn't matter who; fear had found its dwelling place in his loud voice. That teacher was the voice for many in terror.

I approached the vice-principal, who was attempting to calm the group, and said,

"How could you? Anthony is one of your own and nine of Josephine's children have graced these halls. Do you have any idea what you've done?"

I had lost my center, my cool, and I could only imagine what Anthony was feeling. This was a place where he had shone, where he was a true star. One stellar achievement after another belonged to him. I was so angry, wanting to strike out at those who had hurt him. Just as I was about to seek out and verbally attack that insensitive teacher, a gentle inner voice spoke to me.

"Forgive them, Father, for they know not what they do."

I was stopped squarely in my tracks. Although my instincts had become like a mother bear prepared to defend her cub, I knew the voice was right. *Chill, Karla,* I spoke to myself, *breathe.* There is a better way to handle this. Thank goodness there was only one more class to go. I did my best to work with the kids for the remaining forty minutes.

The last bell rang, offering me the first opportunity to call Jo. As she answered, it was evident that she had been crying.

"Jo, what happened?"

"Before you or Margo could get down to the cafeteria, the vice-principal had us escorted out. I guess he was afraid the red spots would jump on him. Anthony thought he was coming to say hello as he approached. Karla, he is just devastated.

He's up in his room sobbing and he won't let me in."

"I'm on my way, Jo."

The house was only a few minutes from the school. As I drove, I prayed that Anthony would settle down and let me help him. Pulling into the driveway, I glanced up at his second-floor bay window, as I always did when arriving at his home. This day the blinds were closed. Never had I seen that during the day, for he so loved the light. I ran in. Josephine was furious, pacing back and forth like the wild bear I had been just an hour before. She screamed,

"Haven't they read any of the articles? Don't they know they can't catch this? Are they crazy?"

"It doesn't matter," she cried, "Look what they did to him. Isn't it enough that he has to go through this horrible ordeal, this ugly disease? How could he be betrayed like this? And Billy, poor Billy, he has to go to that school every day."

"Oh, Jo, I'm so sorry," I said reaching out to her. After moments of vicious verbal attacks on the school staff, Josephine dropped heavily down into the chair. Her shoulders slumped, a visible portrayal of defeat.

"Can I go up?" I questioned.

"No, Karla, he said he doesn't want to see you or anyone. He asked me to leave, too."

As I spoke to Jo I thought I heard the muffled sound of his sobs. My heart was breaking.

"It's so hard not to be with him, Jo. I'll come back in a little while."

"You better call first," she responded.

My vision was blurred from the tears flowing down my cheeks as I made the twelve-mile drive home. My always active mind began to analyze and question. I knew that everything happens for a reason, and I knew we had opened a door wide for backlash. I just never expected it to happen at a place where he had been so loved, admired and respected.

"What do I do with this, Lord?" I cried out loud.

Relaxation did not come at home. Once in the house I found it hard to focus. Even a walk along the beach couldn't calm my frayed nerves and meditation became an impossible task. I did all I could do just to stay out of anger. I must have called Jo five times to check on Anthony, but she continued to say he was incognito and inconsolable. A restless night besieged me, my thoughts granting me no rest. Then finally, in the middle of the night, I turned to Reiki to calm myself, and then to send distant healing to Anthony. Daylight was only a few hours away when I wearily succumbed to sleep.

Groggy in the morning at the rude 5:30 a.m. alarm jolt, I dragged myself out of bed. It's too early to call Jo, I thought. But I knew I couldn't wait until a respectable hour, so at 6:45 I made the call. Jo's heavy voice answered.

"Jo, I'm so sorry, but if I didn't call now, I would have to wait for my first break. How is he?"

"Karla, Anthony attempted suicide last night."

"What?" I screamed.

"Yes, with pills. He took an overdose, but he's all right now. Last night he wouldn't let me into his room, and somehow, he got a hold of some pills. I don't know where they came from. He threw up all night long."

"Does he need to see a doctor or go to the hospital?"

"He won't go. He feels too ashamed. After all the publicity, he doesn't want anyone to know how he crumbled."

"Josephine, I was ready to commit murder yesterday, and I'm not going through the horrific pain he is. Something has to be done about this. I don't know what, but I will get back to you. Tell him I'll be there after school no matter what he says."

"I'll tell him, Karla, and I'm sure he'll want you to come."

"Jo, get some rest. I'll see you later."

First break at school I made my way to the other vice-principal's office. Thank God she was appalled about what had happened and had been unaware of it until after the damage had been done. She stood up to greet me.

"Betty," I started, "What I'm going to tell you must remain with us. Do I have your word on that?"

"Of course, Karla," she responded.

Knowing this fine person to be a woman of integrity, I shared what had happened with Anthony during the night.

"Oh, dear God," she gasped, bringing a hand to her heart and falling back into her chair.

"I'm so sorry." Tears welled up as she spoke. "How is he?"

"Well, he was weak to begin with so this didn't help. He's been throwing up. He won't go to the hospital, but Josephine thinks he's out of harm's way."

"What can we do?" she asked.

"I think we need to educate the teachers."

"Will you speak to them, Karla?"

Without a chance to ponder it, I answered,

"Of course. I'll get brochures from Hyacinth Foundation and news articles, all I can to ease their fear. I know it's not truly malice, just fear."

"Great!" she said. "Is tomorrow after school all right? I will post the meeting in the morning bulletin."

"The sooner the better," I responded, "while this is still fresh. I will find out from Jo and Anthony how much I can share about the attempted overdose. I'm so glad you are who you are, Betty."

"You too, Karla. You too."

Our emotions raw with outrage and compassion, we embraced one another. As we hugged, I knew her to be an important player in the bigger picture of awakening human hearts to love.

After school I raced north to the Hyacinth Center in order to secure enough handouts. Many pats on the back were given as volunteers piled pamphlet after pamphlet into my outstretched hands along with excited exclamations of,

"You Go, Girl!" And, "Way To Go!"

"Do you want me to be there for you?"

A kind, gentle and very visibly gay man asked. Al was a dedicated Hyacinth buddy. He had befriended Anthony and played an important part in Anthony's need for humor. They would dramatically camp around like flagrant queens, over emphasizing everything and mimicking the sometimes outrageous behavior of "swooshy" gay men, those that you found on the stage. It was hysterical to watch them goof on themselves and the sexual role that they found themselves in. Anthony and Al would engage in conversations, prancing around, making full use of the dropping limp hand and high pitch effeminate voice as one of them would say,

"Now, honey, listen to me," or "Hey, dearie, have you heard the news?" then sashay off.

We would all laugh uproariously at the grand performance.

But now all I could think of was, *oh great you come with me and I'll have to hold you behind my back so you don't get thrown to the lions.* Instead I said,

"Thanks, Al, you're a dear, but I need to do this by myself."

"All right," he said. "But please call me if you need to."

"I will, Al, I promise, thanks so much."

Driving back, I knew I had to stop at Anthony's to explore his feelings about my telling the truth regarding the overdose. Jo and he still didn't know what I had planned. As I pulled into the gravel driveway the sound of the moving stones pulled me out of my ongoing internal dialogue. My spirit lifted as I saw the blinds in their familiar position, open and allowing light and life in. *Thank God,* I thought.

"Jo, Jo," I called, as I banged on the door.

"Come in," she hollered. "Where have you been? We thought you'd be here hours ago."

"Sorry. Here's the scoop." I told her what had happened with Betty, and that a meeting was scheduled for the next day.

"I need to speak with Anthony. I told Betty about the overdose."

"Yeeks," she said, then, "okay, girlfriend, you know those teachers are gonna eat you alive and spit you out like tobacco."

"No, Jo, I can handle them. As bad as this looks, I believe it has happened for a reason. This will be a huge wake-up call for many."

"Ya think?"

"I have to see Anthony." I made a mad dash up the stairs and tapped lightly on his door.

"Anthony," I called, "Can I come in?"

"Come on in," was his weak response.

"I feel disgusting," Anthony said. "I can't believe I did something so stupid. Me . . . Mr. Courageous. What a joke."

"Hey," I said, as I sat down on the bed next to his small frame and reached for his hand.

"It's okay. I overreacted too. I wanted to kill some of those teachers."

"I just never expected it," he murmured. "Of all places."

"Fear lives everywhere, Anthony. Isn't that what this is all about—transmuting fear, opening minds and educating the public? Look, I have something to ask you. I spoke to Betty Rebarick. She's outraged over what happened. She has asked me to speak to the entire faculty tomorrow in an effort to educate them."

"Really?" he responded, amazed.

"Yes, and she wants them to know just how dangerous their actions were."

"What do you mean?" he questioned.

"I told her what happened last night."

"WHAT?" He bolted upright and said, "YOU DID WHAT?"

"Anthony, before you get mad, Betty is an honorable woman. She won't say anything without your permission. She feels it's important to startle them. A statement that will shock those stuck in righteousness and fear. Perhaps it will clear their clouded minds."

"Whew . . ." Anthony audibly blew out his breath with focus and intent and then, moving his head side to side, "Whew . . ." again.

"Look, we won't do it. I understand your being uncomfortable and embarrassed."

He took in a slow and deep breath, letting this one clear his mind.

"No, Karlina, this must be part of it. Go ahead. What are you going to say?"

"Well I have tons of literature, quotes from Elisabeth Kübler-Ross about the atrocities she experienced as she attempted to help babies with AIDS. I've been going over and over it in my mind."

"Are you scared?" He asked. "Yesterday felt like a lynch mob to me."

"No, my love, I'm not scared. They are."

"You're right," he responded.

"I have to go, are you okay?"

"Yeah, just drained."

"I'll do a little Reiki and then go."

I placed my hands on his upper chest and stomach, asking that the flow of Reiki bring him just what he needed. In no time, he was resting comfortably, a deep sigh escaping from his weathered form.

"Bye, my love," I kissed his cheek and quietly exited his room. Quickly I told Jo what was up and raced home. For the rest of the night, I planned and practiced my talk. I was definitely ready.

As the following school day unfolded, my stomach tightened. The meeting had been posted in the morning teachers' bulletin, an emergency meeting regarding compassion, as Betty had titled it. All staff must attend. Wow! There was that word again—compassion. Suddenly I felt the soft envelopment of the Blessed Mother all around me. She had not been part of my earlier spiritual devotion, but was entirely present for me now, as well as for so many others affected by AIDS. *Is it any wonder,* I thought, as an image of the Pieta came to mind. How many mothers were losing their children, their sons and daughters, to this violent and insatiable disease?

"Thank you, Madonna," I prayed. "Help me soften hearts today."

The last bell sounded and I made my way to the library, pamphlets in one hand, water in the other, for I feared my mouth would go dry.

As I walked in, *A Course in Miracles* reading came to mind.

"I don't have to worry about what to say or what to do. For He who has sent me will speak through me."

Taking a deep breath I opened the large double doors to the library. Teachers were filing in one by one; those already there were engaged in serious conversations. Some looked my way with open smiles and reassuring nods; others merely looked the other way. My school chums, David, Margo, Carlo, and

Bill, the school psychologist, my newest and dearest comrade, stood together directly across from the podium. I wondered if they had planned that? Their collective energy poured out to me. I felt loved and supported. As soon as the rest of the staff gathered and were in their seats, Betty came to the podium. I noticed that my four friends remained standing at the back of the room directly across from me. That felt so good. As I took a stand for Anthony, so would they.

Betty began in a loud and booming voice,

"Last night, Anthony DeVizia attempted suicide."

Oh my God, I thought, *a bullet straight to the heart.* Gasps filled the room. She had everyone's attention. I saw the panic rise up in Margo. I mouthed to her,

"It's okay."

Betty went on,

"We are teachers. We are here to set an example for our children, to prepare them for the world. A world often filled with injustice. What happened the other day was a grave injustice, and to one of our very own. Thank God, he's alive, but I am certain weakened by this horrific blow. Those of you who are in fear about this, open your ears and eyes, listen to Karla, for she knows far more than anyone here about this disease." Calling my name she motioned for me to come to the podium.

Heart in my throat, I rose. Margo's smile felt like the equivalent of a standing ovation. I took a deep breath.

"Fear," I began, "is our enemy, not this AIDS virus. We can no longer blame the gay community. We can no longer blame the drug users or the many women now infected. We cannot blame the hemophiliacs or the babies born with this vicious virus. It is no one's fault. It has come into our midst, perhaps by accident, perhaps by design. It offers us an opportunity to be greater than our little selves, to put prejudice aside and to help one another."

"For the most part, this town of Matawan has done just that. As you all may know, fundraisers and benefits are occurring, many people want to help. So what happened here two days ago? Fear took over, and a young man and his mother were ridiculed, devastated in our midst. Only one person made that call to the front office, but fear has found a dwelling place in many of our hearts. But it's not only fear, it is ignorance. Don't get me wrong; I'm not calling anyone here stupid, you just don't know the facts. You cannot! I repeat, you CANNOT contract this disease by sitting next to or hugging or eating with a person with AIDS. Only blood or semen can pass this virus."

"There are many people like myself doing hospice work, sitting at bedsides, washing, feeding, holding those suffering, and know that many suffer alone. They are not lepers; they cannot hurt us. You need only look at the many brochures here and reports from the AMA. Know that this is just the beginning; this disease is spreading like wildfire. Soon, we will all know someone who has AIDS. We will not be able to shun another, for it may come knocking on our own back door. I understand your fear, I experienced it too, until I investigated. You need to do the same. Here are numbers you can call, and I am available, if you wish, to answer your questions, as well as the staff at Hyacinth. There is a hotline number that you can call as well. It's right there on the brochures."

"Let us not be like the ignorant farmers who torched Dr. Elisabeth Kübler-Ross's farm because she was going to bring AIDS babies home. We are greater than that. For those of you who don't know of Elisabeth, she is a brilliant woman, one of the greatest pioneers in working with death and dying. Elisabeth started the hospice movement many years ago. A beacon of hope and kindness, she has brought Light and a new understanding into a darkened world. We are not the rural farmers in Virginia who allowed fear and ignorance to rule them. We are intelligent and loving people. Together we can set an example right here in this community for others to follow. Let that example be one of courage, support, and compassion."

"Anthony wants you to know that he understands your fear, that he is all right, and hopes you will open your hearts and minds. I thank you for listening."

A deafening applause rose up. Margo rushed over, still beaming, with tears flowing down her cheeks and said,

"Karla, that was great. You know we are so proud of him. Tell him, would you?"

Hugging her, I responded, "Just as soon as I leave here."

There were many thumbs up and the brochures were all taken. The majority of the room, that is all but a few, had chosen the camp of compassion. The teacher who had made the panic call kept his head down in an effort to avert my glance. Before I could approach, he quickly made his way out of the room. I understood and truly felt compassion for him. Perhaps this was his wake-up call.

On the way back to my classroom, Mr. Lloyd, our most respected and dignified English teacher stopped me. He looked me squarely in the eye and said,

"It's really good what you're doing. Really good."

I don't know why, but his remark stood out above all of the other accolades. Perhaps because, in all of the years I had been teaching, he had never spoken a word to me. Mr. Lloyd was a quiet, reserved man who kept to himself, offering only a friendly nod as we passed in the hall. His selected words had great meaning for me.

Glad it was over; I made my way through many more well-wishing teachers and friends. One said,

"I'm still not sure how I feel about this, Karla, but I'm glad you spoke. I've learned something."

Ah, I thought, one in the neutral camp. I believed he

would investigate further on his own, before he plummeted into fear. Yes, this was about awakening consciousness.

I couldn't wait to get to Anthony's house. In the short amount of time it took to get there, Jo had received tons of calls. Many teachers as well as Betty, our fearless vice-principal, phoned. They were honoring the courage of Anthony and his family and wanted to know what they could do to help.

Anthony was downstairs when I arrived, looking far better than he had the day before.

"Hi!" I exclaimed, grinning from ear to ear. "How goes it?"

"Pretty good, Karlina. I hear you were a hit. The phone has been ringing off the wall. I could feel Margo beaming right through the line. It's still uncomfortable, but I'm becoming more at ease with it. Just look at all these new cards and checks. I'm so glad that the burden has been taken off my family, but you know, it's still very hard to receive this."

"I know, Anthony, this is God's way of letting you know how special you are, what a gift you are to others. How many people would have the courage to do what you're doing?"

"Oh I don't know, Karlina, I didn't plan it, it has just all happened."

"But at some level you did Anthony, we both did a very long time ago before we came into this life experience."

Anthony reached over and touched my hand,

"Yes, you're right. But at times it all feels so huge."

I gently squeezed his hand, "I know, it's *humongous*."

"Would you like some Reiki while I'm here?"

"No, I do feel good, and Bruce is stopping by in a little while."

Bruce, Anthony's partner, was a loving, caring, and supportive man who was willing to share Anthony with me through the countless hours we spent together. Like Anthony, Bruce was quite handsome, but the resemblance ended there. He was much taller than Anthony and sported a full head of red hair, while Anthony's dark hair had begun to thin quite early. He and Anthony had been together for over four years. I admired his patience and his gentle loving spirit.

"Okay, then, I'll be off."

I gave him, Josephine and Ron a hug. Ron, Jo's husband, was such a good man, a quiet, yet stable and strong presence. He reminded me of a single mute stone in the midst of wild-flowers. As the bright flowers bobbed in the breeze, Ron remained steady, a silent and good balance to their passionate natures. He was present when there was a need, with strong shoulders for Jo, and a good rudder for the adventurous, gallant ship that was exploring uncharted seas.

Life was calm for a while, and before long, May was upon us. Plans for the fundraiser were in full swing. Anthony and I spent a lot of time together, traveling weekly to New York City for chemotherapy treatments. The doctors and staff were accustomed to us by then. As Anthony held a crystal in the hand that received the treatment, I guided him through an imagery journey, suggesting that it was Christ's hands that guided the nurses, and that the medicine was the Light from God entering into his body, completely shrinking and disintegrating the Kaposi's Sarcoma while it also protected his good cells. We played music in the background, and the sterile, cold treatment room became our sanctuary. Although there were side effects, he didn't suffer as badly as some did.

We studied, laughed and sang at our *Course in Miracles* weekly meeting and birthed the Miracle Singers, our very unprofessional group that would sing at the benefit. Anthony grinned and chuckled as he watched us rehearse after each meeting.

However, as we got closer to the benefit, Anthony's health took a dive. The fatigue was enormous, and the diarrhea gave him no rest. Jo told me he was spending hours in the bathroom. Reiki gave some relief, but I feared there was something more to this.

On the day of the benefit, I went to the house and found Anthony in bed.

"You don't *want* to do this, do you?" I questioned.

"Oh, Karlina, I feel awful. I don't think I can go."

"You don't want to, do you?" I added.

"Nooooo . . . " came the agonized response. "It's just too much. I feel like a spectacle, all eyes on me, and with these red spots. What am I supposed to say? Am I expected to have some great wisdom? You know the representative from Hyacinth isn't coming, and I can't talk about AIDS like he can."

"You don't have to," I responded. "Let it just be a party."

"People are paying money to come to this, and it's for me. I'm so embarrassed."

"I know, baby. Look, people are coming because they love you. They want to celebrate your life and your courage, but you do what you need to do. I want you to come, but I will support whatever decision you make."

"Thanks, Karlina."

I kissed him and went down to Jo and said, "Well I didn't get the emphatic 'No,' that's a good thing. Let's just see what happens. I'll tell folks he's having a bad day and we'll go from there."

"Good," Jo said. "I won't push him. I'll just wait down here for a little while."

Jo was sitting nurturing a cup of coffee as Ron sat like the rock he was at the head of the long kitchen table. I kissed them both. Ron nodded to me in an assuring way as he said,

"It will be fine."

Chapter 20
Camp of Compassion

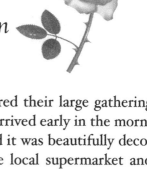

Saint Clement's Church had offered their large gathering hall. The shop owners in town had arrived early in the morning to set up. By the time we arrived it was beautifully decorated with flowers everywhere. The local supermarket and variety stores had supplied decorations, soda, and snacks. Local restaurants had donated delicious food and even the workers to serve it. No task was left unattended. Matawan, a spectacular community, was embracing its own at a time when many AIDS sufferers were being treated as outcasts and left alone to die in shame and disgrace. This was a celebration.

Anthony's sisters were hustling and bustling. Ann Marie greeted people at the door and Linda guided them to their seats. I embraced all of the sisters—Josie, Mary, Christine, Kathy, Patty, her husband Deiter, and their little boys Aaron and Matthew. DeVizias were everywhere. The children were running around yanking at balloon strings and the band was tuning up their instruments. All was in readiness for the birthday boy.

"Is he coming?" asked Billy, with Linda and Ann Marie chiming in right behind him.

"I don't know, kids, he's feeling pretty bad."

Billy moved in closer, placing an arm around me and whispering in my ear,

"I think he's really nervous, Karla."

I grabbed his hand.

"Yes, Billy, he is. Let's just wait and see. Our job is to get this party rolling. Anthony wants us to have fun, remember? No matter what."

"You're right, Karlina," and off he went.

Two hundred and fifty people arrived, laden with gifts and donations. Family, friends, and even strangers wanted to support Anthony and the cause he represented. Many teachers and administrators from the high school as well as Anthony's grammar school were there. Newspaper reporters milled about, asking the question that was on everyone's minds.

"Where's Anthony? Is he coming?"

"We're working on getting him here," Jo responded. "He's been sick for the past few days."

As I observed the hungry press and heard Jo's answer, I sent out a mental message to Anthony,

Come on, baby. You can do it. This is your day!

Then, to our absolute delight, just as *Illusion*, a rock band from the high school, was setting the party hopping, a smiling Anthony appeared at the entrance. He looked elegant in a tan silk jacket with cream colored pants, blue shirt and tie. Ron was right behind him. I wasn't at all surprised that it was Ron who brought him. Overjoyed, I gave Ron the "thumbs-up."

The well-wishers erupted into outrageous applause, whistles, hoots, and yahoos. Anthony looked just beautiful. As our eyes locked across the crowded room, he winked, and I was sure I saw a brilliant light emanating from him. Josephine rushed to his side, then Billy with all seven sisters right behind him, showering Anthony with hugs and kisses. The group continued to hoot and holler, unable to contain themselves. What a moment in God's masterful plan of celebration! Words cannot adequately express the joy, the jubilee, that was present in my heart and the hearts of all those attending. Anthony was beaming.

Something miraculous happened that day. We were all transformed. In that moment incredible suffering had become incredible joy. There was a reason for the madness in the world. I knew that as our minds and hearts rejoiced and chose love, the energy of that love would go out and transform others. Like a pebble tossed into a lake, its ripples spread out, touching and changing far more than we could ever know. This was one of those moments. Our journey, Anthony's, Jo's and mine, was to awaken others, to make a difference in the world. How glorious it was. Something higher was in charge of this and I knew that we were all held in the arms of God, in the arms of Divine compassion.

As I watched Jo with her Anthony, my thoughts went to Tom, away in chiropractic college. I missed him terribly and wished he could be with me to witness this loving family. As I thought of my handsome son, I smiled and sent out a blessing of love to him. Tom and I were healing, and for that, I was so very grateful. I wondered if he would ever meet Anthony.

Abruptly, I was pulled out of my reverie as the pastor of Saint Clement's, began the opening prayer. He had been a close companion to Anthony and Jo and knew firsthand the family's struggles and triumphs. His sentiments captured the feeling present in the hearts of all of us. He said,

"Each of us is a part of the One body of Christ—Jews, gentiles, slaves and priests. Isn't it God's way to make many parts of Himself? If God was present here this is what He would say. We are all needed. For if one part of the body suffers, all parts suffer with it. If one part of the body is honored, all parts are glad. That is what this is about today."

I knew he was speaking about Anthony's lifestyle and the terrible disease that afflicted him and so many others. My heart was gladdened.

The sweet sounds of Anne Hannah's high school Madrigal Singers then graced the room. So many had volunteered to entertain. There weren't enough hours in the day to accommodate everyone. But Anne was Billy's choir director and had been one of Anthony's favorite teachers. We were blessed to have her for Anne was deeply admired and respected by all of us. Billy joined the Madrigals on stage and their sweet voices filled the room.

Then it was my turn. Since the representative from Hyacinth had been forced to cancel at the last minute, it was left to me to speak. It didn't feel necessary to address the AIDS issue itself, as there were plenty of brochures and information packets. Instead, I spoke about Anthony.

As I reached the stage and took the microphone in my hand, the family went nuts, hooting and hollering, yelling,

"Hey, Ooogity-Boogity Woman!" referring to my unusual healing methods and spiritual beliefs.

All in good fun, it was a nickname that I had grown to love. I addressed the group.

"Two years ago I attended an intense Life, Death and Transition Training with Dr. Elisabeth Kübler-Ross. Elisabeth is the originator of the hospice movement and a champion for patients and babies with AIDS."

"At the end of that very grueling week I decided that I would not work with the AIDS crisis, for it was just too big for me. However very soon after that decision Christine called and asked if I would see Anthony. Fate had intervened.

When I later heard Anthony's voice on the phone, I felt like I was welcoming home a long-lost friend. Anthony is the most courageous man I know. He came to my door and said,

'I really feel that I can lick this thing. I have heard all of the scary stuff in the newspapers and on TV and I'm not buying into it. Can you help me?' "

"So we started working together. I have seen him go through excruciating and horrible things, feeling like he can't make it through another day, and then he breathes deeply and turns the pain around. He has turned stumbling blocks into stepping-stones. That is why we are all here today."

"As I've worked with Anthony I've come to realize that this process is not about getting ready to die, that's not it at all folks. It is celebrating life, every single moment, being grateful for each day that we wake up and for each moment when we can go for the gold. It's reaching out to create and to receive all that we can, and if in that day you fall flat on your face, well you fall flat on your face. I have watched Anthony fall flat on his face and then get up and say, 'Where's the gold?' I have seen him in a hospital where people gave up on him and said, 'He's going home to die.' "

"Well guess what, folks? He didn't. Then I saw Kaposi's Sarcoma wreak havoc on his body and people said, 'There's no cure for that.' Well guess what? Those lesions are fading and shrinking and he is still here."

The crowd erupted with applause.

"There is a terrible fear in our society that needs to be transformed and you people are doing just that. Everyone here who has reached out and said I want to help, I want to give, and I want to love is making a tremendous difference. You are transforming that fear."

"There is no such thing as a death sentence. No such thing. There is life. Where there is breath, there is life. If you have faith, if you have hope, and if you can stop for a moment, get

243

centered and take a deep breath as Anthony does, then you can go for the gold."

"I have seen Anthony, this wonderful young man whom I love dearly, go into the hard scary stuff, the pain. I have seen him go into it and say 'I can't do it.' Then he takes another breath and says, 'There's a gift in here for me. What is the gift? What can I take out of this? How can I help people? What can I say about it?'"

"He turns it around. Anthony takes those stumbling blocks and turns them into stepping-stones. He is going for the gold everyday. So we need to get out there and say we don't accept fear and we don't accept a death sentence. We accept life, we accept healing, and Anthony is healing. This is not a process of getting ready to die, folks. This is a celebration of life, and there is no order of difficulty in miracles."

The crowd went wild; loud shouts and declarations sprang up.

"Hoo! Hoo! Hoo!," and "Go, Anthony!" Then, over the wild noise of the crowd a DeVizia voice bellowed out.

"Yay! For Ooogity-Boogity!"

As the laughter subsided, I continued.

"So with that I would like to suggest that we celebrate his life today. That we remember that each moment we are together we have the opportunity to love. We are brothers and sisters in God, and together we take each other Home, hand in hand. That's what this is all about. Today we celebrate Anthony's birthday. We acknowledge his courage and we acknowledge your courage to move past the fear that is in our midst. We acknowledge all of us as brothers and sisters one in Spirit."

Wild applause exploded from the crowd.

"Now let's all join together and sing happy birthday."

We sang and then the exuberant crowd began yelling.

"Speech! Speech!"

An enormous birthday cake was making its way toward a blushing Anthony.

"Make a wish," chanted the ecstatic crowd.

Anthony was visibly moved. He leaned over the cake, took a deep breath and successfully extinguished all twenty-nine candles. Applause rose up again.

"Speech! Speech!" the crowd roared.

As I watched Anthony from the stage I saw him turn to Billy and say "*No!*" It was the curt and very definite response that signaled the end of the matter.

Then with elegance and grace, he stood up and said,

"Thank you all, thank you so much for coming." He was visibly delighted.

Sandy, a nurse who had tended to Anthony when he was in the hospital with pneumocystis pneumonia, was called to the stage. Reluctantly she took the microphone. In her shy demeanor she seemed to be searching for the right words when Josephine shouted.

"If we can do it so can you. You go, girl. Go Sandy!"

She looked at Jo with genuine tenderness and then with a soft, sweet voice and tears in her eyes she began,

"For the most part working with AIDS patients has been a very trying and disappointing experience because the family and community does not gather around the victims. Very often it is just the nurses and doctors that visit the patients. This community is an exception."

As a smiling Sandy left the stage, deafening applause surged from the crowd. They truly had good reason to applaud her and themselves. They were the camp of compassion.

Addressing the group again, I said,

"I have brought with me the Ooogity Boogity Singers. We are not a professional group, folks. We hang out together after our *Course in Miracles* meeting and we sing and play. So what we want to offer you is our simplicity, our joy, and our love. Just tell us to stop when you have had enough."

"We are the Miracle Makers, perhaps the Cosmic Clowns and most definitely the Ooogity Boogity Singers."

As the crowd wildly applauded, the impromptu *Course in Miracles* group came to the stage. Without background music we belted out *That's What Friends Are For*, with Anthony and nearly half of the audience joining us on stage.

"More, More!" they shouted. "Encore!"

On to our shining moment, *Amazing Grace*. Our baritone Ron, acting very gooney, started with a low, drawn-out, very off-key note.

"AAAAAAAAAAAAAAAAAA"—sounding much like an animal groaning.

"MMMMMMM......AAAAAAAAAA"

How is he still holding that note? I was amazed. We certainly had the crowd's attention. All eyes were riveted on Ron, who was still holding the excruciatingly painful, discordant note, head down looking like he was ready to collapse.

"ZZZZZZzzzzzzzzzzzzzzzzzzzzz.....iiiiiiiiiiiiiiii......

nnnnnnnnnn......gggggggggggggggggggg"

Oh, God, this is so bad, I thought to myself. *How did I let my Miracle friends talk me into this?*

"Grrrrrrrrrrrrrrrrrrrrrrraaaaaaaaaaaaaaaaaaaa accccccccccccccceeeeeeee."

Then just as you thought the agony must be nearly over for the baritone, for he looked like he was ready to croak, the cue was given. In a cappella style the rest of the singers joined in. It was a rousing, wild, hand-clapping, jubilant rendition. People jumped out of their seats. Anthony ran up and grabbed a tambourine.

Oh how sweet the sound. That saved a soul like me. I once was lost, but now I'm found, was blind but now I see.

Our harmonies were incredible. All of the DeVizia's were on the stage—Josephine, Linda, Kathy, Mary, Billy, Ann Marie, Patty, Josie, Christine, Bruce and half of the audience. We were going nuts! Anthony was in his glory. What a rush! We repeated the verse and ended with tambourines and arms held high in the air.

At the end of our song, the crowd again hooted and hollered for Anthony.

We then wowed them with a puppet show featuring our one truly great and professional voice, Mary, singing the children's song *Yellow Moon.*

Many songs were sung, all acknowledging our oneness and our love for Anthony and for each other. We finished our performance with everyone singing and swaying to *Let There be Peace on Earth.*

As we completed the peace song, a recording of *That's What Friends Are For* began playing through the sound system. Anthony moved into my arms with Christine right behind him and the three of us gently swayed back and forth to the music, lost in gratitude and the wonder of the day. But not for long, Ron came up to the stage and moved Anthony into the center of the large hall. First his mother danced with him while all gathered around in a circle. Then one by one others cut in, sisters and friends, then Ron and Anthony's brother-in-law Deiter. There wasn't a dry eye in the house. Love was present in all of its beauty and splendor, and we were all swept up in it.

After a final standing ovation for Bob Shuey for making it all happen, we made our way to the door to go home. The waiting press clamored around Anthony, asking for a statement. He spoke to the very patient newspaper reporters.

"It's easy to get caught up in the idea of having a fatal, incurable disease, when people point their fingers and say,

'You deserve this because of the life you've led.' But I can't buy that. I try to be positive. AIDS is not a death sentence. It's important to educate people so they can deal with it. Help them understand how it is transmitted, so they can feel safe. Fear is not the way to go. If I can get that message out, it will be worth it."

"Hyacinth Foundation offers their time and energy to be with people who need support and understanding. When I'm stronger, I would like to donate time to them. All people need to do is to show they care. It goes a long way toward healing me. I'm here and alive and each day, no matter how difficult, is an affirmation of life. I am incredibly grateful for what this town has done for me."

I stood a slight distance away as he spoke, bursting with admiration and gratitude for him and for the family that had adopted and embraced me, and for the town of Matawan, for all who had offered their time and talent. The day of fear at the high school felt like an eternity ago, and this day of love had managed nearly to erase it from consciousness. What a very proud moment this was for us all.

Chapter 21
Opening of the Veil

Time galloped along and as the hot and sultry summer arrived, Anthony was completing his chemotherapy treatments and working with Margo, directing *Crimes of the Heart*, which was to open in September. I was thrilled. Here was the manifestation of his imagery journey from five months earlier. He was tired a great deal of the time, but managed to assist Margo regularly. The diarrhea still plagued him. We anticipated it subsiding with the end of chemotherapy but it didn't. In spite of it Anthony continued to live in a remarkable way. His dedication to life and his family was an inspiration to us all. Instead of whining, he held everyone else up, assuring them that all would be well, even if he were to pass. Of course there were moments when he crumbled. But his courageous spirit remained intact, and was what most people saw.

I was spending the last days at my small riverfront sanctuary. Unable to stay through the summer, I found a great house on a tranquil lake in Asbury Park. Ducks, geese and swans swam lazily by, basking in the sun's glow; herons perched themselves atop pilings, their long necks lifted up to the sky in a gesture of seeming adoration. Even the turtles crawled up onto the rocks and stretched their heads up high in a salute to the sun. All of the wildlife was celebrating creation and I was in my glory.

My multilevel deck and dock offered a panoramic view of the lake, and an old brick mansion across the water. Rumor had it that it had belonged to Clark Gable during prohibition. Water planes transported celebrities to his very popular speakeasy. Filled with nostalgia, it was a tranquil spot, and I was engrossed, basking in the beauty and settling into my new home.

Something felt different between Anthony and me, even though he appeared to be fairly well; I had a sinking feeling that something was coming. I tried to shake it off. Then late in August, one of my dearest friends, Michael, tragically died from a car accident. Michael was a minister deeply loved by all who knew him, including me. In all of the years since Lucky's death, he was the man that I could have seen myself with in a committed relationship, a true partner. Spiritually we were in tune in every way. We had studied the Native American wisdom together, laughed contagiously at each other's struggles and shenanigans, and shared many passionate kisses. However something within would not let me take the next step in our relationship.

As attracted as I was to Michael, I was also repelled, and his fervent requests for my love only pushed me further away. I had always questioned why, and now, here was the answer. At some level I must have known that he was going to die. That which guided my life guided me away from the tragedy of burying another lover.

I recalled one of his tender notes,

"Dear Karla,

I read somewhere that the pygmies live in the rainforest that is so thick and dark that they cannot walk abreast together. And so when they walk, they whistle to one another to be sure that the other one is still there. Our recent experience was a whistle in darkness that each of us answered back to one another. You and your life are for me a story like the wind. You come from a far off place and I feel you."

Almost immediately after his passing, Michael began communicating with me in the dream state, and during the day I would hear a whistle from out of nowhere and begin whistling myself. It was Michael's way of reaching out to me, of letting me know he was still present.

Thinking of Michael, I felt a deep comfort fill me, a familiar knowing that love never leaves its own. I knew that he would help Anthony and me through whatever loomed before us.

As the days progressed Anthony looked more frail and the diarrhea had not stopped. When I visited I asked,

"What are you going to do? Shouldn't you tell the doctor? Aren't you due for a liver test?"

"No!," came that curt and adamant response. He continued,

"Karla, we've done all we can here. You know I chose not to take the AZT, and that was the right decision, but I'm going to die. I can feel it. And I'm beginning to question again if Christ really loves me and if I am pure enough. I'm wondering if there really is another side, a heaven state."

As he sat on the living room couch with a blanket tossed across his small slouched shoulders, I dropped down on my knees and took his hands into mine. Tears welled up in his eyes as he spoke,

"I'm afraid, Karlina."

"Anthony, look at all that has happened here, from the beginning a Wisdom and Light has been guiding you, guiding us. We know we are not strangers to one another. How else can we explain our visions, our knowing? Just recently, my dearest friend Michael from Virginia Beach died. Anthony, he has repeatedly come to me since then. I hear him in my waking moments and I dream of him at night. He was a priest, a beautiful man. I hear him say, 'Yea, though I walk through the valley of the shadow of death, I fear not, for Thou art with me.' "

"Michael continues to assure me of life beyond death. Anthony, don't you know how precious you are to God? He is with you every moment. You are pure in heart and you are safe. I know that Michael is also watching over you, for he knows just how dear you are to me."

Anthony's eyes were huge, dark, round pools that drew me in. One single tear began to flow as I spoke the words to him. I knew those words came from truth, but I was also aware of a tightness and a clinging within me. I wanted to hold him here. I wanted him to stay. After all of the personal work I had done and the training with life, death and transition, I thought I'd be ready, but I had lost my objectivity. There was no professional boundary. *How could there possibly be a boundary?* I thought. *Look what we have been to one another.* But now the ease that once was with us felt a bit strained, as if we were both holding back and beginning to separate from one another. Anthony's steady gaze penetrated into me.

"Most of the time I am in that knowing, Karla. I feel and

believe it all, but there are other times when I crumble."

"How could you not my love? This is uncharted territory, at least for this life. It's okay to feel all of the feelings, the fear and the knowing. It's all part of it."

Yet in my heart of hearts I wanted to believe that his passing was still far off.

A few nights later Anthony and I shared a powerful experience at an Alan Cohen workshop. We gathered with a group of *Course in Miracles* students who had been studying with Alan for over a year, living the principles and lessons of the "Course." Alan opened our hearts with his wisdom and joy and we sang songs of God to one another. Anthony and I partnered; looking deep into each other's eyes we sang a *Course in Miracles* song by Michael Stillwater.

Master, come to me, teach me how to see. You know who I am so well.

Alan then brought us into a guided meditation where we were to move to a peaceful and holy place. My meditation, as always, brought me to the sacred inner garden where I rested against an old grandfather tree and felt the hand of Christ Jeshua upon me. At the close of our meditation, Alan suggested we share our experience with our partner. Anthony, completely at peace, looked compassionately at me, took my hands and softly said,

"Karlina, in my meditation, I am moving down a tunnel toward a great Light, rushing as fast as I can, when a hand comes out and stops me. It's yours."

I was looking into the eyes of love, love that is not of this earth, far from romantic love. It was *The Love.* I knew he was right. I blurted out,

"Anthony, I don't want you to go. I'm so sorry. I'm supposed to be your guide here, but I just don't want you to go, not yet."

I certainly was not the counselor in that moment, just a

soul mate who loved him, one who had walked a high and holy path with him, yet one who was very human.

"I know," he responded. "It will be fine, my Karlina. You'll see, it will be fine."

We were quiet as we drove home. It was clear that something had shifted. Anthony had stepped up to the plate. He was in a good place, for fear no longer walked by his side. Anthony was ready and now I needed to get ready. The phrase, "conscious living, conscious dying" came to my mind. Elisabeth Kübler-Ross had been through this and she was my teacher. Both Elisabeth and Ram Dass had taught me well, they knew how to do this, and I prayed that I could do it too.

We shared a tender embrace as we parted. Anthony shot me a brilliant smile as he exited the car and jokingly said,

"Hey, clean those car windows, they're filthy. You can't see a thing."

"Yeah, yeah," I responded.

Chuckling, I pulled out of the driveway. As I drove home, I remembered Anthony's mandala, nine flowers. Could it be? I tried to stop my thoughts, but they would not give me rest. Nine flowers grew underneath the cross, with no earth beneath them. I counted the months from January, when he had done the drawing. Oh God, September would be the ninth month. It was already the end of August. *Are we that close?* I wondered. *But why the two birds in flight?*

It still perplexed me. As I drove, a quiet peace laid itself down upon me. It was Lucky. *For time and all eternity, love never dies,* I thought, and continued home whispering, "Thank you Lucky, for reminding me. Please stay close."

During the next couple of weeks I was caught up painting my new house. Though fatigued and plagued by the diarrhea, Anthony came over and helped me paint the dining room. He offered decorating tips and was determined to add his creative touch to my walls and home. The now ninety-eight pound remarkable man teased me about my lack of fine-painting ability.

"You need to paint to music, Karlina. Let yourself become one with the brush." Then he added,

"Oh I wish I could do the whole house for you in beautiful faux designs and colors. We could do beige and cream tones here in the dining room and add dramatic touches to the living room. But I can't stay out of the bathroom long enough."

"I just love that you're here with me." I replied. "I'll even hang out with you in the bathroom."

"Now that's just a little too close, Karlina."

We laughed and he then shared how astonished he was at the amount of money that had been raised on his behalf, nearly $10,000. Anthony now felt that he could rest easy, knowing his mother would not be burdened with the enormous bills. We spoke daily on the phone.

"I feel good, Karlina. Life is good."

"How's that diarrhea?" I asked.

"Oh you know, the same. It's pretty disgusting, but I'm hanging in there."

"Anthony, I'll come do Reiki tonight."

"No, you rest. I know you're tired and I'm fine, honestly."

Once again I felt the subtle separation.

"All right," I said reluctantly, "Talk to you tomorrow."

The phone rang again a few hours later.

"Karlina," his voice sounded as if he was in deep prayer.

"Yes?" I said.

"Something extraordinary just happened. Our pastor was here tonight to pray with me. As he walked through my bedroom door, Christ followed him. Karla, I saw Christ as clearly as I saw the pastor. A peace began to fill the room as Father prayed with me. Christ was right next to him looking at me with such love."

I could hear the emotion in his voice. Chills ran through my body.

"Oh, Anthony."

"And, Karla, Father left and Jesus stayed. He sat right on the bed and told me how much He loves me and what a good job I've done."

At that point we were both crying.

"He loves me, Karlina, and He forgives me."

"Oh, Anthony. He has always loved you. Never have you been out of His heart. I'm just so happy for you."

"Karla, I need to put some things in order. I'll call you tomorrow."

"I love you, Antonio."

"I love you too, Karlina."

I was flying on cloud nine. He finally knew, finally accepted how special he was, one of God's dearest teachers. I recalled something Josephine had shown me, a paper Anthony had written in school when he was only seven-years-old called "Priest."

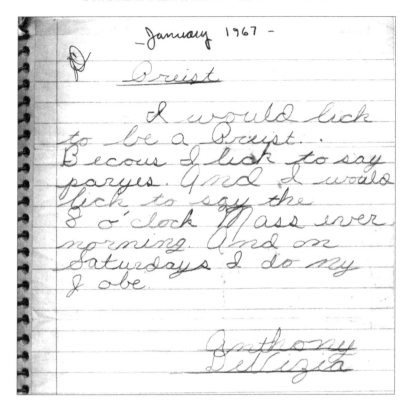

I could envision a tiny Anthony adorned in altar boy vest-
ments, a love for God deep in his tender heart. I rested for a
long time in gratitude. We never know how our ministry will
unfold. There was no doubt that Anthony was fulfilling his
destiny. The priesthood had eluded him, but his Divine purpose had not. I reveled in my memories, the early visions that
blessed my life, Lucky's death and the profound awakening I
experienced from that, his visitations and ever-present love,
and all of the miracles from the past year. My heart was full.

With the transcendent music of Vivaldi playing and brush
in hand the following day, I delicately painted the lovely bay
window, remembering Anthony's creative style. Each stroke

felt like a meditation. I was in a heavenly place. But the phone invaded my reverie and pulled me into ordinary consciousness.

"Hello?"

"Hi, Karla, it's Jo. I thought you should know, Anthony had a great deal of pain in his stomach last night and the diarrhea is constant. He asked to go to the hospital."

"What? He asked?"

"Yes," Jo said. "And, Karla, last night after our pastor left, something happened to Anthony. When I went up to see him, he was ecstatic. He told me Christ had been with him, that he is forgiven. Karla, he was preparing his funeral, all of it, the music, what kind of flowers, whom to call. He's orchestrated the whole thing. He's getting ready now to go to Saint Vincent's Hospital, but first, he wants to stop at his friend Michelle's wake. You know how much he loved her. She died of cancer a few days ago."

"What?" I questioned. "She just died?"

"Yes, and he insists on going. He's so weak from the diarrhea, Ron and I will have to hold him up."

There it was. My breath caught in the back of my throat as I remembered the little black bird from Anthony's mandala, the one that had lifted up in flight just ahead of the bird that I felt represented him. *Oh this is it,* I thought to myself. *Jo and I are the black birds left here in the feeder under the strong cross, the symbol of Christ above us, that which had fed and upheld each of us.*

How is it that we know at that deep level? Yet my life had shown me over and over just how thin the veil is. My full breath returned inviting me into peace.

"Can I talk to him, Jo?"

"He said he'd call you after he got settled in at the hospital. He said not to worry. He wants to get to the wake before it's over."

"All right, I can live with that. Jo, how are you holding up?"

Almost sounding child-like, her voice dropped.

"I'm a little scared."

"Hang in there, Jo. You know God's with you. You are not alone. Please call me as soon as Anthony is settled. And Jo, what are they going to do, try to stop the diarrhea, get him on IV's to hydrate?"

"I don't know yet, but I'll call you just as soon as I can. Love you, Karlina."

"Love you too, Jo."

The day dragged on and on. Knowing it would take hours, I attempted to busy myself with painting and a long walk at the ocean. New York City was an hour and a half away in easy traffic, and hospital admission could take forever. I wondered how Jo would do traveling into the city. She had panic attacks going over bridges and tunnels. This would be a major challenge. Thank goodness Ron was with her.

Attempting to busy myself I fixed my housemate Marty and me a home-cooked meal. Marty had been one of the Ooogity Boogity Singers and at dinner, he joined me in a prayer of gratitude for Anthony and his family.

"Thank you, God for watching over your dearest child. Thank you for his safety and peace. Thank you that his mother and family are held in your tender care. Bless us all, Lord."

Then at nearly eleven p.m. the phone rang. It was Jo.

"Anthony's safely settled in, Karla. His room phone isn't hooked up yet. He said he'd call you tomorrow."

"Oh I just hate not talking with him. Please tell Anthony how much I love him. Are you all right?"

"Yes," she responded. "He seems comfortable. I'm coming back up tomorrow. He said for you to wait until he calls. He really seems okay."

"I hope it's early tomorrow. I want to see him. It's only been a few days since he was here painting with me, but it seems like forever. Have a restful night Jo."

"I'll try, Karlina, talk with you tomorrow."

Physically and emotionally fatigued I slid into my bed. I thought I heard Michael's whistle and soon felt like I was being held. Thank you Michael, thank you Lucky, and thank you all who watch out for me, thank you God. All is in Your hands, Lord. A deep sigh and I drifted off into sleep.

Saturday was a bright, shiny day, and I didn't have to wait too long. At nine a.m., Anthony called. His sweet melodious voice caressed me through the airwaves.

"Hi, my Karlina."

"Antonio, are you okay?"

"Yes," he replied. "Just here for a little rest. I need some hydration."

"I'm going to come up. When are visiting hours?"

"No! Karlina," he answered. "Wait until Monday."

It was the emphatic "No!" that I had heard all too often before.

"Monday?" I questioned. "It's Saturday. Why do you want me to wait until Monday? Anthony, that's too long."

"Just do what I ask," he implored. "And Karlina," his voice dropped slightly, "Do you remember the burning building?"

For a moment I couldn't speak. In a whisper, I responded, "Yes, Anthony."

"You couldn't get me out. You tried, you thought it was your fault. You committed suicide soon after that. My dear Karlina, it wasn't your fault. It is finished . . . "

"Oh, Anthony, I've always known about the burning building. I knew it the day you first appeared at my door and long before that. I love you so much. Please don't shut me out now. Please don't keep me away, let me come." I begged.

"No, Karlina, I will see you on Monday."

I couldn't move. He had known all along. A myriad of questions filled me. How did he know? When had it come to him? I had never uttered a word but none of it really mattered. Again the veil had been rent asunder, and love spoke through lifetimes to heal us, to transport us. We come together again and again to bring each other Home, to be way show-ers, lovers, and ministers for one another.

Marty walked by as I sat looking somewhat dazed.

"What's the matter?" he asked.

I started to open my mouth in an attempt to share what had just happened, but it was deeply personal, deeply intimate, and I felt as if I was only partially present. I was much more in touch with the other side, the side of knowing.

"I need to be quiet just now Marty, I'm fine."

Feeling I would dilute the blessedness of the moment, I retreated and let that sacredness sink in. It wrapped all around me. I was filled with an amazing peace and floated through the remainder of the day.

Sunday arrived. Jo and I spoke in the early afternoon before she left for the hospital.

"Jo, I know he doesn't want me to come. I don't know why, but I have to honor his wish."

Then an idea came.

"Jo, how long are you going to stay?"

"Until they kick me out, Karla."

"Then I'll come to be with you. He doesn't even have to know I'm there. How's that?"

"Sounds great to me," she replied.

"And, Jo, while you're there maybe you could ask him again if I could visit."

"All right, I will. I'll see you later."

I felt like I was in a lucid dream, a déjà vu, as if all of this had been revealed to me long before. *Okay, Karla, ground yourself, get centered and then go.* When I arrived at the hospital, Jo was sitting in the visitors' lounge. I approached her.

"Hi. How is he?"

"He seems fine," she responded. "The IV's are helping. The doctors think he'll just be here for a few days."

"Whew! Thank God." I blew out a long breath. "Did you ask?"

"Yes, Karlina." Her voice softened as she looked at me sadly. "He said you could come on Monday."

"Oh, Jo, this is so strange. I just want to . . . "

Feeling my pain she gently reached out for my hand. "I know, he's funny with me, too. I sit by the bed and hold his hand but he firmly moves my hand away. He told me to go home. Bruce is with him now."

Wow, I thought, *he's pushing us both away.* Josephine and I just looked at each other. We were two women who loved him unconditionally. One had birthed him into the world, watched him grow, marveled at his accomplishments; the other remembered a distant past and relished a present rich in soul growth and spiritual accomplishment. Holding hands, Jo and I sat in front of a large window overlooking the lights of the New York City skyline, two mothers deep in thought.

Finally, near midnight, a nurse approached us and said,

"Anthony's doing fine. Why don't you two go home and get some sleep?"

My dear soul friend Jo went into the room to kiss her son goodnight. I waited on the other side of the door aching to open it, yet knowing I could not. It was agonizing. I did all I could do to contain myself. Silently Jo and I went down the elevator to the parking lot for our long trip home.

"Call me tomorrow, Jo. Anthony said I could visit on Monday. I want to go early so I can spend lots of time with him. Maybe we can go together."

"That would be good, Karlina."

We shared a loving embrace and parted.

Chapter 22

Bring My Mother a Rose

The drive home from the hospital fatigued me; exhausted I stumbled up the stairs and into my bed. But sleep wouldn't come. My thoughts were with Anthony as I tossed and turned, constantly looking at the clock. Did I make a mistake by not going into his room? As agonizing as it was, I knew I needed to honor his wishes and wait until he called for me. He did say he would see me on Monday. Tomorrow I will go. As I looked at the clock it was already Monday, would I ever get to sleep?

Prayers were edging me into welcoming slumber, but just as I was drifting into a peaceful sleep the phone rang, startling me into alertness. It was nearly two in the morning. This could only be the worst of news. I was afraid to answer.

"Hello." My heart was racing; as I had feared, it was Josephine. I could hear the terror in her voice as she cried.

"We've been called back to the hospital."

"Oh my God, we just left," I stammered. "What do you think has happened? They said he was fine when we left just two hours ago."

Josephine replied, "The nurse said a turn for the worst, we have to hurry."

"Okay, I'm on my way," I blurted into the phone as I nearly fell out of bed.

Fear began to grip me. For a moment I lost it entirely as I screamed out for my housemate Marty, waking him from sleep.

"Marty, I'm scared, please pray. I am afraid that Anthony has died."

With a supportive and loving hug he assured me, saying,

"Karla, you know it will be all right no matter what has happened. Just take a deep breath."

"Thanks for the reminder, Marty, please pray."

Throwing on my clothes, I rushed out, knowing that Josephine was also on her way. This brave woman who at one time could not make it over the South Amboy Bridge because of her fear was now racing to New York City. Of course she would do this; she would do anything for her son. Her love propelled her over bridges and through tunnels in the depth of the dark night.

I felt a strange mixture of feelings. Would I be too late? Did he know I had been there earlier right outside his door? Had he waited for me? Had he asked for me? I knew that if he had passed he was safe and in God's Light, finally Home. But the human emotion erupted.

"Please let me be with you. Let me say goodbye."

I raced up the Garden State Parkway, feeling the cool air against my skin from the open window. The wind seemed to be hinting that he was already with Spirit. All at once many feelings moved through me: fear, sorrow, joy, and gratitude.

I heard myself pray, "Lord, he is Yours, I surrender, whatever is best. I give him up, I give him back to You."

But maybe he is still here, my mind raced, moving back and forth, in and out of all the possibilities, until a lovely peace hovered around me, inviting me to be still. With a deep sigh I let myself sink into it.

There was hardly anyone on the road so late at night and as I relaxed the drive became easy. As I drove through the Holland Tunnel the lights seemed unusually golden and bright, almost surrealistic. The closer I came to the hospital the quieter I felt inside. That lovely peace had enveloped me. Then I remembered that I was to hurry so I quickly parked my car and made a mad dash for the entrance.

Billy was the first person I saw standing outside Anthony's room. We immediately embraced; the tears were flowing as our bodies fell into one another, filled with love, filled with sadness.

"He's gone," Billy wept.

Anthony's words rang out. "I will see you on Monday."

He knew when he called me on Saturday that he would already be with Spirit today. This is how I would see him for the last time; there would be no chance of my trying to hold him here. Neither Jo nor I could be the hand that stopped him from rushing to the Light. The student certainly had become the teacher. He no longer needed us; in the end it was we who needed him.

I looked into the room and saw Jo. She had climbed into bed with her son and was cradling him in her arms. Not wanting to disturb her I waited until she motioned for me to enter. I watched Josephine in awe as she let go of her child and rose from his death bed to the tallest five feet I had ever seen. She was steady and strong yet completely present to her deep feelings. An unseen strength and peace emanated from her dark eyes and filled the room. Her beauty shown now more than ever.

I felt Anthony's presence, the presence of Christ, and the Blessed Mother, and I felt certain that Lucky, Michael, and a host of angels were there. The small hospital room felt rich with a love that was almost tangible. In that moment we were all at peace for Anthony had prepared each of us so well to walk the path of letting go. He had become the master teacher.

Those attending to Anthony were very kind, allowing us to stay in the room for as long as we wanted. He looked incredibly peaceful. One by one each member of the family spoke to him, held and loved him. Here was my child from long ago, my dear soul friend and my love from a distant past. I kissed his cheeks and caressed him as I would my own son, then gently kissed his still warm and tender lips.

Anthony had been so much to me, meant so much to me. He was my teacher. My work with him through the journey of life and death had helped me to further heal the unbearable trauma of my husband's passing. As I had not with Lucky, this time I was able to be the midwife, nurturing Anthony and bringing him closer to God as he prepared to go Home. I was finally at peace with death. What a gift he had given me. What a gift we had been for one another. Being with him and with this powerful and blessed family was a deep honor for me. Together we had walked through the greatest of all journeys.

His dearest partner Bruce and I had time to speak. He had been with Anthony during the last moments.

"The doctors were shocked," he shared. "He didn't seem sick enough, they didn't expect him to die, in fact they were considering releasing him as soon as he stabilized."

There was a beautiful, peaceful look behind the glistening tears in Bruce's eyes as he spoke. Anthony had told him that the Blessed Mother, Christ, and his father had entered the room, and with them a magnificent, brilliant Light. Anthony said that it filled him with great comfort and peace. He had smiled at his long-time friend and cherished lover as he said, "Go rest, Bruce, everything is fine."

Bruce went on to tell me how, as he sat back in his chair, letting the sweetness of Anthony's smile envelop him, he began to have an unusual and strange awareness. He looked over at Anthony's bed and thought he saw his spirit begin to rise. Bruce rubbed at his eyes, thinking he was just overtired and imagining it. He walked to the bed.

Anthony was very still and serene. The smile still graced his delicate face.

"Anthony?" Bruce called, but there was no answer. Ever so gently and quietly Anthony had slipped away. Bruce indeed had seen Anthony's spirit rise up from his body.

My heart was overflowing as I heard the words. Anthony chose to leave with no one clinging to him, or even holding his hand. He had sent his mother home and made sure that I would not come until after he had left his body. He made the decision to easily let go. My dear teacher Elisabeth Kübler-Ross would call that *The Good Death*.

Deep in thought and at peace, I returned home. As I opened the front door I heard the phone ringing. It was Jo.

"Karlina," she began, "When I came home from the hospital I went upstairs to Anthony's bed. I got in and began to scream into his pillows. Then I put my arms underneath one of the pillows and found a little booklet our pastor gave him, the Stations of the Cross. The page was opened to the Fourth Station, where Christ, carrying the cross, stops to look at his mother. Karlina, at the bottom of the page Anthony drew a happy face and wrote the words, 'I love you.' " Amazement showed through the clouds of sorrow in her voice. "Karla, he must have known he wasn't coming home. He must have left it there for me to find."

"Oh, Jo, he prepared us all."

"Yes, and you know before he died he arranged everything, all the do's and don'ts. He even sent me to the store to buy a beautiful black suit. Anthony said his friends from New York City would come to his Mass and he wanted me to look just right. If that's not the nuttiest thing for me to do, but I did it and when I came home from the store he asked me to put it on, and I did. When he saw me he said, 'Mom, you're so beautiful.'"

"I'm so glad no one saw us upstairs in the bedroom with me in my black suit going over the plans for his funeral. They would never understand. But you do, Karlina."

"Yes, Jo, I understand and I think it's wonderful."

Jo continued. "You know he's planned the selection of flowers, everything, even the music to be played, and he told me not to worry, that he would be okay. He said, a great gift was coming to him. The gift of love from Christ, and he said, 'That love gets passed along. You will get that gift too, Mom.' We talked about death, Karla; we were really at peace. Yet my heart is still breaking."

"How could it not, Jo? Mine too, but something so holy has transpired here. We both know it, don't we?"

"Yes, dear Karlina, we both know. I just didn't think he was going to leave us this soon."

"I didn't either, Jo. He really fooled us didn't he?"

"Yes. And as sick as he was, he was determined to finish the faux painting in his bedroom. He said it would be my room, a place where I could feel close to him and to God. As he did a little at a time I knew he was in pain. I had all I could do to keep my mouth shut and not interfere. Then finally, as he completed the beautiful artistic design, he asked me to help him clean up. I said a short prayer to the Lord thanking Him for letting Anthony finish the project and I thanked Him for the strength He had given me to just sit back and watch."

"You are so wise, Jo, but that must have been really hard."

"It was, but I knew I had to let him do it by himself. He needed that. Now his room with its colors of blue and white feels just like heaven. It will be our room, just like he said, where I can feel him and feel God."

"And you know that last week he spent a great deal of time with Linda, Billy and Ann Marie. Billy even took him to a Liza Minelli concert."

"Wow, it's mind blowing, just amazing what he did in these last few days. You know Jo, he just closed his eyes and went Home. He slipped out when no one was looking. I've witnessed other deaths from AIDS; they can be horrible, filled with suffering. You have seen it too. This whole journey is just awe-inspiring."

"It is miraculous isn't it?" she added.

"Yes, Jo. There were many things that Anthony did and said to me too. So many completions, I am still in awe. I'm so glad that we can speak freely. Soon I will share with you more of my intimate journey with your beautiful son. You see, I too was his mother in some distant lifetime."

"Yes, I know, Karlina. I was a little jealous at first, especially when we went to the Easter all-night Mass during Holy Week. Anthony was holding your hand, not mine, but I realized that he needed you for some things and me for others. I am so grateful that you have been with us through the thick and thin of this. We are all family now. Toward the end when Anthony and I weren't crying so much we just held each other. We talked about death and about your journey with him."

"Then you know."

"Yes, Karlina, I know a lot of it, but perhaps not all."

"Then soon we will sit together. Jo, I keep being shown that it is to be shared with others in a book. I have even seen it as a film. The voice that speaks to me is saying, 'It will open many hearts and help others to see that there is no death, only a change in form. It is to help awaken consciousness, to let people know that we are all One in God. There is truly no separation.' "

"I envision Anthony's journey as the completion of my memoirs, for he has brought me full circle. I am so at peace with his passing and the afterlife. It is so very different from when I first lost my husband, Lucky."

"None of that would surprise me, Karla."

Josephine and I were just two souls sharing moments of incredible joy and sorrow and in our hearts we knew all of it had been pre-ordained. We were part of a Masterful plan of love and awakening.

In the days that followed his death, Anthony's handsome face graced many newspapers. The various articles acknowledged his amazing courage and his gift to society. Some of the headlines read,

"Matawan V/S Arcadia – DeVizia's AIDS Evoked
Courage and Compassion."

"Compassion Counts"

and

"AIDS Patient Bore Courage to Death."

The article that touched me the most was released on September 9, 1987, just two days after his passing, the day of his memorial service. It was a review of *Crimes of the Heart*, which had just opened. It read,

"Crimes of the Heart - Moving Slice of Life"

By Seamus McGraw

"Because of its humanity, its contradictions and its often broad humor *Crimes of the Heart* can be a very difficult play to be staged but Margo Crupi and co-director Anthony DeVizia balanced the contradictions with grace, skill, and sensitivity. Their production was almost flawless, their timing superb."

"Subtleties in the script are brought out gently and the directors displayed a remarkable eye for detail . . . *Crimes of the Heart* is not to be missed . . . As I was writing this review I learned that Anthony DeVizia, 29, had died on Sept 7, at Saint Vincent's Hospital after a long battle with AIDS. A resident of Matawan, DeVizia became the object of media attention. I interviewed DeVizia at the time and found him to be a sensitive, courageous young man. His strength was an inspiration to me. He will be missed."

Unbelievable, I thought, just days before he leaves this earthly existence he is painting my house, directing a great play, and while en route to Saint Vincent's Hospital pays his final respects to his cherished friend Michelle.

As I listened to a favorite piece of music that Anthony had gifted me with, *He is Sailing,* by Jon and Vangelis, I let it all sink in. I was feeling amazed and in awe, awe for God's Divine plan and for the joy and deep peace that I felt in my heart.

"Oh, Anthony, I know that you know now just how precious you are and what an important mission this was. I am so proud of you."

As I called out to him I felt his presence and his love. His shining spirit descended upon me. It felt as if he lifted me up from the chair and invited me to dance.

I moved in a circle, my arms lifted up to heaven, completely feeling Anthony and the sacredness of our mission. From the first memory of floods given to me when I was a small child, to the moment of the gunshot and Lucky's death, the many visitations and visions that followed and then the moment Anthony appeared at my door—all of the many miracles that had graced my life were present as I danced in celebration and thanksgiving. As the words of the song caressed me I knew that Anthony was with Christ, he was sailing, lifting higher and higher. Filled with peace and gratitude, I knew that the scream that had once been within me was gone now, and in its place was a song of joy.

How can you describe a memorial service as wonderful? The church was packed to overflowing and all of Anthony's wishes had been carried out. There were beautiful wildflowers everywhere, a symbol of his unconfined spirit. And near the altar, on a small round table sat a single red rose in a crystal vase; beside it was a beautiful photograph of Anthony, a close-up. His radiant yet tender smile seemed to put you at ease, while his sparkling brown eyes held a wisdom far beyond their years.

Along with Billy, Anne Hannah and her Madrigal Singers sang Anthony's requested songs: *Ave Maria* and *The Our Father.* The touching lyrics of Jon and Vangelis' *Polonaise* played during the service, leaving a final message to those left behind.

Anthony graced us with that final sentiment, a song that acknowledged the community that had supported him, that spoke of his sacred journey and of his desire for the world. The song echoed throughout the church.

274

...There is strength in the common people
For the people is all we really are
Young and old, the wisest and the lowly
Each indeed is 'Holy' in the 'Light of Love'

When the 'Word' comes I will be waiting
Like the dove that shines he prays for peace
Some have waited what seems a lifetime
Some are waiting now to be released

For the moment we have this freedom
We will choose the way our hearts will move
All the people lost will find their way
Give that chance today
Hear, and I will pray...

For tomorrow another morning
For tomorrow another day
In our children there's that sense of freedom
Help them use it wisely I will pray

I had a sense of him looking down upon us, showering us with Light and blessing, a hopeful prayer in his heart that humanity would continue to awaken to compassion.

After the Mass we feasted, sang and danced, celebrating his

life. The family and close friends, those that had closely walked the walk with him, were in a place of peace. How do you explain that to onlookers and mourners? Weren't we supposed to be forlorn and devastated with sorrow?

"Job so well done, Anthony. Go in peace, until we meet again my dearest one."

I was without grief.

Returning home I felt complete, and ready to take a needed rest. Putting on some soft music I slid into bed. Just a moment had passed when I heard someone running up the stairs. It was Tom. He rushed into the room and as soon as I saw my handsome boy, I was moved to tears. We had come so far in our own healing and I was beyond grateful to have him there with me, alive and well. I got up to greet him.

"I wanted to get here sooner. I'm so sorry, Mom," he said, as he pulled me into his strong arms.

Tom began to sob and immediately my own sobs released, blending with his. I knew that we were letting go of our old grief. It was the grief of Lucky's death, the grief of many years of our unspoken pain when we were emotionally separated from one another. The moment was tender, celebrating a bond of love, the bond of mother and son, of my greatest joy. Then before we knew it, in the midst of our raw emotion the force of our racking sobs caused us to stumble and we fell onto the bed. Tom's rock hard, massive form had landed on top of me, nearly crushing the breath out of me.

"Get up. Get up," I tried to move him. The raspy sounding words could barely make it out of my nearly crushed voice box.

"Tom, I can hardly breathe."

Still sobbing, he rolled over and then we exploded into laughter. In just a few moments, we had moved from deep sorrow to wild laughter and joy. Joy and sorrow had wrestled together once again and joy was victorious. Still laughing, we shook ourselves off and more seriously I said,

"Tom, I am at peace with Anthony's passing. It was an incredible journey we shared. I am so sorry that you didn't get to meet him."

"Me too, Mom, but I did see some raven-haired beauties at the DeVizia's. I went there to look for you. I'm so sorry that I didn't get home in time for the service. They're Anthony's sisters, right? That Linda is gorgeous. In fact they all are."

"Oh boy, what are you thinking?" I asked.

"Hey, you never know. They are a great family aren't they?"

"That they are, and wouldn't it be a wonderful turn of events if you and Linda liked each other. I guess only time will tell."

"We'll see," Tom added, giving me a kiss. Then just as quickly as he had bolted up the stairs to support me he dashed off.

Just days after Anthony's passing, as I was returning home from school, I heard a voice. It was positively Anthony's. His voice was very clear and very distinct. He said to me,

"Bring my mother a rose."

I was immediately taken with that, as the rose had been the symbol of love and confirmation from Lucky as well. I was delighted.

Smiling at my invisible friend, I answered, "Of course, my dear one."

Thrilled that Anthony had chosen to communicate with me in that way I quickly drove to the closest florist and bought the rose.

Standing at Josephine's doorstep, I held the beautiful long-stem red rose in my hand. I was so excited to have this gift for her. Would she believe me when I said that Anthony had told me to bring it to her? I was not ready for what she was about to say to me.

A surprised, yet knowing and beautiful look came over her face as she opened the door.

"Anthony just told me to bring you this. He whispered in my ear," I said excitedly.

Josephine took the rose and with a haunting smile on her face took me by the hand and led me into the dining room. There on her table stood another magnificent long-stem red rose. I began to feel something well up from deep within as tears came to my eyes and chills covered my body. I knew I was in the presence of *The Love*. The veil had opened once again.

She looked into my brimming over eyes and said,

"You just missed Margo. She came to tell me that she had a dream last night. Anthony came to her and said,

'Bring my mother a rose.' "

Epilogue

Time has marched forward. After Anthony's death Josephine became a volunteer for the Hyacinth organization as a speaker on AIDS, helping others to heal as she shared her own journey in a program entitled *Let it Be*. She was also active in The Names Project, the display of the AIDS Memorial Quilt. Anthony's mandala is part of the AIDS quilt, as are three other panels created in his honor, one a beautiful star created by Josephine, another hand stitched by his sister Patty and the third from a loving friend. For a while Anthony's sister Linda and my son Tom shared a very loving relationship. They continue to be good friends.

New Jersey has been very good to me since my return. Miracles have continued and the outpost has proven to be a wonderful place to serve, grow, and flourish. That flourishing includes a beautiful relationship that Tom and I now cherish. He is a successful chiropractor and clinical nutritionist with a dynamic personality and highly spirited approach to health and personal transformation. Because of our past pain we both chose transformative paths that have helped us to heal and become way show-ers for others.

Since the first printing of this book Tom met and married Mandi, the love of his life. We are deeply blessed with the addition of precious Sophia. Life is joyous.

To my absolute delight the early hidden phenomena that I experienced have found their way out of the spiritual closet and into the mainstream world. The media is rich with stories, specials, and movies about the unseen, reincarnation, and encounters with angels and those who are on the other side. I am a closet mystic no more. What was once obscure is now readily available for those with inquiring minds and open hearts.

In the 1970's, Dr. Raymond Moody, in his ground-breaking book *Life After Life*, shared with us the phenomenon of NDE's, near-death experiences. Dr. Moody, the leading authority on this experience, is responsible for launching the amazing paradigm shift that has occurred around death and dying and the spiritual experience. Now a new term has emerged: ADC, an after-death communication with a loved one without the help of a medium. This has been beautifully researched in Bill and Judy Guggenheim's book *Hello From Heaven*, which was based on an ADC project of 3,300 first-hand accounts of people who have been contacted by a deceased loved one. ADC's are experienced in many ways dependent upon how the receiver taps into that place which is beyond the veil.

Many who are clairsentient can feel their loved one. This can come as a strong feeling, a presence, a warm or cool surge of air with an inner awareness that they are not alone. It may be as simple as goose bumps erupting all over the body. Often the sweet scent of flowers fills the room. At times the feeling of love is indescribable. Others who are clairaudient may hear the voice of their loved one. The voice may seem to come from within or even outside of them. Those who are clairvoyant actually see their dear one. In my work I have discovered that encounters of this type are most prevalent close to the time of death. Objects such as radio dials and television stations being moved as well as lights flickering on and off are not uncommon. Often this type of connection is needed to capture our attention, as Lucky captured mine when he repeatedly changed the stereo dial to his favorite station. He indeed stopped me in my tracks.

Our loved ones are as close to us as our heartbeat, watching over us, whispering in our ears just waiting for that moment when we are open to hear, feel, or see. When those sensations come it is helpful to stop and take a full breath, to allow the mind to be still and the heart to expand. Even if the communication is not clear, the presence of love can be felt and absorbed.

The dream state is yet another way our loved ones attempt to reach us. A year before my mother passed over we had a conversation. I asked her to promise that she would find a way to communicate with me after she left this dimension, to let me know what it's like on the other side. Very soon after her death in 1992 I had a dream.

I was in her apartment lying on her bed weeping. Her body was spooning mine, as she softly said,

"Karla, don't cry."

Immediately I sat up and while sitting next to her saw that she was brilliant, clearly luminescent, looking no more than thirty-years-old with no evidence of any illness or handicap. She was completely whole. Filled with joy I asked,

"Mom, what's it like?"

"Oh, Karla," she responded, "It is so beautiful here, and all I need to do to be with you is think of you and I am at your side."

The love that I felt was indescribable and continues to be

as I remember that moment with her. Mom has continued to stay present in my life. Most often I hear her when I am engaged in negative thoughts. Her voice cuts through my thinking process as she says,

"Karla, cut that out!" I still can't get away with anything. Our dear ones are closer than we can imagine.

Not only is the media coming to the forefront with messages from the other side but science as well. New discoveries have revealed a quantum hologram also called the web of life, that connects all living matter. As Edgar Cayce said, "We are all corpuscles in the One body of God." Having left the physical form does not break that Oneness.

The scientist and visionary Gregg Braden refers to the quantum web as "the heaven state," the place where the soul resides when not in body, a place where we are all connected. As our thoughts change from fear to love to an awareness of something far greater than our mortal bodies we can tap into that web, that state of higher consciousness. Not just to touch those who have left their bodies but to touch greater wisdom, the place of Heaven, the God Self.

The more we quiet our minds the more the veil can open. There are many ways to achieve that precious quietness: meditation, *A Course in Miracles*, transcendent music, deep journeying, and the transforming power of Qigong can help transport us into higher realms of awareness. We simply need to get out of our own way, out of the ego that keeps us in the past or in the future. Heaven state resides in the moment of now and can be accessed by gratitude and the open heart.

We are not alone; loved ones, guides, masters and angels travel close, urging us to awaken and transform, to live our lives joyously. In each moment we can decide what we will serve—love and joy or fear and suffering. We can learn how to see the issues in our lives differently and to open to the guidance that is ever present.

One of the finest techniques I have learned is from Gregg Braden. He reveals that scientific discoveries have shown that we can actually change our own DNA. In a 1993 military laboratory experiment a person concentrated on deep gratitude. A sample of the subject's DNA taken from white blood cells was contained in a device in an adjacent room. The DNA actually changed from its tight corkscrew shape, unwinding until the strands were completely open. Think of what that does to the trillion cells *within* the body.

It is not surprising that when the person concentrated on hate or anger the DNA, without any lag time, returned to its very constricted form. Even distance did not slow down the process. The subject was removed from the building to see if the cells would still change, and again the DNA responded immediately. The experiment was concluded after a distance of 50 miles was reached. The DNA still responded.

We are not only affecting our DNA but water as well. In *The Hidden Messages of Water* by Japanese scientist Masaru Emoto we learn that water can be changed by our thoughts, words and feelings. His revolutionary work with high-speed photography and ice crystals clearly indicates that love and gratitude form the most beautiful and perfect crystals, while negative thoughts and words create deformed crystals. The earth and our bodies are composed primarily of water. Emoto shows us that appreciation supports our greater health in body, mind, heart and spirit, and can be a building block for greater peace and global environmental renewal.

We are creating all of the time with each thought and most especially with each feeling. It is now clear that high emotion, such as love, joy, and particularly gratitude can open us to greater healing. Cayce said that we are all co-creators with God. We are far more powerful than we know.

How can this be put into practice in order to create a greater life? Gratitude! By coming into that high emotion we change our state. This is the time to envision our lives as we desire them to be. Remember my running image. As I saw myself running to the group of people I was whole, perfect, and free of pain. That image seeded my body and created healing. It was just a matter of time and faith before the actual vision manifested *exactly* as it was created. How then can we get to gratitude? It is actually quite easy.

While allowing yourself to be quiet, go in your memory to a moment in time when you felt complete gratitude and joy, perhaps to the birth of a child, the touch of a loved one, a time in nature or the felt presence of God.

As soon as you feel the gratitude and joy breathe deeply, allowing every cell in your body and mind to receive the high emotion. You may feel chills, or a light or full feeling in the heart. This heart activation can bring up powerful emotions of love.

On the energy of that deep gratitude allow an image to come to mind of yourself whole, perfect, and at peace in every way, doing something you love to do. As you envision this you are seeding the cells of your body and the future and you are immediately changing your state of consciousness. It is best to complete each breath and gratitude exercise with, "Thank you, God, that this is already done in me and through me." Gratitude by far is the most powerful form of prayer.

Albert Einstein, surely a mystic in our midst, said, "We can't solve problems by using the same kind of thinking we used when we created them." We must go to a higher level, and high emotion is the vehicle that can alter the DNA, giving it a jolt thus creating a new reality. Those that I work with who are experiencing major health challenges perfect their image as they breathe into gratitude a number of times throughout the course of the day. We need not meditate long hours or study exotic disciplines to achieve a more aligned state. It is as close as our breath, our joyful memories, and our open loving heart.

Ancient wisdom and science are finally merging, as revealed in Gregg Braden's powerful books *The Isaiah Effect* and *The God Code*. This wisdom that speaks to the power of emotions has been retrieved from the ancient Isaiah scroll discovered in 1946 in the caves of Qumran, Israel. It tells us that by activating the feeling state of the heart we move into high states of emotion and create a new life. In addition, recent high-level research has documented a donut shape of energy around the body that is affected by our feeling states. Current technology has measured this field, called the *Torus*, at six to eight feet. However, leading physicists suggest that as our technology widens the field will be found to extend far further, perhaps into infinity.

The Institute of Heart Math in California has also demon-strated the innate ability we have to affect our lives by high feeling states. It is refreshing to know that we can quickly and easily spend a moment in joy, seeding that joy into our cells and our world. As we do this we cannot help but create a change in our energy field that can then go out like ripples in a lake to change the states of others. The six to eight feet heart field around us is already reaching others. Let us touch one another with gratitude and love. We can make a differ-ence in the world. We can program who we are destined to become, co-creators with God and joyous beings.

This heart field activation can also be used to connect with those beyond the veil. In Robert Grant's wonderful book, *The Place We Call Home, Exploring the Soul's Existence after Death,* he offers an exercise which I have adapted to include the high feeling state.

Before going to sleep at night write in a dream journal that you wish to connect with your loved one if it is right and per-fect for both of you. Then allow yourself to go to gratitude, perhaps a joyous moment in your memory with the one you wish to contact. Let the feeling rise up and repeat your desire once again—that if it is right and perfect for both a communication will take place.

It may take a while but the process can eventually open the veil. If your dream life has been dormant a simple statement affirming that you will remember your dreams long enough to write them down in the morning is helpful. After the dream life becomes activated you may receive a communication. Remember to restate your desire for that communication. It is important to be patient as a frequency must be established between you both. Your loved one may be operating at channel thirty-three and your channel may need a little tweaking. Persistence and patience is most definitely the key.

Just a few years ago, on Thanksgiving Day, I spent many prayerful moments in loving gratitude thanking all in my life for their love, support, and many lessons. When I came to my husband Lucky I said to him,

"If we are to be together again I need to know that we are at the same level of spiritual awareness. I need to be assured that you know Christ as I do."

Going off to sleep that night I repeated my dream affirmation, asking to connect with him. To my absolute delight a vivid dream came. Standing in a large room I noticed a sign that said, "Lucky LaVoie will be making a guest appearance at *A Course in Miracles* meeting." *Not bad*, I thought. As the dream continued Lucky appeared and told me that he had been with Christ. He assured me that he had moved from the first to the sixth level. I remembered Christ's words, "In my Father's house are many mansions. I go to prepare a place for you." I was overjoyed! Lucky then showed me his work on the other side. He was helping those who were contemplating suicide and assisting those who had already crossed over from that manner of death.

On this level of existence I was helping people who were very ill to recover and assisting those who were crossing over. It seemed as if we were on parallel journeys. There was no doubt in my mind that our connection was still intact. I know that our soul work continues; we grow and continue to be of service to one another no matter what dimension we are living in.

A mother who had lost her nineteen-year-old daughter to a terrible car accident a few months prior attended one of my *Beyond The Veil* presentations. This was a woman who had no prior experience with meditation or understanding of after-death communication. She had read an article that I had written and in deep despair over the loss of her child decided to come to the talk and workshop. I received a beautiful letter from her soon after saying the following.

"I had just been to your presentation at Unity Church on Friday night. I did the heart activation and dream incubation as I went off to sleep. I did not have a dream but on the next day I was sitting in my living room on the sofa when all of a sudden I felt cold air on my left side. I immediately said to myself. 'Where is this draft coming from?' Then I remembered what you said about a change in the air. I began to talk to my daughter Allison. However being the black and white person that I am, I needed to disprove all the things that could be making this cold air. I told her not to go away, to stay right there and then said, 'I will be right back.'"

"I closed my basement door then came back to the sofa and waited. The blast of cold air returned. Again I told her to stay right there and stood on a chair to see if the air vents from the air conditioning were closed. They were. I sat back down and waited. Again the cold air came just on my left side—my right side was a normal temperature. Then I remembered my son Danny had taken a shower about twenty minutes before all this started. So I went to see if he had left the bathroom window open. He hadn't. I came back and waited and the ice cold air began flowing upon me again. My fourth and final time to disprove what was happening was when I moved to the other side of the sofa. I waited and the cold air followed me."

"I knew then that I needed to speak to Allison. I told her that I loved her, that I missed her terribly, and asked her to watch over her brother and keep him safe for me. I then asked her if she was with her Nanny and Pop Pop. After each question I waited and each time the huge blast of cold air flowed on my left side. Each time I took that as a yes! I didn't look at a clock but I am sure it was a good ten or twenty minutes that I felt her answering my questions with that cold air. Her timing was perfect too. Just before my son's friend was to come by she was gone. I have never felt such love, she was completely present with me, and I now know that she is safe and not far away."

"Thank you, Beth Lynam."

Here we have the amazing persistence and patience of a loving daughter waiting for her mom to trust what was happening. I can't help but think that Allison was giggling as her mother raced around the house closing the vents and windows. Saying, "Just wait, I will be right back."

Along the way we meet immortal friends, and I know that love never leaves its own for we are joined heart to heart and soul to soul, and once we have come together nothing can separate us, not even death.

I pray that my journey will help you open the door to greater consciousness, connection, and wisdom, and that it will help you to remember the truth and beauty of who you really are. May your journey be filled with the awe and wonder of a child, God's grace and infinite joy, and deep and abiding gratitude for all of life.

Resources

Awakening Earth Center for Natural Healing and Empowerment
www.karlalavoie.com

• To learn more about Karla's work or to schedule a phone consultation, presentation or workshop visit www.karlalavoie.com.

• Customized healing, imagery and empowerment recordings to meet your personal needs can be ordered as well as healing meditations and books.

• *Garden of Light,* by Karla Lee LaVoie and Mahoteh A journey to the inner temple. Deep relaxation, guided imagery and peaceful music create a sacred garden for meditation and healing.

> *"A powerful moving experience, highly recommended."*
> —Association for Research and Enlightenment

• *Earth Mother,* by Karla Lee LaVoie and Mu D'Akimbo A soothing meditation with enchanting instrumental passages guides you into the heavens, through the earth, deep into the rainforest and oceans on a mission of healing.

> *"Rich and luscious guided imagery affirms healing and peace for the earth."* —Leading Edge Review

> *"Gorgeous music it is truly beautiful."*
> —Elisabeth Kübler-Ross

The Association for Research and Enlightenment (A.R.E.) in Virginia Beach, Virginia is the international headquarters for the work of Edgar Cayce. The A.R.E. offers conferences and educational activities in Virginia Beach and around the world. Visit www.edgarcayce.org.

A Course in Miracles, published by The Foundation for Inner Peace is a unique, universal, spiritual thought system that teaches the way to love and forgiveness. Visit www.acim.org, and www.miraclecenter.org for study group information.

The Bonny Method of Guided Imagery and Music (GIM) is a contemporary, experiential, psychotherapy centered around the fine art of music. It can lead to insight, emotional release, and core integration of body, mind and spirit. Visit www.ami-bonnymethod.org to locate a GIM guide and www.atlantisicm.com.

Genesis Spiritual Life Center, in Westfield, Massachusetts offers hospitality and holistic programs to persons of all faiths, cultures and lifestyles. Visit www.genesiscenter.us.

Omega Institute, located in Rhineback, New York, offers over 250 workshops, retreats and wellness vacations each year. Other locations include Austin, Texas, Costa Rica, Virgin Islands, and California. Visit www.eomega.org.

Qigong is the ancient Chinese art of self-care and health promotion that cultivates energy flow, inner peace, and harmony within the body, mind and spirit. Contact www.FeeltheQi.com for books, training and videos.

Ram Dass books, tapes and the video *Fierce Grace* can be ordered at: www.ramdasstapes.org.

Elisabeth Kübler-Ross books can be found at www.elisabethkublerross.com.

Alan Cohen's books, courses and workshop schedule can be found at www.alancohen.com.

Credits

Music has been a vital part of this story and my life. I grate-
fully acknowledge the following artists and writers for their
talent and inspiration, and the publishers for their generosity.

The Traveler, by James Dillet Freeman
Reprinted with kind permission of Unity www.unityonline.org.

The Twelfth of Never, by Paul F. Webster and Jerry Livingston
Reprinted with kind permission of Webster Music Company
and Spirit Music Group.

And When I Die, words and music by Laura Nyro
© 1969, EMI Blackwood Music Inc, USA
Reproduced by kind permission of EMI Music Publishing
Ltd, London WC2H OQY.

Awakening and *Master Come To Me*, by Michael Stillwater
Arc In Time: A Retrospective Anthology www.musicheals.net
By kind permission of Michael Stillwater.

Polonaise, words by Jon Anderson and music by Vangelis
© 1983, Evangelos Papathanassiou / EMI Music Publishing
Ltd, London WC2H OQY (EMI control 50% on behalf of
Vangelis) Reprinted with kind permission.

Polonaise, composed by Jon Anderson and Vangelis
© Opio Publishing / Warner - Tamerlane Publishing Corp.
By kind permission of Warner/Chappell Music Limited.

Crimes of the Heart – Moving Slice of Life, by Seamus McGraw
Reprinted with kind permission of Greater Media Newspapers.

CPSIA information can be obtained at www.ICGtesting.com
Printed in the USA
BVOW11s0012200814

363467BV00007B/118/P